Ritual Innovation in the Hebrew Bible and Early Judaism

Beihefte zur Zeitschrift für die alttestamentliche Wissenschaft

——

Herausgegeben von
John Barton, Ronald Hendel, Reinhard G. Kratz,
and Markus Witte

Band 468

Ritual Innovation in the Hebrew Bible and Early Judaism

Edited by
Nathan MacDonald

DE GRUYTER

ISBN 978-3-11-037273-1
e-ISBN (PDF) 978-3-11-036871-0
e-ISBN (EPUB) 978-3-11-039267-8
ISSN 0934-2575

Library of Congress Cataloging-in-Publication Data
A CIP catalog record for this book has been applied for at the Library of Congress.

Bibliographic information published by the Deutsche Nationalbibliothek
The Deutsche Nationalbibliothek lists this publication in the Deutsche Nationalbibliografie;
detailed bibliographic data are available in the Internet at http://dnb.dnb.de.

© 2016 Walter de Gruyter GmbH, Berlin/Boston
Printing and binding: CPI books GmbH, Leck
♾ Printed on acid-free paper
Printed in Germany

www.degruyter.com

MIX
Papier aus verantwor-
tungsvollen Quellen
FSC
www.fsc.org   FSC® C083411

Preface

All but one of the essays in this volume originated as papers given for a special unit on "Ritual Innovation in the Hebrew Bible and Early Judaism" at the Society of Biblical Literature international meeting held in St Andrews in July 2013. I am grateful to my erstwhile colleague at St Andrews Kristin De Troyer who invited me to organize the special unit, and to all who participated in those sessions. The idea of examining ritual innovation had arisen in my own research on the Pentateuch a few years earlier and resulted in an essay entitled "Ritual Innovation: The Feast of Weeks from the Covenant Code to the Temple Scroll", which was awarded the inaugural *David Noel Freedman Award for Excellence and Creativity in Hebrew Bible Scholarship* in 2011. A revised form of the essay is to be found in this volume and I am grateful to Bernard Levinson and Theodore Hiebert who responded to an oral version of the paper at the Society of Biblical Literature's annual meeting that year in San Francisco, as well as the awards committee. Finally I would like to thank the then editors of the *Beihefte zur Zeitschrift für die alttestamentliche Wissenschaft*, Professors John Barton, Ron Hendel, Reinhard Kratz, and Markus Witte for accepting the volume into their fine series, and for their confidence then and since.

Nathan MacDonald
St John's College, Cambridge

Table of Contents

Nathan MacDonald

Strange Fire before the Lord: Thinking about Ritual Innovation in the Hebrew Bible and Early Judaism

At first blush "ritual innovation" would appear to be an oxymoron. What is ritual, if not a stereotyped behaviour that has to be practised consistently in order to be effective? This common-sense view of ritual is not without some justification, for rituals frequently appear to have a timeless quality. As Catherine Bell observes,

> Rituals tend to present themselves as the unchanging, time-honored customs of an enduring community. Even when no such claims are explicitly made within or outside the rite, a variety of cultural dynamics tend to make us take it for granted that rituals are old in some way; any suggestion that they may be rather recently minted can give rise to consternation and confusion. Indeed...part of what makes behavior ritual-like is the way in which such practices imply the legitimacy of age and tradition.[1]

Nevertheless, Bell (along with other ritual theorists) insists that rituals can and do change, and they can even be invented.[2]

The possibility that rituals might be invented or that ritual innovation might occur has sometimes been treated by biblical scholars as counter-intuitive. Biblical legislation of ritual practice has often been assumed to be descriptive of actual practice. The Israelite cult was inherently conservative and when ritual change occurred it was a process so slow as to be entirely imperceptible to those participating in its rites. Such a perspective is found in Soggin's reflections on the "conservative function of the cult".

> Given the traditional character of any form of public cult, we should not be surprised that its function is eminently conservative. É. Jacob rightly pointed out that not only does the theological element of "the great affirmations of the faith" support the cult, but there are also "the eminently conservative forces which the rite and the tradition preserve with particular tenacity, a long time after the thought which has inspired it has disappeared".

---

1 Catherine M. Bell, *Ritual: Perspectives and Dimensions* (New York: Oxford University Press, 1997), 210.
2 See also Ronald L. Grimes, *Reading, Writing, and Ritualizing: Ritual in Fictive, Liturgical, and Public Places* (Washington, DC: Pastoral Press, 1993), esp. 1–22.

That is also true of Israel (and much later for the church) where, as far as we can see, "the cult has not escaped the paralyzing power of the tradition".[3]

Such ideas are also evidenced in the occasional references to "(linguistic) fossils" or "vestigial elements" in scholarship on the priestly literature, our most important source of information on Israelite rituals.[4] On the other hand, the recognition of ritual change is deeply embedded in critical discourse about the Old Testament. In his *Prolegomena* Julius Wellhausen critiques those whose arguments "derived all their force from a moral conviction that the ritual legislation *must* be old".[5] A comparison of the presentation of Israelite worship in the constituent sources of the Pentateuch allows Wellhausen to develop a historical schema for how Israelite religion changed throughout its history. Thus, an account of cultic innovation in ancient Israel provides Wellhausen with the critical foundation for establishing the history of traditions, and on that basis a history of Israel.[6]

As a result of these divergent perspectives on ritual innovation, there exist unresolved disagreements within Hebrew Bible scholarship about the nature and development of ancient Israelite religion, and fractures within American scholarship, and between Israeli and continental European scholarship. Focussed attention on the issue may, perhaps, help to remove some impasses, or at very least clarify the nature of the differences. It is in such a context and with such aims that the essays in this volume may be assesed.

Ritual Innovation in the Eyes of the Hebrew Bible's Composers

The instinct that the cult is conservative and that ritual innovation is rare or unusual is a perspective deeply ingrained in western culture and it has often been reflected in anthropological literature.[7] The idea is already found in culturally

---

3 J. Alberto Soggin, *Israel in the Biblical Period: Institutions, Festivals, Ceremonies, Rituals* (Edinburgh: T&T Clark, 2001), 80–81.
4 See, not least, the works of Jacob Milgrom.
5 Julius Wellhausen, *Prolegomena to the History of Israel with a Reprint of the Article Israel from the "Encyclopaedia Britannica"* (trans. John Sutherland Black and Allan Menzies; Edinburgh: Adam & Charles Black, 1885), 11.
6 Wellhausen, *Prolegomena*, 12–13.
7 See the discussion in Bell, *Ritual*, 210–52. Kreinath, Hartung and Deschner observe that ritual theorists have usually been concerned with the static and enduring aspects of ritual (J. Krei-

significant texts, including the Bible. A surface reading of Israel's historical narratives in Exodus–2 Kings and 1–2 Chronicles suggests that the Israelite cult had
its hoary origins in words from God at Mount Sinai mediated through Moses. A
number of biblical narratives portray the negative consequences that result when
the Pentateuch's prescriptions are set aside. Nadab and Abihu's experiment in
ritual innovation, or "strange fire" (אש זרה) as the biblical text has it, is met
with immediate and devastating punishment (Lev 10:1–2). Jeroboam's thorough-
going attempt to create a cult in the north with its own cult places, priesthood
and festivals is emphasized through the repeated use of "he made" (עשה). His
novelties are unambiguously rejected by a deuteronomistic writer (1Kgs 12:25–
33; 13:33–34), and he becomes the archetypal ruler of the rebellious north,
whose conduct ultimately leads to exile (2Kgs 17). Ahaz's alterations to the architecture and furniture of the Jerusalem temple contribute to his portrayal as a
king who did not follow in David's footsteps (2Kgs 16), whilst Uzziah attempts
to burn incense on the altar of incense result in him being struck down with lep-
rosy (2Chron 26:16–21).

In his essay Saul Olyan examines a number of narratives that portray and
condemn the usurpation of another party's ritual privileges, such as that of
King Uzziah. Olyan reminds us of the importance of attending to the question
of who gains through such acts of ritual innovation, and by the portrayal of
them in this way. "Such attempts at ritual innovation through usurpation are
typically condemned by our texts, whose authors seek either to defend exclusive
priestly claims against challenges posed by others, or cast priestly or other adversaries as corrupt and therefore, illegitimate, on account of their practices." Stories condemning ritual innovation guard existing structures of power, and point
to the way that Pentateuchal rituals serve certain priestly hierarchies.

Olyan identifies a second form of ritual innovation that brings benefit to the
manipulator of rituals. These involve the manipulation of mourning rites to
shame and humiliate another party. Unlike the usurpation of priestly privileges,
such ritual innovations are not inevitably rejected. When Shimi throws dirt on
David, the humiliated king does not protest. Astonishingly he allows that Shimi's
actions may be due to divine impulse (2Sam 16:11). Nehemiah's act of pulling out
the hair of those who were intermarried forces them into an act of mourning and
humiliation. Nehemiah justifies his actions by appeal to the Pentateuchal law

---

nath, C. Hartung and A. Deschner, "Introduction", in *The Dynamics of Changing Rituals: The Transformation of Religious Ritual within Their Social and Cultural Context* [Toronto Studies in Religion, 29; New York: Peter Lang, 2004], 2–3). Grimes complains that few theories "accommodate the facts of ritual change, ritual innovation, and ritual performance" (Ronald L. Grimes, "Ritual Theory and the Environment", *The Sociological Review* 51 [2003]: 34).

and stories from Israel's ancient history. He is the hero of his own narrative and his actions are clearly regarded as justifiable and appropriate. Olyan's examples demonstrate that some forms of ritual innovation were held to be acceptable by the Bible's narrators. Further examples would include the institution of Purim, whose historical origins in the Persian empire are clearly indicated in the story of Esther, the institution of fast days to memorialize the fall of Jerusalem (Zech 7:5–6), or the mourning of pilgrims after the destruction of the temple (Jer 41:4–5). Olyan's identification of two forms of ritual innovation pose an important question for us: why were some rites viewed as improvisable, but others not?

Disguising Ritual Innovation

The very fact that ritual innovation was portrayed in some texts – and even more so, the fact that it was condemned – is unambiguous evidence that ritual change *did* occur in ancient Israel. There are good grounds for thinking that those innovations that were successfully promoted by leading priests were integrated into the Pentateuch. In this way their innovations were given warrant by projecting them onto the figure of Moses. Indeed, Bell argues that some invented rituals seek to conceal their recent origins and attribution to an august figure from the past is a good way to achieve this. It is for this reason that the Pentateuch provides such fertile ground for some of the essayists in this volume. Since new rituals conceal their origins and are presented as though in essential continuity with earlier rituals, analysis is not without its challenges.

In his essay James W. Watts examines the ways in which the iconic focus of Israel's worship was shifted from the ark of the covenant to Torah scrolls. Since the ark had a role to play in some of the Pentateuch's ritual acts, such as the performance of Yom Kippur, its absence entailed a change in ritual practice. It also marked an important shift in perspective from esoteric to exoteric. The sacred texts were no longer hidden and visible only to God, as the stone tablets in the ark of the covenant had been, they were taken out and read at regular intervals. Despite these far-reaching innovations, Watts observes that iconography and rhetoric disguise the change as continuity: in synagogues the Torah scrolls are stored in arks. But already in the Pentateuch the distinction between the stone tablets and Torah scrolls is being effaced so that readers are encouraged to equate the two. The fact of innovation is disguised and an equation of later readers and the early Israelites is effected.

Jeffrey Stackert's examination of the Sabbath in the Priestly and Holiness strata of the Pentateuch shows how the same calendrical rite can be understood in different ways. The Priestly Sabbath is understood as a reminder to Yhwh. When Yhwh sees the Sabbath being observed he recalls his promise to grant agricultural blessing. In the Priestly Code it is specifically agricultural work that is prohibited, for it is this that reminds God about his commitment. In the Holiness Code, however, agricultural blessing is not the result of the Sabbath observance, but rather facilitates it. Sabbath observance in the Holiness Code is consequently more demanding: requiring a complete cessation from any work. Stackert's analysis draws attention to a number of subtle changes that are easily lost on any but the most carefully trained eye. The Holiness Code's adaptations fundamentally reconceptualize the Sabbath, but the Holiness writer perhaps successfully concealed that fact from many of his readers.

Nathan MacDonald's essay on *Shavu'ot* traces the development of that feast over more than half a millennium. From the time of the Holiness Code, MacDonald shows how the biblical editors sought to harmonize the various divergent sources available to them. From our perspective such attempts to blend different versions of the feast result not in a festival calendar with all the problems resolved, but in a festival calendar significantly different from its precursors. Thus, through a process of harmonization a single harvest pilgrimage festival was bifurcated and became two distinct days separated by fifty days to mark the firstfruits of harvest and the offering of the new grain. At Qumran and amongst Philo's *Therapeutae* the multiplication of festive days separated by fifty-day intervals continued apace giving rise to a feast for new wine and new oil. As MacDonald demonstrates harmonization provides a particularly fruitful avenue for scribes wishing to obscure the origins of their novelties. Indeed, it is possible that by coordinating two existing traditions, and not introducing any obvious new elements, scribes were themselves unaware of the novelties they were introducing.

The book of Numbers provides one of the best laboratries for thinking about ritual innovation.[8] The ritual material in the book has been identified as supplementary material in a priestly style (P^s). In many cases it has a close relationship to ritual material in the book of Leviticus and apparently develops it. It claims authoritative status by being attributed to Moses, but the revelation takes place during the wilderness wanderings and not on Mount Sinai. Both Roy Gane and Christian Frevel examine Numbers for examples of ritual innovation.

Gane describes the *Sotah* ritual as "one of the most innovative rituals in the Pentateuch". There is a unique combination of civil and cultic legislation for a

---

8 See already N. MacDonald, "The Hermeneutics and Genesis of the Red Cow Ritual in Numbers 19", *HTR* 105 (2012), 351–71.

ritual in the sanctuary produces a judicial verdict. A number of other features are distinctive, including the recipe for the grain offering, tousling the woman's hair, the recitation and writing down of the oath, and the potion containing sanctuary dust and the words of the oath. Gane argues that by drinking the potion the woman takes the holy water into her body. If she is guilty of adultery as her husband suspects, this encounter of the holy and the impure will bring harm to her reproductive system. By depending on an ethical idea of impurity, the *Sotah* ritual signals its dependence on the Holiness Code, and in particular Lev 18:20. Frevel examines Num 5–6 for examples of innovation. Cases of defrauding by means of an oath, the ritual treatment of the wife accused of unfaithfulness (the *Sotah*), and the instructions for the Nazirite are all shown to develop aspects of Lev 5. They concern issues of impurity as well as how to handle "unseen jeapordy by concealment and responsibility through confession and compensation". In Num 5:5–10 the instructions about various forms of property fraud in Lev 5:20–26 are generalized and confession is required prior to restitution. In the case of the *Sotah* the instructions about the *ḥaṭṭa't*-offering are applied to a wife who does not incriminate herself, whilst the Nazirite legislation applies the *ḥaṭṭa't*-offering in Lev 5:1–13 to the Nazirite who has inadvertently annuled his vow through contact with a corpse.

The analyses of Gane and Frevel mark important departures from earlier scholarship which tended to see the unusual elements in the rituals prescribed in Numbers 5–6 as evidence of their antiquity. The fact that generations of scholars could be convinced into believing that these rituals had pre-Israelite roots is testimony to the ability of rituals to pass themselves off as ancient. Importantly, the innovative elements are not entirely new, for as both Gane and Frevel demonstrate they improvise on ritual elements known from Leviticus.

Ritual Changes Inspired by Events

But what drives ritual change? Olyan's essay gathers evidence for some ritual change being driven by acquisitive individuals who sought to reengineer a recognized ritual practice for their own benefit. A change in social circumstances might also force a change in ritual practice.[9] The recognition that this is the case has played an important role in biblical scholarship. The destruction of the Jerusalem Temple and the forced migration of many elites to Babylonia in 587 BCE necessitated considerable alterations to Israelite religious practice. Sab-

---

9 Bell, *Ritual*, 210–23.

bath, circumcision, and prayer have often been pointed to as practices that come to particular prominence in a world without a sanctuary. The story of the pilgrims in Jer 41 provides an interesting case study. The timing of their journey suggests that they were coming to the sanctuary for the annual feast of booths. They come prepared with grain offerings and incense, but they appear as mourners – beards shaved, clothes torn, bodies gashed – not as celebrants. Thus, an innovative practice results from combining two apparently distinct practices.

The essays by Reinhard Achenbach and Watts show the effect that the destruction of the First Temple had on ritual practice. Achenbach traces the notions of divine presence beginning with the time of Josiah, a few decades before the fall of Jerusalem. Emphasizing the intellectual reconceptualization that took place as a result of the drastically changed conditions for the cult, Achenbach's analysis describes how shifting theological ideas result in changed cultic practice. With the cherub throne and the ark removed, the penitential liturgies at the ruined temple in Jerusalem elevated the name as a mode of presence. In the conditions of exile the theology of a mobile divine glory promised a spiritualized presence even outside the land. When the temple was rebuilt, this idea endured and made the refabrication of throne and ark superfluous.

In the post-exilic period Achenbach identifies a process of spiritualization and abstraction. The language of ritual begins to be applied to human interiority. The inscribing of amulets is used to speak of the alteration of the human will: the covenant will be inscribed upon the hearts (Jer 31:33). Similarly, the purification of the conscience is presented as an act of circumcising the heart (Deut 10:16). This process of spiritualization and abstraction also has implications for the perception of divine exteriority, and resulting ritual practice. The divine name, Yhwh, is no longer to be enunciated even in the temple, and in the collection of cultic songs, known as the Elohistic psalter, the divine name is replaced with the common noun *elohim*.

Watts also addresses the disappearance of the ark of the covenant, and notes the existence of metaphorical and spiritual replacements. But in contrast to Achenbach, Watts insists that there was also a physical replacement for the ark: the Torah scrolls. It is for this reason that the post-exilic priestly source can address the fabrication of the ark despite the fact that there was no ark in the Second Temple. The Pentateuch's ark contained texts, the stone tablets, but these are frequently conflated with the Torah scrolls, such that readers are apt to identify them, or at least think of them in similar ways. Nevertheless, as Watts demonstrates, the texts functioned quite differently. Both texts were venerated as holy objects. But whilst the stone tablets were concealed in the ark, which functioned like a reliquary, the Torah scrolls were read out to the people.

Thus, alongside the spiritualization and abstraction that Achenbach identifies, we also have a shift from the esoteric to the exoteric.

Stackert's essay on the Sabbath in the priestly and holiness legislation discerns a similar shift from esoteric to exoteric. In the priestly literature the Sabbath and circumcision are envisaged as reminders for God that he has promised to bless the Israelites. As Stackert argues the Israelites' cessation of work reminds God of his own resting on the seventh day and his blessing of what he had made (Gen 2:1–3). In the Holiness Code, however, the Sabbath is a raminder to the Israelites to reverence Yhwh who sanctifies them. The occurrence of the Sabbath is a weekly reminder to obey the rest of the Torah and achieve the promised sanctification. In other words, the Sabbath has a practical function related to its visibility to the Israelites, just as the same is true of Watts' description of the Torah scrolls. In contrast, for earlier texts the Sabbath and the tablets of stone were important because of their visibility to the deity, whether or not they could be viewed by the Israelites. The parallels between Watts and Stackert's arguments raise the possibility that H's development of the Sabbath was an exilic or post-exilic development. The shift towards lay holiness and the land, rather than priestly holiness and the temple precinct, would be comprehensible innovations in light of the destruction of the First Temple. In his essay, however, Stackert avoids a precise dating of either the original priestly document or the holiness revision.[10]

Ritual Changes Resulting from Textualization

In ancient Israel it was not just events like the fall of Jerusalem that give rise to ritual changes. We must also attend to the wide-reaching effect of textualization (even if this was a process that may have been propelled in significant ways by the fall of Jerusalem and its aftermath). As has long been observed, a text is not a ritual.[11] Not only is it the case that a text only represents aspects of ritual prac-

10 In his *Rewriting the Torah: Literary Revision in Deuteronomy and the Holiness Code*, FAT 52 (Tübingen: Mohr Siebeck, 2007), Stackert discusses the range of dates that would be conceivable for H given his argument that H is dependent on D. "Proposed dates for this corpus prior to the very end of the seventh century or even the beginning of the sixth centuert B.C.E. are thus untenable, while a late exilic or even a post-exilic date for the Holiness Legislation is not excluded" (17–18).
11 David P. Wright, "Ritual Theory, Ritual Texts, and the Priestly-Holiness Writings of the Pentateuch", in *Social Theory and the Study of Israelite Religion: Essays in Retrospect and Prospect*,

tice, but also texts are often produced for different purposes than those that animate the performance of a ritual. In addition, textualization of a ritual often creates new connections and relationships. In other words, the act of translation is simultaneously one of transformation. Or, as Catherine Bell puts it,

> the relationship of texts and rites evokes wonderful complexities for us...What is the significance or functional effect of writing ritual down, both vis-a-vis ritual and as a written text? How does writing a text or depicting ritual in a text act upon the social relations involved in textual and ritual activities? Ultimately, how are the media of communication *creating* a situation rather than simply reflecting it; how are they restructuring social interactions rather than merely expressing them?[12]

Christian Frevel's examination of Numbers 5–6 is particularly attentive to the complex interrelationship of ritual and text. The writing down of a ritual might well serve the purpose of authorizing a tradition, but also results in systematization and homogenization. He also offers a theoretical consideration of the different ways in which ritual texts might relate to ritual practice, and by doing so opens up new possibilities that have usually been overlooked by biblical scholarship. It has often been assumed that the biblical texts reflect antecendent ritual practices in the Jerusalem temple. Another possibility is that the Bible's ritual texts established ritual practice – a view that would comport with traditional attribution of the rituals to Moses's encounter with God. But Frevel observes that we should not exclude a third possibility: that the biblical rituals resolve scribal problems, the purpose of which was not ritual practice.

Frevel insists that since we cannot move confidently from text to the rituals it is difficult to observe ritual innovation beyond the textuality of the rituals themselves.

He examines Num 5–6 for examples of innovation that may take place primarily on a textual, rather than a practical, level. He demonstrates that all of the rituals in Num 5–6 have Lev 5 as an antecendent text. Yet if the antecedent text of Lev 5 has a sophistication and complexity that raises questions about its relation to practical performance, this is even more the case with the rituals in Num 5–6. We may have here examples of Frevel's third category where the biblical rituals are primarily an exercise in scribal erudition.

The development of the Israelite festival calendar presents similar problems according to MacDonald. From at least the time of the Holiness Code's compo-

ed. Saul M. Olyan, SBL Resources for Biblical Study 71 (Atlanta: Society of Biblical Literature, 2012), 195–216.
12 Catherine Bell, "The Ritualization of Texts and Textualization of Ritual in the Codification of Taoist Literature", *History of Religions* 27 (1988), 366–92 (here 368–69).

sition, there is evidence of harmonization and schematization, the justification for which appears to be textual. Did Leviticus 23's harmonization of various instructions about firstfruits offerings exist as a ritual complex before the Holiness Code? And was it subsequently practiced? MacDonald's inclusion of the Temple Scroll within his analysis brings these issues into sharp focus. The various first-fruit ceremonies in the Temple Scroll appear to have no relation to the agricultural seasons, and are only explicable as a rigid application of a fifty-day cycle. Yet, if the scribes who composed the Holiness Code are the very same group who are controlling the temple worship, we may have to reckon with a complex two-way interaction between textual innovation and ritual practice.

Challenges to Discerning Ritual Innovation

The arguments of Frevel and MacDonald trouble the task of recovering rituals in ancient Israel and early Judaism. It is not just that texts are not rituals, but that even the texts purporting to describe rituals may not be describing a ritual that was ever practiced. In the words of Frevel, it is perhaps not a matter of ritual innovation, but of ritual *and* innovation. Ian Werrett's essay raises a different set of troubling issues for the relationship between ritual and innovation. Werrett assesses the arguments that the distinctive burial practices evidenced at Qumran stem from the sect's disctinctive ritual positions on impurity or aspects of its theology. Evidence from other cemeteries in the region shows that the shaft-style burials at Qumran were not unique. It seems increasingly likely that the sects' manner of burying their dead was not due to any cultic, ritual or religious reason.

What Frevel, MacDonald and Werrett's essays have in common is an insistence that we carefully examine the evidence that we have and that we refuse to allow ourselves to be contrained by existing intellectual paradigms. The potential of thinking in terms of ritual innovation lies precisely at this point: it encourages us to think about possibilities beyond those presented to us on the surface of the text. If we allow for the possibility of ritual innovation, new interpretive possibilities and new intellectual questions are opened up.

Saul M. Olyan
Two Types of Ritual Innovation for Profit

Though rarely discussed, biblical representations of ritual innovation are relatively commonplace. There are examples of innovation through ritual non-
conformity, as in 2Sam 12:15 – 23, where David ceases mourning at the death of
his child because, as he explains to his astonished courtiers, nothing is to be
gained from mourning after a death.[1] There are cases of ritual innovation
through the fusion of diametrically-opposed and normally incompatible rites,
as in Jer 41:4 – 5, where lacerated pilgrims with torn garments and shaved beards
travel to the site of the destroyed Jerusalem temple bearing offerings.[2] There are
instances of ritual innovation by means of elevating established, regional sanctuaries to national status and changing the date of an established festival, as Jeroboam is said to do in 1Kgs 12:25 – 30 and 32; or by including otherwise excluded
foreigners in the cult, as Yhwh does according to Isa 56:6 – 7.[3] In some cases, ritual innovation is clearly instrumental, producing something of value for the ritual innovator, as in Jeroboam's cultic actions, the stated goal of which is to divert
pilgrims away from Jerusalem and thereby preserve his new kingdom's inde-
pendence. In other cases, the innovative ritual action profits the actor directly
in no evident way, as in the case of the pilgrims mourning the destruction of
the temple in Jer 41:4 – 5. (Though the ritual actors in this instance do not benefit
personally from their actions, these nonetheless realize and signal cultic collapse, so they are not without a purpose.[4]) Some attempts at ritual innovation
are represented as successful; others are resisted effectively according to our
texts. Of the many types of ritual innovation with an instrumental purpose in

---

1 A second example of ritual innovation through ritual non-conformity is 2Sam 19:1 – 9, in
which David privileges his personal feelings over his ritual obligations, mourning for his dead
rebel son Absalom even though rejoicing after the army's victory over Absalom's troops is
expected.
2 On the pilgrims' combination of the antithetical rites of mourning and rejoicing in their persons and its effect of signaling the collapse of the cult, see my argument in Saul M. Olyan, *Biblical Mourning: Ritual and Social Dimensions* (Oxford: Oxford University Press, 2004), 126 – 29.
3 Some of the claims made by the Deuteronomists about Jeroboam's innovations are doubtful
and even ludicrous (e.g., attributing Yhwh's saving acts in Egypt to bull gods), while others
make sense for a newly established king of a newly independent state (e.g., establishing national sanctuaries to keep pilgrims and their wealth in his kingdom). On the Deuteronomistic polemic against Jeroboam, see Frank Moore Cross, Jr., *Canaanite Myth and Hebrew Epic* (Cambridge,
MA: Harvard University Press, 1973), 73 – 75.
4 On this, see Olyan, *Biblical Mourning*, 126 – 29.

biblical narrative, I shall focus on two, both of which profit the ritual innovator at the expense of others if they are successful: (1) Innovation through the usurpation of another party's ritual privileges, as in 2Chr 26:16–21; Num 16:1–17:5; 1Sam 2; and Mal 1; and (2) innovation by means of the creative manipulation of established rites, as in 2Sam 10:1–5; 16:13 and Neh 13:25. That which is gained through successful ritual innovation might include material items of value such as high-quality meat or less tangible goods such as enhanced social or cultic status, honor, or holiness. Failed attempts at ritual innovation for profit might result in disgrace, marginalization, or even death for the would-be innovator.

Innovation by means of attempting to usurp the ritual privileges of another party is a relatively well-attested theme in biblical narratives concerning the cult. In some texts, the would-be innovator is a non-priestly or allegedly non-priestly outsider seeking to secure distinct priestly privileges such as the right to present the incense offering or exclusive priestly qualities such as holiness. In other texts, innovators are priests attempting to withhold from Yhwh that which is rightfully his or remove Yhwh from his preeminent place in the order of the distribution of sacrificial portions. Such attempts at ritual innovation through usurpation are typically condemned by our texts, whose authors seek either to defend exclusive priestly claims against challenges posed by others, or cast priestly or other adversaries as corrupt and therefore, illegitimate, on account of their practices. The condemnatory voice of Yhwh and the often violent punishments he is said to impose on offenders are not infrequently utilized in these narratives to underscore the claims of their authors, with attempted usurpation cast as a crime warranting cursing, disease, or death as a punishment.

My first example of ritual innovation through usurpation is the narrative of Judean King Uzziah's attempt to present the incense offering in the Jerusalem temple (2Chr 26:16–21). As a result of pride to the point of destruction, Uzziah is said to commit sacrilege (מעל) against Yhwh by entering the temple in order to burn incense on the incense altar. The priests of the temple challenge the king as follows: "It is not your privilege, Uzziah, to burn incense to Yhwh, but that of the Aaronide priests, who are sanctified to burn incense. Go forth from the sanctuary for you have committed sacrilege...".[5] In response to their words, Uzziah becomes enraged, but Yhwh causes skin disease (צרעת) to break out immediately on his forehead and he is removed from the temple in haste, a dire threat to its sanctity. The narrative concludes by noting that Uzziah remained afflicted with skin disease, and therefore separated from the temple, for the rest of his life. According to this text, Uzziah's attempt to burn incense

---

5 All translations in this essay are my own.

in the temple constitutes sacrilege, a crime against a holy item; unlike the Aaronide priests who are sanctified and therefore privileged to manipulate holy items such as incense, Uzziah has no such holy status and therefore no business attempting to usurp priestly privilege.[6] Though not stated directly, the narrative is likely suggesting that Uzziah has made a tacit claim to priestly holiness by his actions, a claim the text clearly rejects. That Uzziah's punishment is severe and comes from Yhwh buttresses the exclusivity of priestly privilege advanced by the narrator: even kings cannot successfully claim it. The punishment, perpetual skin disease, renders Uzziah unfit not only for the priesthood, but even to function as a worshiper in the temple complex. Thus, by claiming cultic status and privileges that he was not entitled to, Uzziah ends up with far less than he had to begin with. What did Uzziah stand to gain from his attempt to usurp the incense offering? If he had been successful, his claim to priestly holiness and priestly privileges would have been upheld and the honour that accrues to priests would also have been his. But he was not.

The story of Korah's rebellion in Num 16:1–17:5 is much like the narrative of Uzziah's attempt to usurp the priestly incense offering. In both texts, it is priestly holiness and the right to burn incense that is at issue, with non-priestly or allegedly non-priestly outsiders making a claim to priestly holiness and privilege. The Korah story, set in the wilderness, pits Korah and other non-Aaronide Levites against Aaron and Moses. Moses suggests an incense-burning contest before Yhwh in order to determine who is holy and worthy of priestly service (16:5,7). Yhwh reacts by destroying Korah and his confederates with fire (16:35) and orders that their censers be made into an altar plate to serve as a reminder to the Israelites that no non-Aaronide may burn incense before Yhwh without suffering the fate of Korah (17:5). P, the text's author, advocates an exclusively Aaronide priesthood and relegates other priestly clans to a subservient status as second-class cultic servants whom P calls "Levites".[7] The narrative serves the interests of P and other Aaronides by portraying Yhwh not only supporting their claims to exclusivity with respect to holiness and priestly privilege, but incinerating anyone who might challenge such claims. Had Yhwh accepted the in-

---

6 Lev 5:14–19 speaks of accidental sacrilege requiring an אשם offering. See also Ezra 9:2,4; 10:2,10,19 for intermarriage with non-Judeans cast as a crime against Judean holiness (מעל) requiring reparation with an אשם (reading *אֲשָׁמָם for the apparently corrupt MT אֲשֵׁמִים in 10:19). In texts such as Josh 7, the penalty for sacrilege is death for the offender and his household.
7 That Korah is the eponymous ancestor of a priestly clan is suggested by Num 26:58a, as others have noted (e.g., Cross, *Canaanite Myth*, 206). For a discussion of attempts to contextualize the conflict of Num 16:1–17:5, see Joachim Schaper, *Priester und Leviten im achämenidischen Juda*, FAT 31 (Tübingen: Mohr Siebeck, 2000), 298–300.

cense offering of Korah and his fellow Levites, the text suggests that their claim to holiness and priestly status would have been confirmed and their social and cultic status would have been elevated as a result. But Korah's claim to holiness and priestly status is portrayed as an illegitimate usurpation and punished with extreme severity.

A different usurpation dynamic is to be found in 1Sam 2:12–17,27–30,31–36 and Mal 1:6–14. In these texts, it is not outsiders or alleged outsiders who are portrayed attempting to usurp priestly privileges through ritual innovation but priests themselves who seek to withhold from Yhwh that which is legitimately his or place themselves ahead of Yhwh in the hierarchy of cultic precedence. In 1Sam 2:12–17, the sons of Eli, who are described as "worthless" and who are said not to "know Yhwh", send their servants to take portions of meat from worshipers at Shiloh before the fat, Yhwh's portion, has been burned to him. The worshiper who objects to this usurping ritual innovation is threatened with force should he not hand over the priests' portion when it is demanded. Thus, says the text, the servants of the priests have "despised the offering of Yhwh" and their sin "is exceedingly great before Yhwh". First Samuel 2:12–17 seems also to suggest that the priests take more than their share of meat and their demand that the meat they receive be raw is also presented as a departure from the ritual norm. Verses 27–30, for their part, speak of how Yhwh has been dishonoured by the Elide priests and how his rightful portion of firstfruits has been plundered by them.[8] As a result of this corrupt behaviour, Yhwh promises the Elide priests that they will suffer and that their line will be displaced by another priestly house on which they will be dependent (2:31–36). As with 2Chr 26:16–21 and Num 16:1–17:5, these attempts at ritual innovation through usurpation of the legitimate rights of another—in this case, Yhwh himself— are met with opposition and condemnation from Yhwh, who punishes the offenders and their descendants with shortened life spans (vv. 31–32) and diminution of status and honour in the form of dependency, poverty and marginalization (v. 36; see also v. 30 where Yhwh states, "those who despise me will be diminished"). Although the Elides sought to place themselves above Yhwh in the hierarchy of cultic precedence and enrich themselves materially at Yhwh's expense and, evidently, at the expense of the worshiper, they end up poor and dishonoured as a result. This attack on the Elides evidently stems from circles sympathetic to the claims

---

8 In contrast, other texts maintain that the firstfruits belong to the priests (e.g., Num 18:12–13; Deut 18:4; Ezek 44:30). See further Saul M. Olyan, *Rites and Rank: Hierarchy in Biblical Representations of Cult* (Princeton: Princeton University Press, 2000), 141 n. 111.

of the "faithful priest" whom Yhwh promises to raise up to replace the Elides (v. 35), whoever that might have been.[9]

Like 1Sam 2:12–17,27–30,31–36, Mal 1:6–14 speaks of priests who withhold from Yhwh that which is rightfully his, in this case sacrificial animals that are in good health and are without physical defects (מומים). The priests, described as "those who despise [Yhwh's] name" (v. 6), have instead presented blind, lame, sick and mutilated animals at Yhwh's altar, animals cast as inferior by the text, and not fit for sacrifice to the deity.[10] Like the corrupt sons of Eli and their servants in 1Sam 2, the priests of the Jerusalem temple are presented in Mal 1:6–14 as ritual innovators who profit from illegitimate gain at Yhwh's expense. Not only will Yhwh not accept the inferior offerings they present (v. 10); he curses those who withhold sacrificial animals of superior quality for themselves and offer him damaged animals (משחת) in their place (v. 14).[11] The acts of the priests are cast as an affront to Yhwh's status as a "great king" whose "name is awesome among the nations" (v. 14; see also v. 11). Not unlike the narratives of attempted usurpation in 2Chr 26, Num 16:1–17:5 and 1Sam 2, Mal 1 portrays Yhwh not only opposing the innovative ritual actions of the priests with strong words but punishing the offenders, in this instance by means of a curse (v. 14).

A second type of ritual innovation which profits the innovator at the expense of another party is innovation through creatively manipulating conventional rites, as in 2Sam 10:1–5; 16:13 and Neh 13:25. In the case of this type of innovation, benefit for the innovator may come in the form of humiliating a rival, enemy or oppressor and gaining honour and enhanced status by so doing. The innovating agent may also profit in other, more concrete ways from breaking established political ties, forging new ties or maintaining political autonomy through innovative rites. In some of the examples I discuss, gain is achieved

---

9 The text is not clear about the identity of the "faithful priest" who is to receive from Yhwh "an enduring house" and who will walk before Yhwh's anointed always, but many scholars assume he is Zadok (e. g., Cross, *Canaanite Myth*, 202–3; P. Kyle McCarter, Jr., *I Samuel. A New Translation with Introduction, Notes & Commentary*, AB 8 [Garden City, NY: Doubleday, 1980], 92–93; Deborah W. Rooke, *Zadok's Heirs: The Role and Development of the High Priesthood in Ancient Israel* [Oxford: Oxford University Press, 2000], 57 and n. 27).

10 Mal 1:8,13. The text also casts the rejected sacrificial beasts as "polluted food" (לחם מגאל) in v. 7 and speaks of the pollution of Yhwh's "table" in v. 12, presumably a result of contact with the inferior offerings. The casting of sacrificial animals with defects and other deficiencies as polluted and polluting is apparently an innovation of Malachi, as I have argued elsewhere (Olyan, *Rites and Rank*, 105).

11 In v. 14, it is specifically those who make a vow and sacrifice a damaged animal when they have another available who are cursed.

through coercive, even violent ritual acts.[12] In contrast to the instances of attempted ritual innovation through usurpation of the privileges or status of others, the examples of innovation by means of creatively manipulating established rites for profit do not involve claiming privileges or status belonging to another party, though the enhancement of the innovator's status in other ways (e. g., increased honour through shaming an adversary) is nonetheless evident.

Second Samuel 10:1–5 is my first example of ritual innovation for profit by means of the creative manipulation of conventional rites. In this instance, mourning at a royal court becomes the context for humiliating an ally and thereby terminating a treaty relationship. Nahash, king of Ammon has died, and David, conforming to his treaty obligations, sends emissaries to the Ammonite court to serve as "comforters" (מנחמים) to his son and successor Hanun, thereby honouring the dead king (v. 3). After Ammonite courtiers accuse David's embassy of an intent to spy, his representatives are seized and publicly humiliated: their beards (or half their beards, according to MT) are forcibly shaven and their buttocks and genitals exposed. Then the Ammonites expel them and they return to Judah deeply shamed. The actions of the Ammonites are hostile and creatively manipulate normal mourning rites such as shaving and tearing garments which the comforters would be expected to undertake themselves.[13] Instead of the comforter shaving his own beard, it is done to him by force, and in a grotesque way according to MT; rather than the comforter tearing his own garment, the garment is forcibly cut in half by the Ammonites, exposing the buttocks and genital area to the comforter's shame.[14] David orders his representatives, described as "exceedingly humiliated", to remain in Jericho until their beards "have sprouted" and then return to Jerusalem (v. 5). The Ammonites, for their part, understand that these acts of violent humiliation have made them "odious" (באש) to David and are grounds for war, which follows immedi-

---

12 See further Saul M. Olyan, "Theorizing Violence in Biblical Ritual Contexts: The Case of Mourning Rites", in *Social Theory and the Study of Israelite Religion: Essays in Retrospect and Prospect*, ed. Saul M. Olyan, RBS 71 (Atlanta: Society of Biblical Literature, 2012), 169–80, in which I explore the violent dimensions of the ritual action depicted in 2Sam 10:1–5; 2Sam 16:5–13; Neh 13:25 and Isa 50:4–11 and its social ramifications. A number of observations made initially in this essay are further developed here specifically as they relate to ritual innovation for profit.
13 As in Job 2:11–13, where Job's comforters weep, tear their garments, strew dust upon their heads and sit with Job on the ground.
14 On the shame of such exposure, see Saul M. Olyan, "Honor, Shame and Covenant Relations in Ancient Israel and its Environment", *JBL* 115 (1996): 201–18 (here 213 and n. 37). I note on p. 213 that the Ammonites manipulate and distort conventional mourning gestures in order to shame David's emissaries, thus anticipating to some degree the argument of this essay.

ately according to the text. What might be gained from humiliating an ally in this aggressive manner? The termination of an evidently undesirable treaty relationship, to be sure, and possibly the securing of new and better allies. Furthermore, if the Ammonites can get away with dishonouring David and his embassy, they very likely gain enhanced status and honour for themselves. Just as victory in battle humiliates the vanquished (2Sam 19:4) and increases the honour of the victor (2Kgs 14:10), so humiliation of an enemy or rival in a ritual setting very likely enhances the perpetrator's status. In this instance, the exposure of the "nakedness" of David's emissaries not only represents a manipulation of an established mourning rite, but may also be intended to suggest military defeat for Israel when David responds, given that nudity is not infrequently imposed on vanquished prisoners in ancient West Asia.[15]

Second Samuel 16:13 describes a second example of ritual innovation for profit through creatively manipulating established rites. And as in 2Sam 10:1–5, it is a mourning rite that is manipulated. The context is David's flight from Jerusalem as Absalom's army approaches. At Bahurim, Shimi, a Saulide, appears, cursing David and stoning him and those accompanying him according to 2Sam 16:5–6. As Shimi walks along the ridge above David, he continues to curse and stone the king, and the text adds in v. 13 that Shimi throws dirt at him (וְעִפַּר בֶּעָפָר). Cursing is a ritual act one might expect from an enemy, and Shimi's stoning likely suggests that David is worthy of death for his crimes against the House of Saul.[16] But tossing dirt on David appears to be a creative manipulation of a mourning rite one normally does to oneself when one mourns or comforts the mourner, as Job's comforters do to themselves in Job 2:12. As a comforter, strewing dirt or ashes on oneself is an act of affiliation or confirmation of a pre-existing bond between parties. By tossing dirt on David, Shimi rejects any kind of positive association with him. Were Shimi interested in affiliating or confirming pre-existing bonds, he would have been in mourning himself as is David's loyal courtier Hushay, who has tossed dirt on his own head and torn his garments when he comes to meet David according to 2Sam 15:32. What might Shimi gain from his creative manipulation of the mourning rite of dirt tossing? Certainly, such behaviour, like stoning and cursing, would suggest Shimi's rejection of all ties with David and his stance as David's enemy. Given that it is a contemptuous ritual act, it would likely also add to David's humiliation and enhance Shimi's status if he can get away with it, as Abishay, David's command-

---

15 "Honor, Shame, and Covenant Relations", 213 and n. 37. Isa 20:4 envisions nudity imposed by Assyria on a vanquished Egypt and Kush; Amos 2:16 speaks of defeated soldiers fleeing nude from the scene of battle.
16 See further my discussion in "Theorizing Violence", 175 and n. 26.

er, evidently understands with respect to Shimi's cursing: "Why should this dead dog curse my lord the king? Let me cross over that I might remove his head!" (v. 9).

A third example of the creative manipulation of established rites for profit is to be found in Neh 13:25 and it too concerns the exploitation of a conventional mourning rite. Nehemiah, engaged in a covenant lawsuit (ריב) with intermarried rivals, curses them, strikes some of them, pulls out their hair and forces an anti-intermarriage oath on them. That the context is judicial is suggested by the mention of the lawsuit and the imposed oath. Though it is likely that all of Nehemiah's acts in this setting are ritually significant, one action in particular suggests creative manipulation of an established rite: the pulling out of the hair of Nehemiah's opponents (מרט).[17] Nehemiah's act of forcefully depilating his rivals appears to be yet another case of an aggressive agent imposing a mourning rite on a rival or enemy which is normally performed by a mourner on himself. Thus, it is not unlike the manipulation of mourning rites by the Ammonites in 2Sam 10 and by Shimi in 2Sam 16. In this instance, Nehemiah's pro-intermarriage opponents are forced to adopt Nehemiah's anti-intermarriage position and to assume a ritual stance of penitential mourning on account of their past behaviour, with their new ideological position realized and communicated through their missing hair and anti-intermarriage oath-taking. In effect, the rivals now signal regret for their intermarriages as well as their new anti-intermarriage position through their appearance as penitential mourners.[18] What does Nehemiah gain from his manipulation of the mourning rite of depilation? Through this ritual act and the others he has undertaken, Nehemiah has forcibly turned rivals into allies, thereby strengthening his support network and his ideological position. Though the text does not say so explicitly, Nehemiah has likely also gained honour for himself by humiliating his opponents through imposing penitential depilation on them as well as by cursing them, beating them and forcing them to take the anti-intermarriage oath.

I have addressed here two types of ritual innovation which benefit the innovator at the expense of others if they are successfully undertaken: Innovation by means of usurping another's ritual privileges, as in 2Chr 26:16–21; Num 16:1–17:5; 1Sam 2; and Mal 1; and innovation through creatively manipulating established rites, as in 2Sam 10:1–5; 16:13 and Neh 13:25. Both types of innovation have an aggressive dimension in common: agents either lay claim to ritual priv-

---

17 The verb מרט is used elsewhere for both the pulling out of head hair and beard hair in a penitential mourning context (Ezra 9:3).

18 Some aspects of this argument are anticipated in my essay "Theorizing Violence", 177–78.

ileges not their own, thereby challenging the claims of others, or they manipulate conventional rites creatively in order to enhance their honour or to gain in more tangible ways (e. g., supporters for their agendas) at the expense of another party. The fundamental difference between these two types of ritual innovation for profit is that innovation through creative manipulation of established rites does not involve usurping privileges or status belonging to another party. Instead, the manipulating agent profits by enhancing his status in other ways (e. g., increasing his honour by shaming an adversary, rival or oppressor). These are but two types of ritual innovation which benefit the innovator. Further exploration of this topic is necessary as we seek to theorize ritual innovation in its biblical representation.

James W. Watts
From Ark of the Covenant to Torah Scroll: Ritualizing Israel's Iconic Texts

The builders of Jerusalem's Second Temple made a remarkable ritual innovation. They left the holy of holies empty, if sources from the end of the Second Temple period are to be believed.[1] They apparently rebuilt the other furniture of the temple, but did not remake the ark of the covenant that, according to tradition, had occupied the inner sanctum of Israel's desert tabernacle and of Solomon's Temple.

The fact that the ark of the covenant went missing has excited speculation ever since. It is not my intention to pursue that further here.[2] Instead, I want to consider how biblical literature dealt with this ritual innovation. Why did the Pentateuch, a Second-Temple-era work at least in its final form, describe in elaborate detail the manufacture and use of a ritual object (Exod 25:10 – 22; 37:1 – 9; 40:20 – 21; Lev 16:12 – 16) that did not exist in its own time? How did this Torah support and validate Second Temple rituals that deviated from its prescriptions in such a central way? My thesis is that the Pentateuch was shaped to lay the basis for Torah scrolls to replace the ark of the covenant as the iconic focus of Israel's worship.

1. Ritual Replacements for the Ark of the Covenant

It might appear that the temple replaced the ark as the central focal point of worship, because the ark disappeared into Solomon's temple (1Kgs 8:6 – 8) and never

---

1 Josephus, *J.W.* 5.5.5; Tacitus, *Hist.* 5.9. Note also its omission from the account of the temple's rededication in the second century BCE in 1Macc 4:49 – 51. Josephus and 1Macc insist that the rest of the interior furniture – the menorah, the incense altar, and the table of show-bread – were present inside the Hellenistic-era Temple.
2 For a summary of both academic and popular theories and a sober evaluation of them, see John Day, "Whatever Happened to the Ark of the Covenant?", in *Temple and Worship in Biblical Israel*, ed. John Day, LHBOTS 422 (London: T&T Clark, 2007): 250 – 70. For discussion of how speculations about the lost ark functioned in late Second Temple Judaism, see Steven Weitzman, *Surviving Sacrilege: Cultural Persistence in Jewish Antiquity* (Cambridge, MA: Harvard University Press, 2005), 25 – 28.

re-emerged in stories about later events. The temple clearly stands as a locus of
YHWH's presence in texts relating events of both the First and Second Temple
periods, just as the ark does in stories of earlier times. The temple more obviously, however, replaced the tabernacle. Both the Deuteronomistic History and
Chronicles say so explicitly (2Sam 7:2,7; 1Kgs 5:5; 1Chr 22:19). Stories in which
the ark appears usually also mention the tabernacle or temple, rather than presenting ark and shrine as equivalent to each other (1Sam 3:3; 4:3; 2Sam 6:17; 1Kgs
8:4 – 9; 2Chr 35:3), and 1 Kings implies that the Tabernacle was deposited inside
Solomon's new temple (1Kgs 8:4). The same can be said of Torah scrolls: outside
the Pentateuch, their mention frequently accompanies an emphasis on the temple (e. g. 2Kgs 22:8; 2Chr 34:15; 1Macc 1:54 – 61; Sir 24:10, 23; Acts 7:44 – 53).[3] According to biblical and post-biblical texts, the ritual change between pre-exilic
and post-exilic Israel did not involve the role of the temple, which they claim remained the same. Instead, the change involved the forms of the iconic texts that
were kept inside those temples, and the absence of the ark.

The ark's disappearance necessarily forced changes in traditional ritual
practices. What replaced the ritual functions of the ark? The answer to that question varies depending on which of its ritual functions we consider. P's rules for
offerings require that the blood of bull and goat sin offerings be sprinkled on the
ark's cover every year on Yom Kippur (Lev 16:14 – 15). According to the Mishnah
(m. Yoma 5:2), when Second-Temple-era high priests entered the holy of holies on
Yom Kippur, they performed the blood ritual on the exposed bedrock. This
"foundation stone" (שתייה) was believed to be the place where the ark had previously rested inside Solomon's Temple. (This may be the same outcrop that is
enshrined today in the Dome of the Rock.)

The ark, however, also served other ritual functions. It represented God's
presence in Israel, perhaps as God's throne or footstool as suggested by the
title, "the ark of the covenant of YHWH of Hosts who sits enthroned upon the
cherubim" (1Sam 4:4; cf. 2Sam 6:2; 1Chr 13:6). Like the images and symbols
that represented the presence of gods in other ancient cultures, the ark could
be paraded in public (Num 10:33 – 36; Josh 3; 2Sam 6) and could even accompany
Israel's armies to war (Josh 6; 1Sam 4; cf. Num 14:44). The ark also served as a
repository for Israel's most sacred relics. It contained the covenant tablets written by God (Exod 25:16; 40:20; Deut 10:1 – 5). Either inside or beside it were kept a

---

3 Ezra and Nehemiah complicate this generalization. On the one hand, the books emphasize
efforts to rebuild the temple as well as Ezra's role in bringing the Torah from Babylon and reading it to the people. On the other hand, they separate the ceremonies of Torah reading from temple rituals. For discussion, see James W. Watts, "Scripturalization and the Aaronides", *JHS* 13
(2013). http://www.jhsonline.org/Articles/article_186.pdf.

jar of manna (Exod 16:32–34) and Aaron's flowering rod (Num 17:10), as well as a Torah scroll (Deut 31:9,26; however, 1Kgs 8:9 denies that the ark contained anything but the tablets). These processional and reliquary functions could not be performed by exposed bedrock inside the temple.

Neither the Pentateuch nor any other biblical text addresses the ritual problem of the ark's absence directly. Unlike other rituals modified because of circumstances, such as David and Solomon's decision to build a stone temple to replace the tabernacle (2Sam 7; 1Kgs 5; 1Chr 22; 2Chr 2), or Ahaz's redesign of the temple altar (2Kgs 16:10–18), or the expansion of the personnel for slaughtering offerings to accommodate the large numbers at Hezekiah's Passover (2Chr 30), or the Maccabees' decision to store away the defiled altar and build a new one (1Macc 4:44–47), no ancient narrative describes and explains the decision to leave the holy of holies empty. The account of rebuilding the temple in the book of Ezra emphasizes the Persian rulers' commitment to restore to the Jerusalem temple all "the gold and silver vessels of the house of God which Nebuchadnezzar took" (Ezra 5:14–15; 6:5), but its inventory only includes tableware (1:8–11).[4] The books of Ezra and Nehemiah do not mention the ark or the rest of the temple's special furniture.

We can only speculate then about why the Second Temple's inner sanctum was left empty. It is possible that this decision reflects exegesis of Pentateuchal texts. Deuteronomy insists that God wrote the second set of tablets as well as the first set that Moses broke (Deut 10:4–5, cf. Exod 34:28). On that basis, post-exilic Judeans may have believed that the tablets could not be reconstructed by humans. Of course, the manna and the flowering rod were also irreplaceable. Perhaps they thought that there was no point in rebuilding the ark without these relics to put inside. Second Temple Judeans were apparently willing to tolerate an empty holy of holies, but not an empty ark of the covenant. Their reluctance may indicate that the prevailing understanding of the ark was that it served pri-

---

4 So also 1Esd 2:10–15. Other Second-Temple-period texts (1Esd 4:44,57; 6:17–26; 8:17,55; Dan 1:1–2; 5:2–3,23; Jdt 4:3) frequently mention the Babylonian's appropriation of the temple vessels which the Persians returned. They use the theme of the temple vessels to emphasize ritual continuity between First and Second Temples, but do not mention the ark or the other interior furniture. See Peter R. Ackroyd, "The Temple Vessels: A Continuity Theme", in *Studies in the Religion of Ancient Israel*, VTSup, 23 (Leiden: Brill, 1972), 166–81; Isaac Kalimi and James D. Purvis, "King Jehoiachin and the Vessels of the Lord's House in Biblical Literature", *CBQ* 56 (1994): 449–57; and Isaac Kalimi and James D. Purvis, "The Hiding of the Temple Vessels in Jewish and Samaritan Literature", *CBQ* 56 (1994): 679–85.

marily as a reliquary for sacred texts and, perhaps, other sacred objects.[5] In that case, the reliquary had no purpose without tablets to put inside.

Though biblical narratives never confront the problem of the missing ark directly, several prophetic texts suggest metaphorical and spiritual replacements for the ark. Jeremiah 3:16–17 predicts that the ark will not be remade after its destruction by the Babylonians, and proposes that the city of Jerusalem will replace it as "the throne of YHWH". Ezekiel 1 and 10 depict God's real throne as supernaturally portable and surrounded by cherubim (cf. Isa 6). Isaiah 66:1 casts the sky and the earth in the roles of God's throne or footstool. Later, 4Ezra 8:1–2 coped with the destruction of the Second Temple by arguing that the true temple survives in heaven.[6] Seers in the first century CE envisioned angels making incense offerings ceaselessly in the heavenly temple (*T. Levi* 1:22–23) and even imagined the ark installed in its inner sanctum (Rev 11:19).[7] By and large, God's throne has remained in heaven ever since in Jewish and Christian traditions. Such speculations do not, however, provide a substitute for the ark in earthly rituals of procession nor do they replace its reliquary functions.

Narrative accounts from the late Second Temple and the Late Antique periods indicate another ritual replacement for the ark, namely, Torah scrolls. The evidence for this development in Late Antiquity is fairly abundant from rabbinic literature and the physical remains of ancient synagogues. Jews in Late Antiquity displayed portable arks containing scripture scrolls in public processions (m. Ta'an. 2:1). The traditional name for such scroll boxes or cupboards is "ark" (ארון), just like the biblical ark.[8] From the fourth century CE on, the physical re-

5 C. L. Seow, "Ark of the Covenant", *ABD* 1:386–93 argued that P's depicts the ark only as a book reliquary.
6 Weitzman, *Surviving Sacrilege*, 113.
7 Jewish mysticism identifies the divine presence, the *Shekhinah*, as itself "the ark of the covenant, the container of *Yesod*" (Zohar 1:2a,33b,50b,59b,228b; 2:13a,214b,235b,259a–b [Heikh]; 3:199a; Moses de Leon, *Sheqel ha-Quodesh*, 75 [95]; see Daniel Chanan Matt, trans., *The Zohar: Pritzker Edition*, vol. 3 [Stanford, CA: Stanford University Press, 2006], 377, 544). A tradition of Catholic mysticism that dates back to at least the third century CE provides an incarnational twist to ark mysticism by identifying the Virgin Mary as "the living shrine of the Word of God, the Ark of the New and Eternal Covenant" (Pontifical Council for the Pastoral Care of Migrants and Itinerant People, *The Shrine: Memory, Presence and Prophecy of the Living God* [Vatican City: Libreria Editrice Vaticana, 1999], §18; and United States Catholic Conference, *Catechism of the Catholic Church* [New York: Doubleday, 1993], §2676).
8 The use of "ark" (ארון/ארונא) to describe a cabinet containing Torah scrolls appears in a dedicatory inscription in the Dura Europos synagogue (third-century CE), which calls the aedicula in the central wall a "house of the ark" (Steven Fine, *Art and Judaism in the Greco-Roman World* [Cambridge: Cambridge University Press, 2005], 177). The label appears in rabbinic literature in y. Meg. 73d, "the curtain over the ark containing the scrolls is as sacred as the ark itself"

mains of many synagogues contain permanent installations for arks. Arks also appear in Jewish art from the period that frequently shows the scrolls inside.[9] Rabbinic literature tells us that scrolls of scripture, and especially Torah scrolls, were regarded as holy (m. Šabb. 16:1). They conveyed sanctity to the arks that contained them (b. Šabb. 32a) and the buildings in which they were kept (m. Meg. 3:1).[10]

The evidence from the earlier Second Temple period is not so abundant. The letter of Aristeas in the second century BCE labeled the Torah "holy" (ἁγιός) and "divine" (θεῖος),[11] and remarked on the beautiful gold lettering and excellent parchment of the Torah scrolls sent to Egypt for translation.[12] Second Maccabees 8:23 depicted Judah Maccabee using a Torah scroll in the process of arranging his army for battle. It is not clear whether he consults the Torah as an oracular source or has it read aloud to his troops. At any rate, the writers of 2 Maccabees thought a Torah scroll should be present with the army on this occasion.[13] *Tefillin*

(also y. Šabb. 17c). It is also reflected in John Chrysostom's anti-Jewish polemic, which in the fourth century CE emphasized the ritual discontinuity between the ark of the covenant and an ark of the Torah: "What sort of ark (κιβωτός) is it that the Jews now have, where we find no propitiatory, no tablets of law, no Holy of Holies, no veil, no high priests, no incense, no holocaust, no sacrifice, none of the things that made the ark of old holy and august?" (*Adv. Jud.* 6:7 [PG 48:913], quoted in Eric M. Meyers, "The Torah Shrine in the Ancient Synagogue", in *Jews, Christians, and Polytheists in the Ancient Synagogue: Cultural Interaction during the Greco-Roman Period*, ed. S. Fine [New York: Routledge, 1999], 201–23 [here 207]).

9 Lee I. Levine, *The Ancient Synagogue: The First Thousand Years* (New Haven: Yale University Press, 2000), 351–53.

10 Seth Schwartz, *Imperialism and Jewish Society: 200 B.C.E. to 640 C.E.* (Princeton: Princeton University Press, 2009), 234–36, 241–43.

11 *Let. Aris.* 177.

12 *Let. Aris.* 3,5,31,45,313; see Pieter W. van der Horst, "Was the Synagogue a Place of Sabbath Worship Before 70 CE?", in *Jews, Christians, and Polytheists in the Ancient Synagogue: Cultural Interaction during the Greco-Roman Period*, ed. S. Fine (New York: Routledge, 1999), 18–43 (here 35).

13 2Macc 8:23: καὶ Ελεαζαρον, παραναγνοὺς τὴν ἱερὰν βίβλον καὶ δοὺς σύνθημα θεοῦ βοηθείας, "and Eleazar, for reading aloud the sacred book and giving the watchword, 'the help of God'". For the translation "read aloud", see J. Lust, E. Eynikel, and K. Hauspie, *Greek-English Lexicon of the Septuagint*, rev. ed. (Stuttgart: Deutsche Bibelgesellschaft, 2003), 466. For the association of the name Eleazar with God's help, see Exod 1:4. Robert Doran regarded the appearance of Eleazar as a secondary gloss inspired by this association, and noted that the Syriac text makes it explicit that Eleazar reads the scroll (*2 Maccabees*, Hermeneia [Minneapolis: Fortress, 2012], 169, 177). He wondered: "Are we to imagine the scroll being carried into war as was the ark of the covenant in 1 Sam 4:3–5? Or is Judas's reading from the holy scroll a reflection of the command in Deut 17:19 that the king shall read in the law all the days of his life? Note how, in 2Macc 15:9, Judas encourages his soldiers 'from the law and the prophets'. As Judas and

and their parchments were discovered among the Dead Sea Scrolls, which indicate that using Pentateuchal texts as amulets of this kind, and perhaps as *mezuzot*, was already common practice by the first century BCE.[14] There is therefore some evidence that, by late Second Temple times, scrolls and parts of scrolls assumed the role of relics and the processional functions that had previously been performed by the ark of the covenant and the tablets it contained.

One legend explores the theme of the Torah replacing the ark. Second Maccabees 2:1–8 tells of Jeremiah giving the people "the law" before hiding the ark.

> The prophet, after giving them the law, instructed those who were being deported not to forget the commandments of the Lord…He exhorted them that the law should not depart from their hearts…Jeremiah came and found a cave-dwelling [on Mt. Sinai], and he brought there the tent and the ark and the altar of incense; then he sealed up the entrance…He declared, "The place shall remain unknown until God gathers his people together again and shows his mercy." (NRSV)[15]

Stephen Weitzman observed that 2 Maccabees interpreted Jer 3:16 as a command to the prophet rather than a prediction. Doing so encouraged cultural survival through belief in the ark's supernatural survival.[16] Since the ark has been rendered ritually inaccessible, however, this story also mythically encapsulates Jewish historical experience: Torah scrolls remained readily available for reading and memorizing while the ark disappeared.

Second Temple-era literature also attests clearly to the idea that the Torah is a text of divine and heavenly origin like the tablets of the covenant. This motif appears first in extant sources in Sir 24:23 (early second century BCE). Ben Sira describes personified wisdom present with God in heaven since creation (*à la* Prov 8) as ministering "in the holy tent…and established in Zion". He then identifies wisdom specifically with "the book of the covenant of the Most

---

his men are fighting for the sake of the laws (8:21), it is appropriate that these laws be in evidence." (177). Daniel R. Schwartz, *2 Maccabees*, CEJL (Berlin: De Gruyter, 2008), 340, thought that 2Macc 8:23 refers to oracular consultation of the Torah instead, as in 1Macc 3:48.

14 For a recent discussion, see Yehudah B. Cohn, *Tangled Up in Text: Tefillin and the Ancient World*, BJS 351 (Providence: Brown University, 2008), 55–62.

15 2Bar. 6:7–9 credited an angel with hiding the ark. See George Nickelsburg, "Narrative Traditions in the Paralipomena of Jeremiah and 2 Baruch", *CBQ* 35 (1973): 60–8; Marilyn F. Collins, "The Hidden Vessels in Samaritan Tradition", *JSJ* 3 (1972): 97–116; Doran, *2 Maccabees*, 56–58; and the literature cited in note 4 above.

16 Weitzman, *Surviving Sacrilege*, 25–28.

High God, the law that Moses commanded us" (NRSV).[17] By the end of the Second Temple period, the notion that the Torah scroll originated in heaven was widespread (Bar 4:1; Acts 7:53; 'Abot 3:15; cf. 5:6; Gen. Rab. 1:1).[18] Just as God gave Moses the tablets of the commandments, so God gave Moses the Torah that existed in heaven from before the creation of the world.

2. Scrolls in Place of Tablets

The ritual innovation that replaced the tablets and ark with the Torah was anticipated and encouraged by the Pentateuch itself. Pentateuchal passages that speak of the tablets in the ark or the scroll of Torah tend to conflate the contents of tablets and scroll. These conflations have fuelled many reconstructions of the history of the editing of these texts. The prevalence of this ambiguity in various Pentateuchal texts, however, is evidence for the intentional conflation of tablets and scrolls during the redaction of the Pentateuch.

Deuteronomy distinguishes the tablets from the scroll, but also identifies the two kinds of texts. Deuteronomy 9:9–11 describes the tablets as "tablets of the covenant that YHWH made with you" (v. 9) "written by the finger of God" (v. 10 = Exod 31:18), containing "all the words that YHWH had spoken to you (pl) at the mountain out of the fire on the day of the assembly" (v. 10, referring back to 5:1–22). According to Deut 10:1–7, God also wrote the second set of tablets. The emphasis on completeness in 9:10 appears again in the book's description of the Torah scroll. In Deut 31:9, Moses writes down the law and deposits it "with the Levitical priests who carry the ark of the covenant of YHWH and with the elders". Later in that chapter, he also writes a song of warning (31:19,22), then writes "the words of this law (תורה) in a scroll (ספר) to the very end" (31:24) and orders the Levites to place it "beside the ark of the covenant of YHWH (ארון ברית־יהוה)" to serve as a "testimony" (עד) against the Israelites (31:25–26). Interpreters have struggled to distinguish the song from the law in this chapter that

---

17 Michael A. Knibb, "Temple and Cult in Apocryphal and Pseudepigraphal Writings from Before the Common Era", in *Temple and Worship in Biblical Israel*, ed. John Day, LHBOTS 422 (London: T&T Clark, 2007), 401–16 [here 405].

18 For a discussion of the Bible's place among ancient traditions of heavenly books, see Dorina Miller Parmenter, "The Bible as Icon: Myths of the Divine Origins of Scripture", in *Jewish and Christian Scripture as Artifact and Canon*, ed. C. A. Evans and H. D. Zacharias (London: T&T Clark, 2009), 298–310.

describes both of them as testimonies (cf. v. 28) against Israel.[19] What is clear, at any rate, is that the Torah scroll finds its place beside the ark containing the tablets of the covenant, which the scroll also contains – the one physically, the other literarily.

Exodus identifies scroll and tablets to the point of confusion. In Exod 24:7, the words "book (scroll) of the covenant" (ספר הברית) – which appear otherwise only in 2Kgs 23:2,21 – describe the original written form of the covenant containing "all the words of YHWH" (24:4; cf. v. 3: "all the words of YHWH and the commandments [המשפטים]"). Moses writes down this book of the covenant on a scroll even before God can write it on stone. Interpreters debate whether the Book of the Covenant includes the commandments spoken by God or not, a debate that serves to emphasize the text's ambiguity on this point.[20] A few verses later, God promises to write tablets containing "the law and the commandment" (התורה והמצוה; Exod 24:12). Again, the contents of the tablets are ambiguous and interpreters come to different conclusions: do the tablets contain just the Decalogue (Exod 20:2–17), also the Book of the Covenant (Exod 21–23) or the cultic Decalogue (Exod 34:10–26) or something else?[21] The names of these texts and of the ark meld together "testimony" (עדות), "covenant" (ברית), and "law, instruction" (תורה) in ambiguous ways.[22] Even the textual tradition in Exod 24:12 reflects

---

19 For a thorough discussion of this problem, see Jean-Pierre Sonnet, *The Book Within the Book: Writing in Deuteronomy*, BibInt 14 (Leiden: Brill, 1997), who suggested that the emphasis on the completeness of the book in v. 22 means that it contains the song mentioned in v. 19 (p. 159). Sonnet extended his analysis to the rest of the Pentateuch in "'Lorsque Moïse eut achevé d'écrire' (Dt 31,24): une 'théorie narrative' de l'écriture dans le Pentateuque", *RSR* 90 (2002): 509–24.

20 Those who thought it does include Brevard S. Childs (*The Book of Exodus*, OTL [Philadelphia: Westminster, 1974], 505) and William H. C. Propp (*Exodus 19–40*, AB 2A [New York: Doubleday, 2006], 295. Those who thought it does not include Cornelis Houtman (*Exodus*, HCOT, 4 vols. [Leuven: Peeters, 2000], 3:291) and Thomas B. Dozeman (*Exodus*, ECC [Grand Rapids: Eerdmans, 2009], 566).

21 See the summary of the debate in Houtman, *Exodus*, 3: 300–301.

22 Against those who have tried to distinguish the "ark of testimony" from the "ark of the covenant", Seow argued convincingly that the terms are synonymous (Seow, "Ark of the Covenant"). P's designation for the ark, ארן העדת, plays on a root that echoes in various forms throughout its text, as Propp observed: "'ēdût chimes with P's common designation for Israel: (hā)'ēdâ '(the) congregation'. Moreover, the phrase 'ōhel hā'ēdût 'the Testimony Tent' evokes the Tabernacle's frequent designation 'ōhel mô'ēd 'Meeting Tent' (cf. LXX hē skēnē tou martyriou 'the Tent of the Testimony'). While 'ēdâ and mô'ēd both derive from the root y'd 'to meet', another important Priestly theme word is an anagram: yd' 'to know'...Thus the Testimony ('ēdût) Tablets bear witness ('ēd), admonishing (hē'îd) the community ('ēdâ) to fulfill its covenant obligations

this ambiguity: MT "stone tablets" (לחת האבן) followed by *vav* distinguishes the tablets from the "law and commandment" (התורה והמצוה), while SP's omission of *vav* puts them in apposition and identifies them (similarly LXX).[23] In Exod 31:18; 32:15–16, God finally provides the tablets of the testimony (העדת), which Moses then proceeds to break. Moses re-writes the "words of the covenant (הברית), the ten words" on new tablets, which in Exod 34:27–28 seem to be "these words", i.e. the ritual Decalogue that precedes this statement (cf. the similar language in Deut 4:13; 10:4) rather than the words that the people heard God speak from Mount Sinai (Exod 20).

This survey shows that almost every description of the tablets in the Pentateuch works to connect them with Torah scrolls in one way or another. These links do not appear outside the Pentateuch. Instead, the stories of Israel's early history feature the ark (1Sam) which at least 1Kgs 8:9 insists contained the tablets, while stories of Judah's later history feature Torah scrolls (2Kgs; 2Chr; Ezra-Neh). Only in the Pentateuch do the two kinds of texts get juxtaposed and implicitly conflated.[24] The fact that the Pentateuch, especially its redacted form combining D, P and other sources, works so hard to identify ark and scroll suggests that the Pentateuch was itself the engine for ritually replacing the ark with the Torah scroll in the Second Temple period.

3. Scrolls in Place of the Ark of the Covenant

In contrast to the Pentateuch's descriptions of stone tablets whose exact contents interpreters struggle to identify, the Pentateuch is unambiguous about the scroll's contents. The Torah contains *all* the words of God to Moses (Exod 24:4; Deut 31:22), including everything on the tablets. The Pentateuch therefore removes the need for anyone to open the ark to consult the tablets: the Torah already contains the contents of the tablets. In fact, the Hebrew Bible never depicts

---

('ēd[əw]ōt), since God has made himself 'known' (yd') to them and continues to encounter (y'd) them at Meeting (mô'ēd) Tent" (*Exodus 19–40*, 385).

23 See *BHS* and Dozeman, *Exodus*, 584. Childs (*Exodus*, 499) concluded that "the law and the commandment", which confuses the syntax, was added later, perhaps because Deut 5:28–31 suggests that Moses heard additional instructions than those initially heard by the people.

24 Isaiah 30:8, "write it before them on a tablet (לוח) and inscribe it in a scroll (ספר) so that it may be for the time to come as a witness (עד) forever", may attest to a traditional association between the ideas of tablet, scroll and witness/testimony quite apart from the specific instances of the tablets in the ark of the covenant and Torah scrolls. An original and continuing function of written texts is to serve as evidence for adjudicating legal and economic claims (e.g. receipts).

anyone reading the tablets, while it describes or commands public reading of Torah scrolls on five different occasions.[25] The Pentateuch also contains literary elaborations of the ark's other contents. It describes how a jar of manna (Exod 16:34) and Aaron's staff (Num 17:25 [Eng. 17:10]) were deposited "before the testimony" (לפני העדת) "for safekeeping" or "for observing" (למשמרת), the staff to serve as "a sign" (אות) against rebels.[26] Thus it describes the ark functioning as a reliquary containing not only physical texts documenting the covenant but also the manna as physical evidence of YHWH's rescue of Israel and Aaron's flowering staff as physical evidence of the Aaronides' god-given pre-eminence in Israel.[27] In doing so, the Pentateuch presents the textual evidence for the revelation of Torah, both as Decalogues and as larger speeches, as well as for YHWH's deliverance of Israel from Egypt and for YHWH's appointment of the Aaronides as Israel's hereditary priests. Its blessings and curses (Lev 26; Deut 27–30; 32) serve as testimonies and signs warning Israel of the consequences of breaking the covenant.

In each Pentateuchal case, oracular texts portray YHWH emphasizing the evidentiary function of these objects. The manna must be kept "throughout your generations, in order that they may see the food with which I fed you in the wilderness, when I brought you out of the land of Egypt" (Exod 16:32). Aaron's staff must be placed "before the covenant, to be kept as a warning to rebels, so that you may make an end of their complaints against me, or else they will die" (Num 17:10). The scroll of the law must be placed "beside the ark of the covenant of YHWH your God; let it remain there as a witness against you" (Deut 31:26). In the form of Torah scrolls, the Pentateuch thus functions as the physical testimony to YHWH's rescue of Israel (in place of the manna), to the divine origins of the commandments (in place of the tablets), to the rights and responsibilities of the Aaronide priests (in place of Aaron's rod), and to YHWH's promises and threats to Israel (in place of the Mosaic scroll).[28]

---

25 Exod 24:7; Deut 31:11–12; Josh 8:34–35; 2Kgs 22–23; 2Chr 34; Neh 8; see James W. Watts, *Reading Law: The Rhetorical Shaping of the Pentateuch* (Sheffield: Sheffield Academic Press, 1999), 15–31.
26 For traditional and critical explanations for the position of the statement about depositing the manna beside an ark that has not been built yet, see Houtman, *Exodus*, 2:325, who observed that Exod 16:35 is also explicitly proleptic.
27 Reinhard Achenbach noted the prominence of rod and flower motifs in Persian royal iconography to argue that the flowering rod story reflects Persian-period claims for Aaronide pre-eminence (*Die Vollendung der Tora: Studien zur Redaktionsgeschichte des Numeribuches im Kontext von Hexateuch und Pentateuch*, BZABR 3 [Wiesbaden: Harrassowitz, 2003], 127).
28 The Pentateuch adopts and elaborates the form of a rhetorical argument starting with stories of the (divine) king's past beneficence, lists of obligations governing Israel's present behavior,

The Torah scroll can therefore function as a literary reliquary that replaces the ark's reliquary function of preserving testimony. In the stories of Josiah and Ezra reading a Torah scroll aloud to the people, the scroll functions in precisely this way to convict the people of their sins in failing to observe the festivals it mandates (Passover and Sukkot respectively). The Torah thus serves as "a witness, testimony" (עֵד) and as "a sign" (אוֹת). The Torah scroll functions as a material icon as well, ritually displayed and processed as a legitimizing symbol. Doing so legitimized the regulations of Jerusalem's temple and priesthood. Later its authority gradually spread over Jewish and Samaritan legal institutions and family life.[29] The biblical accounts of Israel's pre-exilic apostasy and post-exilic repentance suggest implicitly that Torah scrolls proved much more effective than the ark in focusing the people's attention on the covenant with God.

Thus attention to the ritual function of Pentateuchal texts that portray tablets, ark, and scrolls shows that the scrolls did not replace the tablets so much as they replaced the ark of the covenant that contained the tablets. Once Moses deposited the tablets in the ark, no story tells of their re-emergence. They are manipulated only within their reliquary, the ark of the covenant, just as medieval Christians in Armenia and Ireland displayed and carried sacred texts within book shrines. These reliquaries simultaneously hid and displayed the texts they contained. Within their reliquaries, sacred books could be processed, venerated, and even lead armies into battle.[30] Only moderns who think textual power comes only from reading would dream of opening them to read what is inside.

In fact, biblical literature may have partly inspired this modern tendency to emphasize the semantic meaning of texts rather than their iconic or performative dimensions. The Pentateuch contains the tablets just as the ark contained them. However, both the ark and the Pentateuch are much more than just the tablets. Just as the golden ark surmounted by cherubim is far more elaborate in Exod 25:10 – 22 then the wooden box described by Deut 10:1– 3, so too the five-book Pentateuch contains far more than just stories about the tablets, manna, rod and scroll. Both ark and Pentateuch appear as baroque elaborations of the orig-

---

and sanctions describing the future consequences of fulfilling those obligations or not (see Watts, *Reading Law*, 36 – 48). The contents of the ark of the covenant can be understood as iconic representations of those stories (the manna), lists (the tablets and rod) and sanctions (also the tablets and rod are described as "a witness" or "testimony" [עֵד / עֵדוּת] and "a sign" [אוֹת]).

29 James W. Watts, "Ritual Legitimacy and Scriptural Authority", *JBL* 124 (2005): 401 – 417 = *Ritual and Rhetoric in Leviticus* (Cambridge: Cambridge University Press, 2007), 193 – 217.

30 See Michelle P. Brown, "Images to be Read and Words to be Seen", in *Iconic Books and Texts*, ed. J. W. Watts (London: Equinox, 2013), 93 – 118 (here 110 – 11).

inal revelation, in iconographic and literary media respectively. Both have repeatedly tempted modern historians to try to reconstruct simpler originals.

The Pentateuch, however, makes the tablets available publicly more than the ark did. The ark was an icon that could be displayed and venerated. A Torah scroll is also an icon that can be displayed and venerated in exactly that way, but the scroll can also be read. Reading the scrolls aloud made the tablets more directly available to listeners and readers than the ark ever could.

In shifting from iconic text hidden in its ark reliquary to displayed text read regularly to all Israel, Deuteronomy changed Judean religious texts from esoteric to exoteric. This was a ritual innovation with long-lasting implications for Western religions. This was not, however, a shift from ritual to text, contrary to a line of interpretation that has prevailed from the ancient rabbis to many contemporary scholars.[31] The contents of the ark already provided textual authorization of the ritual (Exod 34) and, in any case, the ritual continued unchanged (it is claimed) in Jerusalem's Second Temple. What was new was exoteric textual validation of rituals through the regular iconic display and performative reading of the Torah scroll. As a ritualized public text, Torah combined the ritual functions of epic and totem in one and the same thing.[32] The ritual change involved a shift from the iconic ark reliquary to iconic scrolls, which eventually gained their own ark reliquaries.

This shift was not necessitated by changing technologies or ideologies. For millennia, ancient Near Eastern cultures had ritually manipulated scrolls, tablets and the boxes that contained them. The evidence from Egypt is especially clear. From at least the early second millennium BCE on, Egyptians used portable chests topped by statues or images of the god, Anubis, to keep ritual texts as well as cultic implements like scepters and embalming chemicals.[33] Egyptian art also depicts priests holding scrolls aloft in processions and funerary rituals. The Papyrus of Ani (13th–12th centuries BCE) shows a figure holding up an open scroll while the ceremony is performed.[34] A tomb painting from the New Kingdom shows, in the words of David Lorton, "artisans applying the finishing touch-

---

31 For a survey and bibliography, see Watts, "Scripturalization", and Watts, *Leviticus 1–10*, HCOT (Leuven: Peeters, 2013), 517–20.

32 For this conclusion about the effects of ritualizing religious scriptures generally, see James W. Watts, "The Three Dimensions of Scriptures", *Postscripts* 2/2–3 (2006), 135–159 (here 145) = *Iconic Books and Texts*, ed. J. W. Watts (London: Equinox, 2013), 8–30 [19].

33 Harco Willems, *The Coffin of Heqata (Cairo JdE 36418): A Case Study of Egyptian Funerary Culture of the Early Middle Kingdom*, OLA 70 (Leuven: Peeters, 1996), 142–45. The tomb of King Tutankhamun contained a beautifully gilded example (cf. Exod 25:11).

34 Nineteenth Dynasty, ca. 1295–1186 BCE, from Thebes; in the British Museum, EA 10470/6.

es to two anthropoid sarcophagi" while "a man holds an open papyrus on which the words 'performing the Opening of the Mouth' are written".[35] The Brooklyn Oracle Papyrus (651 BCE) depicts a procession of the image of the god Amun-Re in which the chief lector priest reads aloud from a papyrus roll he holds before him.[36]

Evidence like this suggests that tablets, scrolls and text boxes were all subject to ritual manipulation in ancient cultures. Israel's shift from box to scroll exchanged one traditional ritual object for another. This was not what the book of Jeremiah envisioned when it predicted that the ark would not be rebuilt (3:16–17). Jeremiah imagined the ark being replaced by Jerusalem as the throne of YHWH and he dismissed temple worship as ineffective and unnecessary (7:4,12–15,21–23). Elsewhere the book of Jeremiah expects that the covenant will be replaced by one "written on the heart" so that torah instruction is no longer necessary (33:31–34). Though resonating with the elevation of the Jerusalem community in other texts (Isa, Ezek, Ezra–Neh), as the Second Temple period progressed this utopian vision yielded to the pragmatic practice of a textualized torah instruction. Such instruction impressed the covenant "on the heart" through scribal practices very much rooted in textual torah traditions.[37]

Contrary to many reconstructions of religious history that cast scribes as rivals of priests in this period, the priests' monopoly over temple rituals was strengthened by shifting the focus of veneration from the ark of the covenant to the Torah scroll. High priests in Jerusalem rode the rising prestige of both temple and Torah to unprecedented heights of religious and political influence.[38] Only at the end of the Second Temple period did scribal and prophetic challenges to Aaronide priestly precedence gain significant influence in Rabbinic Judaism and early Christianity.

Thus the ark of the covenant evolved into the Torah scroll, displayed and performed for all to see and hear. Both iconography and rhetoric disguised

---

35 David Lorton, "The Theology of the Cult Statues in Ancient Egypt", in *Born in Heaven, Made on Earth: The Making of the Cult Image in the Ancient Near East*, ed. Michael B. Dick (Winona Lake, IN: Eisenbrauns, 1999), 158; a photo of the painting appears in Eberhard Otto, *Die Ägyptische Mundöffnungsritual*, Ägyptische Abhandlungen 3, 2 vols. (Wiesbaden: Harrassowitz, 1960), 2: fig. 13.

36 Brooklyn Museum 47.218.3a–j.

37 See David M. Carr, *Writing on the Tablet of the Heart: Origins of Scripture and Literature* (Oxford: Oxford University Press, 2005).

38 James W. Watts, "The Political and Legal Uses of Scripture", in *The New Cambridge History of the Bible, Volume 1: From the Beginnings to 600*, ed. J. Schaper and J. Carleton Paget (Cambridge: Cambridge University Press, 2013), 345–64; and James W. Watts, *Leviticus 1–10*, 107–19.

this change as continuity, like most other successful ritual innovations.[39] Identification between Decalogue and Torah and between the ark of the covenant built at Sinai and holy arks in every synagogue obscured the transition from esoteric to exoteric sacred texts that took place in the Second Temple period. Fascination with spiritualized arks and the whereabouts of the lost physical ark continues to disguise the ritual innovation by which Torah scrolls replaced the ark as the holiest objects in Jewish worship.

The influence of this ritual innovation reached far beyond Judaism. It shaped the veneration of Gospel codices in ancient Christianity and of pandect Bibles in modern Christian denominations, and provided precedents for the veneration of books of scripture by Muslims and Sikhs as well.[40] Cherished scriptural texts, displayed for all to see and read for all to hear, became a characteristic feature of Western religious rituals.

---

39 On the ubiquity of claims for the unchanging nature of rituals despite constant ritual criticism and change, see Ronald Grimes, *Ritual Criticism: Case Studies in Its Practice, Essays on Its Theory* (Columbia: University of South Carolina Press, 1990), 13–20.
40 See the essays on these traditions and more in James W. Watts, ed., *Iconic Books and Texts* (London: Equinox, 2013).

Reinhard Achenbach

The Empty Throne and the Empty Sanctuary: From Aniconism to the Invisibility of God in Second Temple Theology

1. The Empty Throne in the First Temple

The divine presence in the Solomonic Temple was expressed by two symbols: the empty throne of cherubs, connected to the royal and solar aspects of the Deity, and the ark, the ancient Yahwistic palladium for divination especially in times of war, now described as the "footstool" of God (cf. 2Chr 28:2).[1] In Isaiah's report on the vision of the throne it is already made clear that the shrine itself was not capable of even symbolizing the housing of God, but that it was just a place where the holy *kabôd* (akk. *melammu*) could be imagined and envisioned.[2] There is no proof that in the *debir* there was an anthropomorphic image of the deity; thus we do not know anything about the symbolic representation of divine presence in the inner core of the cult apart from the cherub throne and the ark.[3] However,

---

1 Othmar Keel, *Die Geschichte Jerusalems und die Entstehung des Monotheismus, Teil 1*, Orte und Landschafte der Bibel IV,1, 2 vols. (Göttingen: Vandenhoeck & Ruprecht, 2007), 292–307. A bulla found by R. Reich and E. Shukron close to the Gihon (Reg. 16764, unpublished, cf. Keel, *Die Geschichte Jerusalems*, 304) shows a chair with a solar disc; perhaps this imprint takes up the emblems of the Jerusalem royal temple ideology (Keel, *Die Geschichte Jerusalems*, 302).
2 Friedhelm Hartenstein, *Die Unzugänglichkeit Gottes im Heiligtum: Jesaja 6 und der Wohnort YHWHs in der Jerusalemer Kulttradition*, WMANT 75 (Neukirchen-Vluyn: Neukirchener, 1997); Friedhelm Hartenstein, *Das Angesicht YHWHs: Studien zu seinem höfischen und kultischen Bedeutungshintergrund in den Psalmen und in Exodus 32–34*, FAT 55 (Tübingen: Mohr Siebeck, 2008); Friedhelm Hartenstein, "YHWH und der 'Schreckensglanz' Assurs (Jesaja 8,6–8). Tradition- religionsgeschichtliche Beobachtungen zur 'Denkschrift' Jesaja 6–8", in *Schriftprophetie: Festschrift für Jörg Jeremias zum 65. Geburtstag*, ed. Fritz Hartenstein, Jutta Krispenz, and Aaron Schart (Neukirchen-Vluyn: Neukirchener, 2004): 83–102.
3 Nadav Na'aman, "No Anthropomorphic Graven Image: Notes on the Assumed Anthropomorphic Cult Statues in the Temples of YHWH in the Pre-Exilic Period", *UF* 31 (1999): 391–415; Elizabeth Bloch-Smith, "Solomon's Temple: The Politics of Ritual Space", in *Sacred Time, Sacred Place: Archaeology and the Religion of Israel*, ed. B.M. Gittlen (Winona Lake, IN: Eisenbrauns 2002), 83–94; cf. also Tryggve N.D. Mettinger, "Israelite Aniconism: Developments and Origins", in *The Image and the Book: Iconic Cults, Aniconism, and the Rise of Book Religion in Israel and the Ancient Near East*, ed. Karel van der Toorn, BET 21 (Leuven: Peeters, 1997): 173–204;

this does not preclude the possibility that religious practice was related to a set of deities within a more or less polytheistic pantheon until the time of Josiah and even beyond that, and that they were represented by idols in the hall of the sanctuary (2Kgs 23; Ezek 8; 13; Jer 48). The theology of divine presence in the First Temple was highly synthetic. In the description of YHWH's person, elements of deities related to Uranus, such as El, and of the storm-gods such as Baal or Hadad were combined.[4] In any case the Judahites imagined a heavenly dwelling of the deity with a heavenly throne and a residence on earth for worship and meeting in the horizon of "the face" of YHWH.[5]

2. The Central Sanctuary as the Dwelling-Place of YHWH's Name

Moshe Weinfeld has already seen very clearly that the deuteronomistic theology of the presence of YHWH's name at the place chosen by him seems to be far more

---

Ronald S. Hendel, "Aniconism and Anthropomorphism in Ancient Israel", in *The Image and the Book: Iconic Cults, Aniconism, and the Rise of Book Religion in Israel and the Ancient Near East,* ed. Karel van der Toorn, BET 21 (Leuven: Peeters, 1997): 205 – 228; versus C. Uehlinger, "Anthropomorphic Cult Statuary in Iron Age Palestine and the Search for Yahweh's Cult Images", in *The Image and the Book: Iconic Cults, Aniconism, and the Rise of Book Religion in Israel and the Ancient Near East,* ed. Karel van der Toorn, BET 21 (Leuven: Peeters, 1997): 97 – 156. Aniconic cults were not restricted to Israel *per se*, cf. Silius Italicus, *Punica* 3.20 – 31; Philostratus, *Vit. Apoll.* 5.5; Herodian, *Hist.* 5.3.4 – 5 etc., cf. Tryggve N.D. Mettinger, "The Absence of Images: The Problem of the Aniconic Cult at Gades and its Religio-Historical Background", *SEL* 21 (2004): 89 – 100.

4 Cf. Gen 19:24; 28:12 – 13; Deut 33:26; 1Kgs 8:12 – 13; Isa 6:1; 31:4b; Pss 2:4; 18:10; 29; 68:34.

5 Ina Willi-Plein, "Warum mußte der Zweite Tempel gebaut werden?", in *Gemeinde ohne Tempel: Zur Substituierung und Transformation des Jerusalemer Tempels und seines Kults im Alten Testament, antiken Judentum und frühen Christentum,* eds. Beate Ego, Armin Lange and Peter Pilhofer, WUNT 118 (Tübingen: Mohr Siebeck, 1999): 57 – 73, thinks that the Israelites were aware of the fact that the building was necessary for religious consciousness and human undertakings, not for the deity himself. Keel, *Geschichte Jerusalems*, 2: 799: "JHWH hat schon immer im Himmel gewohnt. Seine Residenz auf Erden war seit je eine Art 'Zweitwohnung'...H. Niehrs Behauptung 'Heaven becomes YHWH's dwelling place only in the period after the exile'...ist falsch." (versus Herbert Niehr, "In Search of YHWH's Cult Statue in the First Temple", in *The Image and the Book: Iconic Cults, Aniconism, and the Rise of Book Religion in Israel and the Ancient Near East,* ed. Karel van der Toorn, BET 21 (Leuven: Peeters, 1997): 73 – 96 [here 71]).

abstract than older priestly concepts of *kabôd*-theology.[6] The formula was known from Mesopotamian and west-Semitic royal monumental inscriptions as well as from other literature; the Deuteronomists used it to express the claim of YHWH's royal authority over the cultic centre of Judah and Israel. The formula was introduced into the deuteronomic text in a secondary, deuteronomistic phase of *reécriture*.[7] The Akkadian parallel expresses a juridical claim of possession. The loss of the temple leads to a more abstract and – perhaps – secularized concept of the divine presence.[8] The change in the temple theology of presence during the Josianic period seems to be from the YHWH-King-Theology of the royal sanctuary to a YHWH-Exodus-Theology that stressed the liberating work of YHWH in the salvation of Israel from the slavery of Egypt, and in the gift of the land to Israel (cf. Deut 16:1,10,13b,14). The Josianic turn, however, was not accepted by Jerusalem and Judean society; the temple theology returned to the old royal, polytheistic shape under Jehoiakim and Zedekiah (cf. 2Kgs 23:37; 24:19 – 20; Ezek 8; 13; Jer 48).

3. The Destruction of the First Temple and of the Divine Throne

The note about the destruction of the Solomonic temple in 2Kgs 25:8 – 9a is very short: "Nebuzaradan, the chief of the guards, an officer of the king of Babylon, came to Jerusalem. He burnt the House of YHWH, the king's palace, and all the houses of Jerusalem." The bronze from the columns and from the large ritual vessels was broken down, and together with the golden and silver vessels it was brought to Babylon (2Kgs 25:13 – 17; cf. also 2Chr 36:18 – 19); Jer 52:17 – 23 mentions

---

6 See Moshe Weinfeld, *Deuteronomy and the Deuteronomic School* (Oxford: Clarendon Press, 1972), 177 and Moshe Weinfeld, *Deuteronomy 1 – 11: A New Translation with Introduction and Commentary*, AB 5 (New York: Doubleday, 1991). For an overview about the discussion of the formula cf. S.L. Richter, *The Deuteronomistic History and the Name Theology: lᵉšakkēn šᵉmô šām in the Bible and the Ancient Near East*, BZAW 318 (Berlin: de Gruyter, 2002); she has shown that the Akkadian "idiom *šuma šakānu* meaning 'to place the name' is a standard element of the literary typology of the Mesopotamian royal monumental inscriptions...The idiom may also be used in an extended symbolic sense to indicate the claiming of territory." (p. 204). She observes that the use in Jeremiah reflects the deuteronomistic use of the formula.
7 Thomas Römer, *The So-Called Deuteronomistic History: A Sociological, Historical and Literary Introduction* (London: T&T Clark, 2005), 61 – 63.
8 Tryggve N.D. Mettinger, *The Dethronement of Sabaoth: Studies in the Shem and Kabod Theologies*, ConBOT 18 (Lund: CWK Gleerup, 1982), 36 – 37; Thomas Römer, *So-Called Deuteronomistic History*, 62.

the plundering, but not the destruction (cf. also Jer 39:8). One reason for the plundering of the temple may be that the chief priest (כהן הראש) Seraiah, and the deputy priest Zephaniah were involved in the rebellion against the Babylonians. Consequently, together with the three guardians of the threshold, who were responsible for the financial administration of the temple, they were condemned to death (2Kgs 25:18–20). The biblical reports avoid mentioning the burning of the ark or the destruction of the cherub-throne.[9] It has sometimes been assumed that in Lam 2:1 the author was thinking of the cherub-throne and the ark when he said that "Yнwн in his wrath has…cast down from heaven to earth the majesty of Israel" (תפארת ישראל) and "he did not remember his footstool on his day of wrath" (ולא־זכר הדס־רגליו; cf. Pss 99:5; 132:7; 1Chr 28:2).[10] The destruction was interpreted as the divine punishment of Jerusalem and Judah (Jer 40:2–3). The worship of Yнwн, however, continued in the form of penitential liturgies at the ruins of the sanctuary (Jer 41:1–9; Zech 7:3; 8:18–19; Ps 74:4–9; Lam 2:1,7; Isa 64:9–11).[11] The deuteronomic formula that described the presence of Yнwн in his name then gained more importance: for those who prayed at the ruins of the holy place, the consciousness of the God who now causes the remembrance of his name (Exod 20:24b!) determined a belief in the cultic presence of the name recalled at the site of the ancient place of worship (cf. 1Kgs 8:29).[12] The temple itself, rather than the reconstruction of the throne and the ark, became the "footstool" of Yнwн (Ezek 43:7).[13]

---

9 The measure was as exceptional as the destruction of the temple of Marduk in Babylon by Sennacherib in 689 BCE, or the destructions of the temples in Susa by Assurbanipal (646 BCE), and the destructions of the Assyrian temples in Assur in 614, Kalhu in 613, and Nineveh in 612, and of the temple in Haran in 610; cf. Othmar Keel, *Geschichte Jerusalems*, 2: 765–68; Rainer Albertz, "Die Zerstörung des Jerusalemer Tempels 587 v. Chr. Historische Einordnung und religionspolitische Bedeutung", in *Zerstörungen des Jerusalemer Tempels: Geschehen – Wahrnehmung – Bewältigung*, ed. J. Hahn, WUNT 147 (Tübingen: Mohr Siebeck, 2002): 23–41; W. Mayer, "Die Zerstörung des Jerusalemer Tempels 587 v. Chr. im Kontext der Praxis von Heiligtumszerstörungen im antiken Vorderen Orient", in *Zerstörungen des Jerusalemer Tempels*, ed. J. Hahn: 1–22.
10 Keel, *Geschichte Jerusalems*, 2: 791.
11 Keel, *Geschichte Jerusalems*, 2: 784–86; for the ruins of the temple cf. Lam 5:18; Hag 1:4,9; Jer 41:5.
12 Karl-Friedrich Pohlmann, "Religion in der Krise – Krise einer Religion: Die Zerstörung des Jerusalemer Tempels 587 v. Chr.", in *Zerstörungen des Jerusalemer Tempels*, ed. J. Hahn: 40–60 (here 47–48), assumes that the deuteronomistic "Name Theology" reflects the conditions of an empty space.
13 Christian Frevel, "Zerbrochene Zier: Tempel und Tempelzerstörung in den Klageliedern", in *Gottesstadt und Gottesgarten: Zu Geschichte und Theologie des Jerusalemer Tempels*, ed. Erich Zenger and Othmar Keel, QD 191 (Freiburg: Herder, 2002): 99–153 (here 107).

4. The Wandering *Kabôd* in the Priestly Theology

The tradition about the prophet Jeremiah shows that during the first period of Babylonian hegemony and even during the early exilic period it was extremely difficult for most priests and the leading classes of Jerusalem to accept the idea that YHWH could renounce his temple and deliver it up for destruction (cf. Jer 26:6–7; 27:16–22). After the destruction of the temple the concepts of divine presence differed between the several Jewish communities. Ezekiel 11:15–16 reports that those who remained in the homeland of Judah stated that the land was given to them now and that this was the signal that YHWH would remain with them, while he was far from those who had to suffer being exiled. The priestly prophet Ezekiel provides an opposing view of comfort for the elders and people around him in an oracle, saying: "Thus says the Lord YHWH: Indeed, I have removed them far among the nations and have scattered them among the countries, but then I have become to them a little sanctuary in the countries, whither they have had to go (ואהי להם למקדש מעט בארצות אשר־באו שם)!" – The presence of God among the exiles replaces (at least to a small degree) the absence of an adequate place of worship and the deficiency of a community with God in the ritual of sacrifice and holy meals. Ezekiel 11:17–21 rejects the claim to legitimacy by the congregation of Judah with the reproof of syncretism and idolatry. The theology of the *golah* culminates in an impressive visionary replacement of the ancient temple theology in Ezek 10:4,7 (18–22); 11:22–25 (Ezek 1–2*), where it is stated that YHWH in his *Kabôd*[14] had left Jerusalem and remains with the *golah* until the time that punishment, retribution, and atonement will be fulfilled. The priestly vision of the new temple, the return of YHWH (Ezek 43:2–5), and the establishment of a new order of the land (Ezek 44–48) is the counter-theory to the theory of the archetypical reformulation of the ancient foundation myths of Israel in the Hexateuch.

---

14 The term has its roots in the YHWH-King-theology of the temple, as a metaphor for a mental iconography designing the fiery splendour surrounding the deity and its presence in the world. To some extent it is described in contrast to the Assyrian concept of the divine *melammu* (Mettinger, *The Dethronement of Sabaoth*; Hartenstein, "Jhwh und der 'Schreckensglanz' Assurs"; Thomas Wagner, *Gottes Herrlichkeit: Bedeutung und Verwendung des Begriffs kābôd im Alten Testament*, VTSup 151 [Leiden: Brill, 2012]).

In accordance with the self-perception of the religious groups in the *golah*, the myth of the empty land was created,[15] and thus the claims of the leading families of the diaspora returning to Judah were formulated to the detriment of those who had remained in Judah and Jerusalem. The theory of the wandering *kabôd* and its legend about the revelation of the desert tabernacle were formulated in the narrative of the Priestly Code (cf. Exod 24:16–17; 29:43; Lev 9:23). Perhaps this legend fits best with the self-perception of those exiled persons who were gathered in the Babylonian "Al Yahudu", i. e., the Babylonian name for Jerusalem given to a colony of the exiled close to Babylon.[16] While many members of the diaspora chose to remain in Babylonia or moved to Persia, some of them went home to Jerusalem after 539 BCE.

The return of the *Kabôd* is a mental symbol for the universal horizon of the notions about the return of YHWH to Jerusalem in Isa 40:5 (cf. Isa 58:8; 59:19; 60:1). In the theology of the second of the Trito-Isaianic oracles the community of YHWH at Zion itself represents the splendour of divine presence (cf. Isa 61:6; 62:2).

---

15 Hans M. Barstad, *The Myth of the Empty Land: A Study in the History and Archaeology of Judah During the "Exilic" Period*, SO Fasc. Supp. 28 (Oslo: Scandinavian University Press, 1996); Bob Becking, "'We All Returned as One!': Critical Notes on the Myth of the Mass Returned", in *Judah and the Judeans in the Persian Period*, ed. Oded Lipschits and Manfred Oeming (Winona Lake, IN: Eisenbrauns, 2006), 3–18; Ehud Ben Zvi, "Total Exile, Empty Land and the General Intellectual Discourse in Yehud", in *The Concept of Exile in Ancient Israel and its Historical Contexts*, ed. Ehud Ben Zvi and Christoph Levin, BZAW 404 (Berlin: de Gruyter, 2010), 155–68; cf. also in the same volume H.-J. Stipp, "The Concept of the Empty Land in Jeremiah 37–43", in *The Concept of Exile*, ed. Ben Zvi and Levin, 103–54; Christoph Levin, "The Empty Land in Kings", in *The Concept of Exile*, ed. Ben Zvi and Levin, 61–90; Jakob Wöhrle, "The Un-Empty Land: The Concept of Exile and Land in P", in *The Concept of Exile*, ed. Ben Zvi and Levin, 189–206; Reinhard Müller, "A Prophetic View of the Exile in the Holiness Code", in *The Concept of Exile*, ed. Ben Zvi and Levin, 207–28.
16 Leane Pearce, "New Evidence for Judeans in Babylonia", in *Judah and the Judeans in the Persian Period*, ed. Oded Lipschits and Manfred Oeming (Winona Lake, IN: Eisenbrauns, 2006), 399–411; Kathleen Abraham, "West Semitic and Judean Brides in Cuneiform Sources from the Sixth Century BCE: New Evidence from a Marriage Contract form Al-Yahudu", *AfO* 51 (2005/06): 198–219; Ran Zadok, "Judeans in Babylonia in Ancient Times", in *Encyclopedia of the Jewish Diaspora: Origins, Experiences, and Cultures, Volume 3*, ed. M. Avrum Ehrlich (Santa Barbara: ABC Clio, 2009): 757–62; Kathleen Abraham, "The Reconstruction of Jewish Communities in the Persian Empire: The Al-Yahudu Clay Tablets", in *Light and Shadows – The Catalog: The Story of Iran and the Jews*, ed. H. Segev and A. Schor (Tel Aviv: Beit Hatfutsot, 2011), 33–36, 261–64; Leane Pearce and Cornelia Wunsch, *Into the Midst of Many People: Judean and West Semitic Exiles in Babylonia*, CUSAS 18 (Bethesda: CDL Press, forthcoming).

After the resettlement and the rebuilding of the temple, the community re-wrote their old foundation myths and thus reformulated the etiologies of Yhwh's presence amongst Israel. The Hexateuch narrative added the legend of the ark from P (Exod 25:10–22) to the legend of the desert wandering (Num 10:33,35–36; 14:44; cf. Deut 10:1–5). The motif of the wandering *kabôd* was pre-served and developed among the tradents of the scroll of Ezekiel (Ezek 1:28; 3:12,23; 8:4; 9:3; 10:4,18,19; 11:22,23; 39:21; 43:2,4,5; 44:4). In the later Pentateuch Redaction, the theory of the wandering ark and the wandering *kabôd* that re-vealed itself at the Tent of Meeting (Exod 33:7–11; Num 14:10,21,22; 16:19; 20:6) was expanded into a theory of the permanent presence of Yhwh in the revealed form of a clouded, fiery column, that wandered together with Israel from the Red Sea to the Solomonic temple (Exod 13:21,22; 14:19,24; Num 10:34; 12:5; 14:14; Deut 31:15; 1Kgs 8:10–11). In this way the theory of Ezekiel and his tradents could be found again in the Pentateuch in a modified shape.

5. The Spiritual Presence of Yhwh in the Sanctuary

The Cyrus Cylinder states that after the conquest of Babylon the kings of the (conquered) lands rendered homage and tribute to the new king (ll. 28–30), and the king allowed the exiles to return to their original living places (l. 32), tak-ing with them the images of their deities.[17] The resettlement and even the return of some of the ancient vessels of the temple in Jerusalem were permitted.[18] The theological basis for the resettlement was the belief that Yhwh was the owner of the land and would now give it back to his people. The temple was not restored during the first period of Persian hegemony, which meant that the cult continued under the exilic conditions at the ruins of the temple mount. It was only during the reign of Darius, when the new imperial order of satrapies with its adminis-trative structure had been established that the renewal of the Jewish temple was possible. The ancient layers of the prophecy of Haggai show that the eco-nomic conditions for the rebuilding were bad, especially after a drought and

---

17 H. Schaudig, *Die Inschriften Nabonids von Babylon und Kyros' des Grossen samt den in ihrem Umfeld entstandenen Tendenzschriften: Textausgabe und Grammatik*, AOAT 256 (Münster: Ugarit-Verlag, 2001), 550–56.
18 The several versions of the special decree of Cyrus for the Jews seems to be a secondary, fic-tional reconstruction of what was believed to have been the contents of the decree (Ezra 1:2–6; 6:3–5; 2Chr 36:23).

bad harvests (Hag 1:6,11). The prophet's motivation and encouragement went to Zerubbabel ben Shealtiel and Joshua the priest. The visions of the later prophet Zechariah reflect the deliberations among the religious leaders about the question how the presence of Yhwh could be expressed. The vision of the lamp with the seven lips in Zech 4:1–5,10b,11–14 gives the first hint to the revival of ancient traditions: besides the incense altar and the table for the bread of display, which represented the adoration and the cultic communion between the congregation and the deity, the lampstands in the Solomonic temple had been a symbol for the presence of God in the world outside the Most Holy. The lamp represents the "eyes of Yhwh ranging over the whole earth" – thus they surpass the control exerted by the Persian administrators of the king, who were called "the King's Eyes" (Herodotus, *Hist.* 1.114; Xenophon, *Cyr.* 8.2.10– 12; 8.6.16),[19] and it was the responsibility of the priest and the governor of Yehud to make sure that this stand permanently had enough oil (Zech 4:12).[20] After Zechariah's attempt to promote Zerubbabel into an office of kingly leadership had failed, the vision of the lamp was not realized. We know, however, that the shape of the seven-armed lampstand in the Second Temple was according to the design that the Priestly Code had given (Exod 25:31–40; 37:17–24; 40:25), and that the High Priest himself took care of it (Exod 30:7b.8; Num 8:1–4).[21] Later reports about the rebuilding of the temple make clear that there were difficult conflicts among the different Jewish groups in Samaria and in Yehud (Ezra 3–6).[22] The oracle in Zech 4:6aß–7, which was added secondarily to the visionary text, states that Zechariah warned Zerubbabel against using any political violence in order to launch the new sanctuary; instead he should only rely on the power of the divine spirit (v. 6: לא בחיל ולא בכח כי אם־ברוחי אמר יהוה צבאות).[23] In Hag 1:14 the formula אני אתכם is followed by the statement, that Yhwh roused the spirit (רוח) of Zerubbabel and Joshua and the 'am ha-araetz to begin the building of the tem-

---

19 Pierre Briant, *Histoire de l'empire perse de Cyrus à Alexandre* (Paris: Fayard, 1996), 355–56.
20 Ina Willi-Plein, *Haggai, Sacharja, Maleachi*, ZBK 24.4 (Zurich: Theologischer Verlag, 2007), 91–96.
21 For further information about the interpretation and function, cf. Rachel Hachlili, *The Menorah, the Ancient Seven-armed Candelabrum: Origin, Form and Significance*, JSJSup 68 (Leiden: Brill, 2001); Jens Voß, *Die Menora: Gestalt und Funktion des Leuchters im Tempel zu Jerusalem*, OBO 128 (Fribourg: Presses Universitaires, 1993).
22 Concerning the discussion about the historical background cf. Gary N. Knoppers, "Revisiting the Samarian Question in the Persian Period", in *Judah and the Judeans in the Persian Period*, ed. Oded Lipschits and Manfred Oeming (Winona Lake, IN: Eisenbrauns, 2006), 265–89; Gary N. Knoppers, *Jews and Samaritans: The Origins and History of their Early Relations* (New York: Oxford University Press, 2013), 102–68.
23 Willi-Plein, *Haggai, Sacharja, Maleachi*, 96–100; for similar glosses cf. Mic 3:8; Hos 9:7.

ple. In Hag 2:4b,5a the prophetic encouragement of Zerubbabel, Joshua, and the *'am ha-'araetz* expands Haggai's message based on the kerygma of the exodus (Hag 2:4b, 5a): "'For I am with you' – says Yʜᴡʜ Sebaoth – the word I promised you when you came out of Egypt!".[24] The language of the formula (אני אתכם), which reminds the audience of God's presence at the time of the exodus and the conquest (cf. Judg 1:3), is used only one other time, in Jer 21:5, where it is stated that God says he was present in the war against Jerusalem!

However scholars may evaluate the sequence in a diachronic sense, it is obvious that the background of this text is affected by the discussion about the mode of divine presence in the process of the rebuilding of the temple. The climax of this development is expressed in Hag 2:5: ורוחי עמדת בתוככם אל־תיראו, "and my Spirit will stand in your midst! Fear not!" This text is a priestly reflection on the prophetic message of divine presence that alludes to the programmatic sentences of the Priestly Code, cf. Exod 25:8 ועשו לי מקדש ושכנתי בתוכם (cf. also Exod 29:45). The Spirit of Yʜᴡʜ that comes over his servants (Isa 42:1; 48:16; 59:21) and (priestly) prophets (Ezek 11:5) is now expected to remain present steadily (עמד, עמדת) in the midst of the congregation, that is the Most Holy of the temple, as Yʜᴡʜ was present in the midst (בתוך) of the cloud and the fire (Exod 24:18; Deut 5:4,22–26). Later scribes wrote: in the column (עמוד) of fire and cloud (Exod 13:21–22; cf. Num 12:5; 14:14). What we can see here, is that the concept of divine presence underwent a metamorphosis from connecting it to sacred symbols to a mode of spiritualization that made the reproduction of the former symbols such as the throne or the ark superfluous.

6. Jerusalem as the Throne of Yʜᴡʜ: Jer 3:13–18

Moshe Weinfeld in his famous study on "Jeremiah and the Spiritual Metamorphosis of Israel" has shown that the process of spiritualization started in the reflections of the book of Jeremiah about the attitudes that will be changed during the time of the exile after the destruction of the sanctuary and its most holy precinct, the ark.[25] (Weinfeld himself thought that all the texts were Jeremianic.) The sentences are introduced by the formula בימים ההמה לא־יאמרו עוד – in those days they shall say no more... (cf. Jer 16:14–15; 23:7–8; 31:29–30,31–34!)

---

24 Hag 2:5a is missing in the LXX, so there might have been older text forms in which this addition was not yet present.

25 Moshe Weinfeld, "Jeremiah and the Spiritual Metamorphosis of Israel", *ZAW* 88 (1976): 17–56.

Jeremiah 3:16 – 17

16 And when you increase and are fertile in the land,	16 והיה כי תרבו ופריתם בארץ
in those days –	בימים ההמה
oracle of Yʜwʜ –	נאם־יהוה
that it shall no more be spoken of	לא־יאמרו עוד
the Ark of the Covenant of Yʜwʜ,	ארון ברית־יהוה
nor shall it come to mind,	ולא יעלה על־לב
they shall not mention it,	ולא יזכרו־בו
or miss it,	ולא יפקדו
or make another.	ולא יעשה עוד
17 At that time, they shall call Jerusalem "Throne of Yʜwʜ" (names for Jerusalem: Jer 33:16; Isa 62:2,4,12; Ezek 48:35),	17 בעת ההיא יקראו לירושלם כסא יהוה
and all nations shall assemble there, in the name of Yʜwʜ, at Jerusalem. They shall no longer follow the willfulness of their evil hearts.	ונקוו אליה כל־הגוים לשם יהוה לירושלם ולא־ילכו עוד אחרי שררות לבם הרע

The fiction of a Jeremianic sermon is used to refer to the circumstances after the end of the exile. It takes up the legend from the Priestly Code's narrative about the fruitfulness and increase of the Israelites under the conditions of their slavery in Egypt (Exod 1:7) and reflects the priestly formula פרו ורבו from Gen 1:22 (cf. Gen 1:28; 8:17; 9:1,7; 17:20; 28:3; 35:11; 47:27; 48:4; Exod 1:7; Lev 26:9 und Jer 23:3; the inverted form ורבו ופרו appears only in Ezek 36:11, a prophecy about the post-exilic time)![26] The fictional naming of the ark as ארון ברית־יהוה is post-deuteronomistic[27] and post-priestly and does not even refer to the pre-exilic precinct. The term יעלה על־לב (= it comes into my heart/mind) is attested rather sparsely,[28] but is typical of parenetic phrasing in Jeremiah (cf. Jer 7:31; 19:5; 32:35; 44:21). The abandonment of the holy object, even the end of its remembrance, seems a radical consequence of spiritualization in Second Temple theology. Instead of the renewal of the artifact, the purpose of the material symbol is transferred to the abstract concept of the presence of the divine *name* that is connected with the city of Jerusalem, and the concept of the throne is replaced by the pure *localization* of the worship on Zion (v. 17). There is no material item to which the divine presence in the holy precinct of the temple is connected, but Jerusalem in general is considered to be the place in the world where the

---

26 For a closer analysis of Jer 3:16 – 19 cf. Peter Porzig, *Die Lade Jahwes im Alten Testament und in den Texten vom Toten Meer*, BZAW 397 (Berlin: De Gruyter, 2009), 222 – 27.
27 Num 10:33; 14:44; Deut 10:8; 31:9,25,26; Josh 3:3,17; 4:7,18; 6:8; 8:33; 1Sam 4:3,4,5; 1Kgs 6:19; 8:1,6; Jer 3:16 and 1Chr 15:25,26,28,29; 16:37; 22:19; 28:2,18; 2Chr 5:2,7.
28 Josh 14:8; 2Kgs 12:5; Isa 65:17.

heavenly throne of God should be attended.[29] Together with the loss of the ark, scribes must have also imagined the loss of the tablets of the Decalogue, which, according to Deut 10:2,5,8, had to be deposited inside the ark. Thus the vanishing of the ark was the narrative foundation for the legend of the tablets of the Decalogue. The Decalogue was the document of the covenant broken (Deut 5:3)! Jeremiah 3:16–18 forms the basis of the spiritual renewal of the covenantal tablets written upon the hearts of Israel (Jer 31:33)! The written Torah – according to the legend of Deut 31:24–29 – had been deposited at the site of the ark, and thus the written Torah was the only witness to the covenantal words of God with a permanent presence among the Israelites. To put the Torah onto their hearts also meant securing a *permanent awareness of the presence of God's word* in Israel!

Jer 16:14–15

14 Therefore: behold, in those days –	14 לכן הנה־ימים באים
oracle of YHWH –	נאם־יהוה
it shall no more be said,	ולא־יאמר עוד
"As YHWH lives,	חי־יהוה אשר העלה את־בני ישראל מארץ
who has brought up the children of Israel out of the land of Egypt!"	מצרים
15 but: "As YHWH lives,	15 כי אם־חי־יהוה
who brought up the children of Israel from the land of the north, and from all the countries, whither he had driven them!" –	אשר העלה את־בני ישראל מארץ צפון ומכל הארצות אשר הדיחם שמה
And I will bring them again to their land that I gave unto their fathers.	והשבתים על־אדמתם אשר נתתי לאבותם

---

29 Cf. Jer 14:21; 17:12; Ezek 43:7; Isa 60:13. For the development of the theology of divine presence in the second temple cf. Keel, *Die Geschichte Jerusalems*, 799, and his critical remarks concerning the *realia, the sacred devices*: "I. Willi-Plein meint zu Recht, dass mindestens für die Klgl die 'Zerstörung der Wohnadresse' JHWH kein größeres theologisches Problem zu sein scheint...JHWH hat schon immer im Himmel gewohnt. Seine Residenz auf Erden war seit je eine Art 'Zweitwohnung', die höchstens für die Menschen, nicht für ihn von entscheidender Bedeutung war. Mit dem Himmel waren sowohl der Sturm- und Wetter- wie auch der Sonnengott engverbunden, beides uranische Gottheiten (vgl. z.B. Ps 18,10; 29; Gen 19,24; 1 Kön 8,12f.)." Also, Keel, *Die Geschichte Jerusalems*, 1033: "Im Allerheiligsten (der Stiftshütte) platziert die Priesterschrift eine Kombination aus 'Bundeslade' und Kerubim ergänzt durch die Deckplatte (*kapporaet*), die bei Sühnezeremonien eine entscheidende Rolle spielt (vgl. 1 Kön 6,23–28 und 8,1–9 mit Ex 25,10–22...Es ist fraglich, ob das Gerät je real existiert hat...1 Chr 28,18 lässt im Allerheiligsten, das David konzipiert, einen komplexen, aus allerhand Traditionselementen kombinierten Gegenstand untergebracht werden, der so nie existiert hat."

The transformation of deuteronomistic concepts of "Heilsgeschichte" into a present post-exilic perspective of remigration to the old homeland includes at the
same time a spiritualization of the traditional foundation myth of the exodus:
it becomes a metaphor for divine action in the future. When stating that even
the oath is connected with the transformative formula of the "presence of Heilsgeschichte", the traditional formula of the deuteronomistic creed is transposed
into a deposit of cultural remembrance as a code and thus achieves a more abstract quality. We can thus observe a *metamorphosis of traditional kerygmatic language* by a method of hermeneutical updating into a new religious interpretation
of the reader's presence in light of a fictive prophetical prolepsis in order to confirm and assure the beliefs of the post-exilic generations. It is the time when the
concept of belief is transferred to the concept of faith – Hebrew האמין, אמונה.[30]

In connection with the affirmation of the divine promise in Jer 23:5–6 that a
new branch of David's line will arise, the same sentence is repeated in a slightly
different version in Jer 23:7–8. The passage concludes the sermon on the kings in
Jer 21:11–23:8, a composition attached to the post-deuteronomistic narrative in
Jer 21:1–10.[31] The sequence of texts referring to the kings followed by a text referring to prophets and priests (Jer 23:9–32,33–40) seems to reflect the sequence
of the laws on kings, priests, and prophets in Deut 17:14–20 and Deut 18:1–8,9–
22. When LXX transposes Jer 23:7–8 to the end of the chapter (after Jer 23:40), it
becomes obvious that the verses reflect a very late stage in the formation of Jeremiah, as we can also see from the late parallel to Jer 23:5–6 in Jer 33:14–26
(MT), which is even lacking in the LXX.[32] In Jer 31, verses 27–30 end the long
speech on the return of the diaspora. Verse 27 takes up 3:16 (see above!), and
v. 28 announces the inversion of the initial message of the prophet (Jer 12:14–
17; 18:7 (1:10); 1:12 + 25:6,29). In addition, v. 29 quotes the proverb of Ezek

---

30 אמונה, cf. Jer 5:1,3; 7:28; 9:2; האמין, cf. Gen 15:6; Exod 14:31; 19:9; Num 14:11; 20:12; Deut
1:32; 9:23; Isa 7:9; 28:16; 43:10.
31 Weinfeld, "Spiritual Metamorphosis", 39–52, believes that the words originally come from
Jeremiah, but this position has not been confirmed by recent scholars; cf. Hans-Jürgen Hermis-
son, "Die 'Königsspruch'-Sammlung im Jeremiabuch – von der Anfangs- zur Endgestalt", in *Die
Hebräische Bibel und ihre zweifache Nachgeschichte: Festschrift für Rolf Rendtorff zum 65. Geburtstag*, ed. E. Blum (Neukirchen-Vluyn: Neukirchener, 1980): 277–99 (here 285); Christl Maier,
*Jeremia als Lehrer der Tora: Soziale Gebote des Deuteronomiums in Fortschreibungen des Jeremia-
buches*, FRLANT 196 (Göttingen: Vandenhoeck & Ruprecht, 2002), 227–28.
32 K. Schmid, *Buchgestalten des Jeremiabuches: Untersuchungen zur Redaktions- und Rezep-
tionsgeschichte von Jer 30–33 im Kontext des Buches*, WMANT 72 (Neukirchen-Vluyn: Neukirchener, 1996), 323–27, even pleads for the originality of the LXX version and dates the redactional layer somewhere in the 3rd century BCE.

18:2–3 and confirms the principle of individual retribution (cf. Deut 24:16).[33] Konrad Schmid has demonstrated that these verses parallel vv. 31–34 and that they belong to a layer that gives the whole of Jer 30–33 a structure in connection with Jer 1–29.[34] Verse 28 refers to chapters 1, 11 and 25 and thus seems to provide an orientation for the reader.[35] In connection with Jer 31:31–34 it prepares for the message of the renewal of the covenant. Verses 31–32a and v. 34 take up the metamorphosis formulas again with respect to the character of the covenant renewal.[36] E. Otto has shown that the text discusses the covenant theology of the deuteronomistic and priestly redactions of the Pentateuch.[37] The covenant of the time to come (הנה ימים באים נאם־יהוה; v. 31a, cf. the same formula above) will not be of the same character as the ancient covenant with the fathers of Israel (לא כברית אשר כרתי את־אבותם; v. 32). The people cannot fail or break this covenant again, because it will, in an abstract way, be "inscribed" onto their "hearts"; this is a metaphorical expression for the way God will affect the fixation of the legal texts in the common consciousness of the Jewish people, a fastening of the oral Torah onto the collective memory of Israel. Thus the scribes of Jeremiah plead for establishing a spiritual, oral teaching of Torah in line with the written tradition of the Torah.[38]

7. The Invisibility of God during the Teaching of the Torah according to Deut 4:10–24

In the Book of Ezekiel the vision of the prophet (Ezek 10) is explained in a broad and colourful extended form in Ezek 1–2. The mental imagination of the prophet

---

33 For references of Jer 31:27–30, cf. G. Fischer, *Jeremia 26–52*, HThKAT (Freiburg: Herder, 2005), 168–71 (including references for further literature).
34 Schmid, *Buchgestalten*, 77–85, 345–46.
35 Schmid, *Buchgestalten*, 300–302.
36 Weinfeld, "Spiritual Metamorphosis", 26–39; Fischer, *Jeremia 26–52*, 171–76. For an analysis of the contextual relationship between Jer 11 and 31:31–34 cf. Schmid, *Buchgestalten*, 295–98; Eckart Otto, "Jeremia und die Tora: Ein nachexilischer Diskurs", in *Tora in der Hebräischen Bibel: Studien zur Redaktionsgeschichte und synchronen Logik diachroner Transformationen*, ed. Reinhard Achenbach, Martin Arneth and Eckart Otto, BZABR 7 (Wiesbaden: Harrassowitz, 2007), 134–82.
37 Otto, "Jeremia und die Tora", 160–78.
38 Otto, "Jeremia und die Tora", 171–82; the scribes of the scroll of Jeremiah thus take up an ancient tradition of memorization and oral performance (cf. D.M. Carr, *Writing on the Tablet of the Heart: Origins of Scripture and Literature* [Oxford: Oxford University Press, 2005]) and oppose the scribal canonization of the Pentateuch as the only measure of Torah and Covenant.

relates to a דמות הכסא דמות כמראה אדם (Ezek 1:26). In the anthropological concept of P the description of an anthropomorphic idea of God is replaced by the concept of the replacement of the king as royal צלם (imago, statue) of a deity through humankind in general (male and female) as representing the messianic existence of humanity, whereas God remains invisible with his *kabôd* hidden (Gen 1:26 – 28).

In the final layers of the Pentateuch we find traces of a discussion about the mode of God's visibility and invisibility. The scribes stress that – in opposition to all other prophets – Yhwh had known Moses פנים אל־פנים – πρόσωπον κατὰ πρόσωπον – face-to-face (Deut 34:10). Thus Moses met Yhwh regularly in the tent of meeting, speaking to him face-to-face as a man speaks to his friend (Exod 33:11). In Num 12:8, in a revelatory speech of Yhwh it is stressed: "With him I speak mouth to mouth (פה אל־פה אדבר־בו – στόμα κατὰ στόμα λαλήσω αὐτῷ), even in a Vision (apparently, ומראה – ἐν εἴδει), not in dark speeches (ולא בחידת – καὶ οὐ δι' αἰνιγμάτων), and he envisions/looks at the similitude/figure of Yhwh (ותמנת יהוה יביט)!" At this point LXX avoids a strictly literal translation – "and he sees the similitude of Yhwh" – but translates: καὶ τὴν δόξαν κυρίου εἶδεν! LXX thus follows a tendency that can be found even within the *Fortschreibung* of the Pentateuch. The reason for the theological hesitative doubtfulness is the prohibition of idols in Exod 20:4 ‖ Deut 5:8 (לא תעשה־לך פסל וכל־תמונה). In Deut 4 we find a sermon about the revelation at Mount Horeb that emphasizes that Israel only heard the voice of Yhwh out of the fire and saw the phenomena of the epiphany, but they did not see any "similitude" of Yhwh (ותמונה אינכם ראים זולתי קול 12 – καὶ ὁμοίωμα οὐκ εἴδετε, ἀλλ' ἢ φωνήν, cf. Deut 4:12,15,16,23,25)! LXX thus expands this view: Moses was in the closest contact with God that one could imagine, but even if this was a face-to-face contact, Moses could not distinguish the shape of the divine figure: he only saw the *doxa* – the sign of his glory (Num 12:8[39]). Thus LXX follows a *Fortschreibung* of Exod 33:7–11 in Exod 33:12–17 with vv. 18–23. When Moses demands that Yhwh should reveal himself to him his *kabôd*, Yhwh describes the delimitation of his revelation, v. 20: לא תוכל לראת את־פני כי לא־יראני האדם וחי – Οὐ δυνήσῃ ἰδεῖν μου τὸ πρόσωπον· οὐ γὰρ μὴ ἴδῃ ἄνθρωπος τὸ πρόσωπόν μου καὶ ζήσεται! In addition we find the teaching about the people's insight at Mount Horeb in Deut 5:24:

---

39 A similar change of text can be found in Ps 17:15 (= 16:15 LXX): the *visio Dei* of David in the Hebrew text – אני בצדק אחזה פניך אשבעה בהקיץ תמתתך – "As for me, I shall behold your face in righteousness, I shall be satisfied, when I awake and see your figure!" – is translated in LXX: ἐγὼ δὲ ἐν δικαιοσύνῃ ὀφθήσομαι τῷ προσώπῳ σου, χορτασθήσομαι ἐν τῷ ὀφθῆναι τὴν δόξαν σου! When speaking about spirits, תמונה is translated by μορφή (cf. Job 4:16).

הן הראנו יהוה אלהינו את־כבדו ואת־גדלו ואת־קלו שמענו מתוך האש היום הזה ראינו כי־ידבר אלהים את־האדם וחי

Ἰδοὺ ἔδειξεν ἡμῖν κύριος ὁ θεὸς ἡμῶν τὴν δόξαν αὐτοῦ, καὶ τὴν φωνὴν αὐτοῦ ἠκούσαμεν ἐκ μέσου τοῦ πυρός· ἐν τῇ ἡμέρᾳ ταύτῃ εἴδομεν ὅτι λαλήσει ὁ θεὸς πρὸς ἄνθρωπον, καὶ ζήσεται!

LXX makes clear that the statement that God had spoken face-to-face with Moses implied the most immediate way of proffering a message and of receiving a response. However, there was – according to later priestly teaching – no immediacy with respect to the visibility of God's תמונה. The revelation of God's word does not include the revelation of God's תמונה.

8. The Presence of the Name in the Blessing of Aaron (Num 6:22 – 27) and Yhwh as the God of Heaven

The priestly blessing has the task of performing the act of God's authoritative claim on the temple-community: when the holy formula is cited, the name of the Holy is laid upon the congregation of the people of God. The priestly task to pass on divine blessings and to bless the people in the name of Yʜwʜ (לברך בשמו, Deut 10:8) is now defined in a new sense (Num 6:23 כה תברכו את־בני ישראל אמור להם, 6:24 ... יברכך; 6,27 ושמו את־שמי על־בני ישראל)! Thus the congregation itself seems almost to embody the sanctuary. To a certain extent the formula replaces the older deuteronomistic formula of "laying the name on a place".

The true dwelling place of Yʜwʜ and thus the origin of the blessing is believed to be in heaven (cf. Ps 115:3,15 – 16; cf. also Pss 2:4; 103:19; 123:1; Qoh 5:1). In late post-exilic layers of the Old Testament from Achaemenid times – especially before other peoples – God is called the "God of Heaven and the God of Earth" (Gen 24:3) or simply the "God of Heaven" (אלהי השמים, Gen 24:7; Jonah 1:9; Ezra 1:2; Neh 1:4 – 5; 2:4.20; 2Chr 36:23).[40] Whereas in pre-exilic times the temple

---

[40] Cf. also Dan 2:18,19,37,44; Ezra 5:(11),12; 6:9,10; 7:12,21,23 (aram. אל שמיא); and אל השמים Ps 136:26; יהי אלה שמיא Cowley, AP 27:15; 30:28; אלה שמיא AP 30:2; 31:27; 32:4; 38:3,5; 40:1 etc.; Cornelis Houtman, *Der Himmel im Alten Testament: Israels Weltbild und Weltanschauung*, OtSt 30 (Leiden: Brill, 1993), 98; for the development of the concept cf. Beate Ego, "'Der Herr blickt herab von der Höhe seines Heiligtums': Zur Vorstellung von Gottes himmlischen Thronen in exilisch-nachexilischer Zeit", ZAW 110 (1998), 556 – 69; Beate Ego, *Im Himmel wie auf Erden: Studien zum Verhältnis von himmlischer und irdischer Welt im rabbinischen*

was described as the cosmological centre of YHWH's reign and activities, in later compositions these activities have their origin in heaven (Ps 57:4); the cosmos itself has become the sacred space, as J. Jeremias and K. Schmid have observed concerning Ps 104: "Ps 104 versucht, 'Jahwes Weltherrschaft und seine Kontrolle über das Chaos *ohne* [irdischen, K.S.] *Tempel* zu umschreiben', dafür erscheint der Kosmos selbst in Ps 104 in *tempeltheologischer Deutung.*"[41] This is the reason why the temple building remains permanently as a symbol for the divine presence; it helps the believers to trust that God is dwelling in the midst of Israel (בקרב ישראל, Joel 2:27), Zion is the cosmic symbol of the holy hill connected to Jerusalem (שכן בציון הר־קדשי, Joel 4:17; שכן ירושלם, Ps 135:21).[42] The belief in the divine presence was rooted in the temple ritual (Josephus, *J.W.* 6.293–99; m. Sukkah 5.4).[43]

9. Spiritual Presence and Spiritual Renewal

An investigation of the term רוח in the Old Testament shows that the word is increasingly applied in anthropological as well as in theological statements. The focus of the reflection on human consciousness is transposed from the organic activity of the "heart" (לבב) onto the spiritual or intellectual activity of the "spirit" (רוח). In late passages of the parenesis in Deuteronomy we find the metaphoric admonition to "circumcise the hearts", purify one's own consciousness in order to learn obedience to the Torah (Deut 10:16). The motif is taken up again in Jer 4:4. In Ezek 11:19–20 we find God's promise to the new generation that will return from exile (v. 17); God will renew their heart and even will give them a new *spirit* (v.19: ורוח חדשה אתן בקרבכם), so that they will follow the commandments. This con-

---

Judentum, WUNT II/34 (Tübingen: Mohr Siebeck, 1989); Beate Ego, "Von der Jerusalemer Tempeltheologie zur rabbinischen Kosmologie: Zur Konzeption der himmlischen Wohnstatt Gottes", *Mitteilungen und Beiträge der Forschungsstelle Judentum der Universität Leipzig* 12/13 (1997): 36–52.
41 Konrad Schmid, "Himmelsgott, Weltgott und Schöpfer. 'Gott' und der 'Himmel' in der Literatur der Zeit des Zweiten Tempels", in *Der Himmel*, ed. Martin Ebner *et al.*, JBTh 10 (Neukirchen-Vluyn: Neukirchener, 2005), 111–48 (here 126–27), with reference to Jörg Jeremias, *Das Königtum Gottes in den Psalmen: Israels Begegnung mit dem kanaanäischen Mythos in den Jahwe-Königs-Psalmen*, FRLANT 141 (Göttingen: Vandenhoeck & Ruprecht, 1987), 45.
42 See also the Temple Scroll 29:7–10; Matt 23:21; G.I. Davies, "The Presence of God in the Second Temple", in *Templum Amicitiae: Essays on the Second Temple presented to Ernst Bammel*, ed. W. Horbury, JSNTSup 48 (Sheffield: JSOT Press, 1991), 32–36.
43 m. Sukkah 5.4: ואמרו אבותינו שהיו מקום הזה אחוריהם אל ההיכל ופנהם קדמה ומשתחוים קדמה לשמש; ואנו ליה עינינו הפכו פניהם ממזרח למערב cf. Davies, "Presence", 35–36; cf. b. Yoma 21b.

cept is expanded upon in Ezek 36:26–28, where we find the promise that God will give his own spirit to the Israelites (ואת־רוחי אתן בקרבכם)![44] Thus, in combination with Hag 2:5b we can observe the formation of a theology of spiritual presence and renewal in the late second temple period.

10. The Invisibility of God in the Sanctuary and the Absence of Symbols in the Most Holy

Josephus' description of the central space of the sanctuary (*J.W.* 5.215–21)[45] proves that the perception of the deity during the Second Temple period had become most abstract, stressing the invisibility of God and the impossibility of an earthly temple hosting the universal deity and God of the heavens. For the Most Holy, Josephus says:[46]

> ἔκειτο δὲ οὐδὲν ὅλως ἐν αὐτῷ, ἄβατον δὲ καὶ ἄχραντον καὶ ἀθέατον ἦν πᾶσιν, ἁγίου δὲ ἅγιον ἐκαλεῖτο.

The concept of holiness connected with the *debîr*, the most inner and most holy place of the sanctuary as known from the older tradition (cf. 1Kgs 6:16; 7:50 ‖

---

44 J. Schnocks, "'Und ich werde meinen Geist in euch geben' (Ez 37,14): Konzeptionen der Rede vom Geist in Ez 36–37", in *Heiliger Geist*, ed. Martin Ebner *et al.*, JBTh 24 (Neukirchen-Vluyn: Neukirchener, 2009): 31–52, assumes: "Es (i.e.: das Geistverständnis von Ez 36:24–28) gehört offenbar in den Kontext einer religiösen Gegenbewegung gegen eine hasmonäische – oder allgemeiner gesprochen: politische – Vereinnahmung der Heilsansage des Ezechielbuches."

45 Josephus, *De Bello Judaico / The Jewish War, Books IV–VII*, ed. by H. St. J. Thackeray, LCL (Cambridge, MA: Harvard University Press, 1961), 5.215–21 (pp. 264–67): "Passing within one found oneself in the ground floor of the sanctuary. This was sixty cubits in height, the same in length, and twenty cubits in breadth. But the sixty cubits of its length were again divided. The first portion, partitioned off at forty cubits, contained within it three most wonderful works of art, universally renowned: a lampstand, a table, and an altar of incense." (The Menorah, cf. also Josephus, *Ant.* 3.144–45, had been depredated by Antiochus IV and was replaced by Judas Maccabaeus, cf. 1Macc 1:21; 4:49). Josephus interprets its meaning cosmologically: "The seven lamps...represented the planets." The table with the loaves (cf. Exod 24:23–30; Josephus, *Ant.* 3.139–42; Philo, *Mos.* 2.104) for Philo was a symbol for the land and its fruitfulness. The incense altar (cf. Exod 30:1–10; Josephus, *Ant.* 3.147–48; Philo, *Mos.* 2.105) signified for Josephus "that all things are of God and for God".

46 *J.W.* 5.221: "The innermost recess measured twenty cubits, and was screened in like manner from the outer portion by a veil." (Greek text see above): "In this stood nothing whatever: unapproachable, inviolable [immaculate], invisible to all, it was called the Holy of Holy."

1Chr 6:34; Exod 26:33–34) has changed: The *debîr* is described *via negativa:* it is unapproachable because of its holiness (cf. 1Kgs 8:10–11), it is immaculate (> χραίνω) because God is imagined in absolute purity (Isa 6:5), and it is invisible (Exod 33:20). It is even a risk to speak out his name to mark his presence.

During the 3rd century BCE we can even observe an increasing hesitation to pronounce the holy name of Yʜwʜ. Using God's name was avoided in front of heathen people, and in order not to pollute it pious Jews started even avoiding the name among their own congregation. The Priestly Code started replacing the name of Yʜwʜ in the context of all narratives about the Israelites in the Abrahamic status of foreignness (בארץ מגורים), with the universal name of אלהים.[47] In the post-priestly additional Elohistic didactic narratives of the Pentateuch the name "Elohim" was accepted as the universal name in front of or even in the mouth of non-Israelites (cf. Exod 1:15–22; 18:12; Num 22–24*). The use of the holy name was successively restricted to the Aaronide Blessing around 100 BCE. It was perhaps only whispered by the High Priest when he entered the Holiest of Holies on Yom Kippur. This tradition seems to explain the highest degree of abstraction in the concept of the divine presence in the theology of the Second Temple period: not even to speak out the Holy Name in the presence of the empty *debîr*, the Most Holy.

In the Elohistic Psalter the name was (almost) completely replaced by "Elohim", so that worship could be shared by both Israelites and those worshipers who joined the worship of the God of Abraham from foreign lands (cf. Ps 47:10).[48] The LXX, translated for Jewish and non-Jewish readers, replaced the Tetragrammaton completely with κυρίος, and in the scriptures of Qumran the holy name was written in paleo-Hebrew letters in order to mark its holiness (as in some LXX manuscripts). After the Qumran community had withdrawn from the Jerusalem temple, a tendency can be observed that even the temple itself was replaced by a more abstract view. The community itself is designated as a בית קדוש(cf. 1QS 8:5–6) and the expectation was expressed that God would let a new temple descend from heaven in a new messianic era.[49]

---

47 A. de Pury, "Gottesname, Gottesbezeichnung und Gottesbegriff: 'Elohim als Indiz zur Entstehungsgeschichte des Pentateuch", in *Abschied vom Jahwisten: Die Komposition des Hexateuch in der jüngsten Diskussion*, ed. Jan C. Gertz, Konrad Schmid and Markus Witte, BZAW 315, (Berlin: De Gruyter, 2002), 25–47.
48 Volker Haarmann, *JHWH-Verehrer der Völker: Die Hinwendung von Nichtisraeliten zum Gott Israels in alttestamentlichen Überlieferungen*, ATANT 91 (Zurich: Theologischer Verlag, 2008).
49 Lawrence H. Schiffman, "Community Without Temple: The Qumran Community's Withdrawal from the Jerusalem Temple", in *Gemeinde ohne Tempel/Community without Temple: Zur Substituierung und Transformation des Jerusalemer Tempels und seines Kults im Alten Testament, an-*

In accordance with the belief of divine presence in the word of the Torah, the sapiential reworking of the book of Psalms focuses on the belief of the divine presence in individual prayer and in the community of non-cultic meetings encountering God in the worship of diaspora congregations.[50] As in the diaspora, so also in Qumran and among other groups during the decadence of the Hasmonean period, the metamorphosis from the ancient concepts of divine manifestation to a completely abstract category of God's unattainability and sovereignty was implemented. Christian worship shared the results of that process believing in a divine presence in the midst of a community of believers (cf. Matt 18:20; 1Cor 3:16 – 17; 2Cor 6:16).[51] After the fall of the Second Temple several rabbinic theories about the modes of divine presence were launched in connection with the ancient holy place, as we still can see from Shemot Rabba 2 on Exod 3:1:

> It is written: *But the Lord is in His holy temple* (Hab. II, 20). R. Samuel b. Naḥman said: Before the Temple was destroyed, the Divine Presence dwelt therein, for it says: *The Lord is in His holy temple* (Ps. XI, 4)...R. Eleazer says: The *Shecinah* did not depart from the Temple, for it is said: *And Mine eyes and My heart shall be there perpetually* (II Chron. VII, 16). So it also says: *With my voice I call unto the Lord, and He answereth me out of His holy mountain, Selah* (Ps. III, 5)... though Jerusalem is laid waste, God had not departed from there. R. Aḥa said: The Divine Presence will never depart from the Western Wall, as it is said: *Behold, He standeth behind our wall* (Song of Songs II, 9), and also: *His eyes behold, His eyelids try, the children of men* (Ps. XI, 4). R. Jannai said: Although His Presence is in heaven, yet *"His eyes behold, His eyelids try, the children of men"*.[52]

---

tiken Judentum und frühen Christentum, ed. Beate Ego, Armin Lange and Peter Pilhofer, WUNT 118 (Tübingen: Mohr Siebeck, 1999), 267 – 84.

50 Erich Zenger, "Der Psalter als Heiligtum", in *Gemeinde ohne Tempel/Community without Temple: Zur Substituierung und Transformation des Jerusalemer Tempels und seines Kults im Alten Testament, antiken Judentum und frühen Christentum*, ed. Beate Ego, Armin Lange and Peter Pilhofer, WUNT 118 (Tübingen: Mohr Siebeck, 1999), 115 – 30.

51 C. Böttrich, "'Ihr seid der Tempel Gottes': Tempelmetaphorik und Gemeinde bei Paulus", in *Gemeinde ohne Tempel/Community without Temple: Zur Substituierung und Transformation des Jerusalemer Tempels und seines Kults im Alten Testament, antiken Judentum und frühen Christentum*, ed. Beate Ego, Armin Lange and Peter Pilhofer, WUNT 118 (Tübingen: Mohr Siebeck, 1999), 411 – 25.

52 *Midrash Rabbah: Exodus*, trans. S. M. Lehrman (London: Soncino Press, 1939), 47 – 48; b.Yoma 21b states that even the elements of the first temple period that had been distincted to symbolize the divine presence as the ark of the covenant, the cherubs, the fire on the altar, the divinity, the holy spirit (of prophecy) and the ephod, were present in a certain sense in the second temple, but without effect. For further literature on the rabbinical concepts of immanence cf. J. Abelson, *The Immanence of God in Rabbinical Literature*, (London: Macmillan, 1912); A. M. Goldberg, *Untersuchungen über die Vorstellung von der Schekinah in der frühen rabbinischen Literatur* (Berlin: De Gruyter, 1969).

Nathan MacDonald
Ritual Innovation and *Shavu'ot*

Ever since Julius Wellhausen's incisive analysis as part of his *Prolegomena*, the differences between the Israelite festival calendars in the Bible have been recognized as an important means of charting religious change in ancient Israel.[1] At least five versions of the festival calendar are preserved in the biblical text,[2] and they provided Wellhausen with an important foundation for his critical account of Israelite religious history. By associating the different Pentateuchal versions of the calendar with the sources of the documentary hypothesis, he could order the sources and trace Israel's religious development. As Wellhausen observed, the differences between the calendars illustrated the changes that he sought to map with "clearness and precision".[3] The centralization of festivals led to the calendar becoming more fixed and sacrifices more tightly prescribed. At the same time the festivals began to be loosened from the seasonal events that had originally occasioned them and took on new, historical associations.

Whilst scholarly interest has focused upon the contribution the different versions of the festival calendar can make to uncovering Israel's religious development, there is also value in thinking about how the festival calendars might contribute to our understanding of ritual change and how we theorize it. This is an important task since differing scholarly accounts of the festival calendar often reflect different assumptions about the possibility and nature of ritual change. We might usefully compare Wellhausen's understanding with some recent interpretations of the festival calendar. Wellhausen discerns an inner logic to Israelite religious development: from nature to history. In his seminal work Bernard Levinson emphasizes the political motives that lay behind Deuteronomy's innovations and the hermeneutical means by which they were achieved.[4] Jan Wagenaar emphasizes external influences in the form of the Babylonian New Year

---

1 Julius Wellhausen, *Prolegomena to the History of Israel with a Reprint of the Article Israel from the "Encyclopaedia Britannica"*, trans. John Sutherland Black and Allan Menzies (Edinburgh: Adam & Charles Black, 1885), 83–120.
2 Exod 23; 34; Lev 23; Deut 16; and Ezek 45. Although Num 28–29 has often been identified as the Priestly Code's festival calendar (in distinction to the Holiness Code's festival calendar in Lev 23), this is mistaken. It is more accurately viewed as a set of instructions dealing with sacrificial offerings throughout the year (Num 28:2).
3 Wellhausen, *Prolegomena*, 83.
4 Bernard M. Levinson, *Deuteronomy and the Hermeneutics of Legal Innovation* (New York: Oxford University Press, 1997), 53–97.

festivals.[5] Wellhausen assumes that the biblical calendars mirror the cultic and social realities of the time of their composition. In contrast, the recent work by Shimon Gesundheit views the calendars much more as midrashic exegesis. In his words, "we are not dealing with the development of the Israelite cultus but with the history of *cultic literature* in Israel".[6] Wellhausen argues that the differences between the festival calendars reveal changing practices and theology. Gordon McConville insists, however, that there are no substantive changes, merely differences in theological emphasis.[7] Jacob Milgrom finds the ancient cultic calendar of Shiloh preserved in the priestly literature of the Pentateuch.[8]

In this essay I will examine *Shavuʿot*, the Feast of Weeks, in the different festival calendars. I will not be seeking to make new claims about the relationships between the different festival calendars, but rather focus on what might be learnt about ritual change. Since I am interested in the dynamics of ritual change, I will not be examining one festival calendar, or how one version of the calendar reworks an earlier one. Instead, I will trace the history of the feast through various festival calendars attested in the Hebrew Bible and at Qumran, a textual development that took half a millennium or more. My investigation will seek to demonstrate not only the ways in which the prescriptions for the festival developed, but even how new festivals were generated. My approach will be to begin with the earliest textual appearance of *Shavuʿot* in the Covenant Code (Exod 23:18). From there I will trace its development through the book of Deuteronomy (Deut 16:9–12), the Holiness Code (Lev 23:9–22), the covenant prescriptions following the Golden Calf incident (Exod 34:22), and the Temple Scroll (11QT 18:1–23:01).[9]

---

5 Jan A. Wagenaar, *Origin and Transformation of the Ancient Israelite Festival Calendar*, BZABR 6 (Wiesbaden: Harrasowitz, 2005).

6 Shimon Gesundheit, *Three Times a Year: Studies on Festival Legislation in the Pentateuch*, FAT 82 (Tübingen: Mohr Siebeck, 2012), 229.

7 J. Gordon McConville, *Law and Theology in Deuteronomy*, JSOTSup, 33 (Sheffield: JSOT Press, 1984), 99–123.

8 Jacob Milgrom, *Leviticus 1–16: A New Translation with Introduction and Commentary*, AB 3 (New York: Doubleday, 1991), 1–52; Jacob Milgrom, *Leviticus 17–22: A New Translation with Introduction and Commentary*, AB 3A (New York: Doubleday, 2000), 1319–1443; Jacob Milgrom, *Leviticus 23–27: A New Translation with Introduction and Commentary*, AB 3B (New York: Doubleday, 2001), 1947–2080.

9 For reasons noted in fn 2 above, I will not included a detailed consideration of Num 28:26–31. Its instructions for the performance of the Feast of Weeks are limited to prescribing the sacrifices required during the festival. Like a number of other Pentateuchal texts, Num 28:26–31 does have a discernible textual influence upon the instructions for the Feast of Weeks in Lev 23:9–22 and 11QT 18:1–23:01. Thus, although Num 28:26–31 will not merit a separate dis-

The choice of *Shavuʿot*, rather than one of the other festivals, is a pragmatic one. *Shavuʿot* has not enjoyed the same level of attention as either *Pesaḥ-Maṣṣot* or *Sukkot*, not least because of the various interpretative challenges that the prescriptions for those festivals pose. An examination of *Pesaḥ-Maṣṣot* or *Sukkot* would need to extend far beyond the bounds of a single essay. Nevertheless, it will still be necessary to place limitations on my investigations. This essay will be restricted to the prescriptions about *Shavuʿot* in the festival calendars. A number of texts provide additional evidence for how *Shavuʿot* was understood prior to the Fall of Jerusalem in 70 CE.[10] In the late Second Temple period precise answers are given to the question of when the feast was to be celebrated and an association with an annual renewal of the covenant is established. The concern of my exegetical investigation, however, is not to provide a complete history of the Feast of Weeks to the end of the Second Temple period,[11] but to explore ritual innovation by means of the festival instructions concerning *Shavuʿot*. With the exception of the earliest stage of the festival's history found in the Covenant Code, for which we possess no textual precursor, each of the festival calendars reworks earlier festival calendars. My five texts, therefore, provide a controlled and tightly delimited case study for the dynamics of ritual innovation.

The Harvest Festival in the Covenant Code

The earliest reference to what would later become part of *Shavuʿot* is found in Exod 23:16 as part of the so-called Covenant Code.[12] The Covenant Code pre-

---

cussion, we will have reason to discuss its contribution to the festival calendar in the Holiness Code and the Temple Scroll. In addition, I will not discuss the festival calendar in Ezek 45. Although 45:21 refers to *Shavuʿot*, this is usually thought to be a tendentious alteration of the text in MT that makes no sense syntactically, and is not reflected in the versions. Wagenaar suggests the change may "be the result of a freak accident in the course of the transmission of the text" (Wagenaar, *Origin*, 101). For a discussion of Ezekiel's calendar and its relation to other festival calendars in the Hebrew Bible, see Wagenaar, *Origin*, 101–124.

10 See, *inter alia*, Jer 5:24; 2Chr 8:13; 15:8–15; Tob 2:1–10; 2Macc 12:31–32; Philo, *Spec.* 2:162–87; Jub. *passim*; Josephus *Ant.* 3.250–57; 13.251–52; Acts 2; 20:16; 1Cor 16:8.
11 For a recent contribution towards that end see Sejin Park, *Pentecost and Sinai: The Festival of Weeks as a Celebration of the Sinai Event,* LHBOTS 342 (London: T&T Clark, 2008).
12 The festival calendar in the Covenant Code is now widely considered to be the earliest Israelite example. For a dissenting view see John Van Seters, *A Law Book for the Diaspora: Revision in the Study of the Covenant Code* (Oxford: Oxford University Press, 2003), 162–71. Van Seters' problematic rejection of redactional activity in the Covenant Code by itself requires him to postulate a late date for the material. For incisive criticism of Van Seters' arguments see Bernard M.

scribes the keeping of three feasts. The first of these, the Feast of Unleavened Bread (חג המצות), is associated with the exodus event (23:15). The other two festivals are related to points in the agricultural year: the Feast of Harvest (חג הקציר), during which the firstfruits of the field crops are offered, and the Feast of Ingathering (חג האסף), after the grapes and olives had been harvested (23:16).[13] At these festivals all the Israelite males are enjoined to appear before YHWH (יראה כל־זכורך אל־פני האדן יהוה; 23:17). The cultic location clearly implies that YHWH is to be offered some part of the harvest. No additional specification is given about the cultic location for these celebrations, but earlier in the Covenant Code no restriction is placed upon where YHWH might be worshipped, provided that offerings are made on an altar made of earth or undressed stones (20:24– 26). Since these are pilgrimage festivals (חג) they were probably celebrated at a regional cultic centre, rather than the local high place.[14]

For my purposes it is not necessary to venture an absolute dating of the festival calendar in Exod 23 or the Covenant Code as a whole. It is sufficient only to observe that the Covenant Code is justifiably understood to be pre-deuteronomic, and in Exod 23 we have the earliest textual evidence of an Israelite festival calendar.[15] The unusual names for the agricultural festivals, חג הקציר and חג האסף, may perhaps be indicative of this early date. Here, there is a rather striking overlap with the terminology of the Gezer calendar, which refers to "two months of gathering" (ירחו אסף), "a month for the barley harvest" (ירח קצר שערם) and "a month for harvesting" (ירח קצר).

Ritual Innovation and the Feast of Weeks in Deuteronomy 16

The innovative character of many of Deuteronomy's practices has long been an established reference point for Old Testament scholarship with the presence or

---

Levinson, "Is the Covenant Code an Exilic Composition? A Response to John Van Seters", in *In Search of Pre-Exilic Israel: Proceedings of the Oxford Old Testament Seminar*, ed. John Day, JSOTSup 406 (London: T&T Clark, 2004), 272–325.

13 For the use of אסף with grapes and olives see Deut 16:13; Isa 32:10; Jer 8:13, although it can be used of the harvest in a broad sense (e.g. Exod 23:10; Deut 28:38).

14 Propp, on the other hand, argues that "a trip to the local High Place probably suffices" (William Henry Propp, *Exodus 19–40: A New Translation with Introduction and Commentary*, AB 2A [New Haven: Yale University Press, 2006], 238).

15 Exod 34:11–26, the so-called *Privilegrecht Jahwes*, is now widely regarded as a late composition, and will be discussed in more detail later.

absence of Deuteronomic ideas providing a key index for determining the date of Old Testament texts relative to Deuteronomy. The principal innovation of Deuteronomy is the restriction of the Israelite cult to a single place, and scholarship has argued that the earliest version of the book, the so-called *Urdeuteronomium*, was primarily, if not exclusively, concerned with those laws that needed reshaping in light of the practice of centralization.[16] A representative instance of the book's novel programme is the Deuteronomic festival calendar. Here, there are two main lines of innovation. First, each of the three Israelite festivals is to be celebrated at the central sanctuary or, in Deuteronomy's parlance, the place where YHWH will place his name. Second, *Pesaḥ* and *Maṣṣot* are combined into a single festival. The combined effect of these two innovations is that *Pesaḥ* is no longer celebrated at the home. This key innovation has resulted in vv. 1–8 receiving the lion's share of critical attention,[17] though the prescriptions for *Shavu'ot* (vv. 9–12) and *Sukkot* (vv. 13–15) also differ from Exod 23:16.

That the present form of Deut 16:1–17 reworks the festival calendar in Exod 23:14–19a has been clearly demonstrated in recent scholarship by Bernard Levinson. The prohibition of leaven in Exod 23:18 is incorporated into the regulations for *Pesaḥ* in Deut 16:3–4, whilst in Deut 16:16–17 the instructions in Exod 23:15–17 are appropriated and hermeneutically transformed.[18] There is continued disagreement about whether the festival calendar in Deut 16 is a composition of the Deuteronomic writer, as Levenson argues, or whether the similarities to Exod 23 are the result of an expansion later than a Deuteronomic law about centralization, as Gesundheit argues.[19]

Although in broad terms Deut 16 can be viewed as a reworking of Exod 23, Deuteronomy's specific instructions about *Shavu'ot* shows considerable freedom in relation to Exod 23:16. This is most apparent in the name given to the festival: the earliest evidence for the familiar name *Shavu'ot* (חג שבעות) is found here in

---

16 "the centralization of the cult...dominates everything...The demand for centralization is the motif which is the impetus towards the amendment of the older book of the law and in fact governs the changes. It is the main law of Ur-Deuteronomy and as such a positive criterion for literary division superior to all other possibilities" (Reinhard Gregor Kratz, *The Composition of the Narrative Books of the Old Testament* [London: T&T Clark, 2005], 118).

17 E.g. Levinson, *Deuteronomy*, 53–97; Shimon Gesundheit, "Der deuteronomische Festkalendar", in *Das Deuteronomium*, ed. Georg Braulik, ÖBS 23 (Frankfurt am Main: Peter Lang, 2003), 57–68; Jan Christian Gertz, "Die Passa-Massot-Ordnung im deuteronomischen Festkalender", in *Das Deuteronomium und seine Querbeziehungen*, ed. Timo Veijola, Schriften der Finnischen Exegetischen Gesellschaft 62 (Helsinki: Finnische Exegetische Gesellschaft; Göttingen: Vandenhoeck & Ruprecht, 1996), 56–80.

18 Levinson, *Deuteronomy*, 81–89, 90–93.

19 Gesundheit, *Three Times a Year*, 96–166.

Deuteronomy.[20] The name derives from the seven-week period that begins with the first ingathering of grain and precedes the festival: "You shall count seven weeks. You shall begin to count the seven weeks from the moment the sickle is put into the standing grain" (Deut 16:9). If Deut 16 is simply a reworking of Exod 23, an explanation is needed for why the expression חג שבעות is preferred to חג הקציר. A frequently ventured solution is that the seven-week period allows for regional differences in the date for harvesting the grain.[21] Such flexibility would only have been necessitated by a centralized celebration, and thus the name must have originated with Deuteronomy.[22] Alternatively, the widespread assumption that חג שבעות and חג הקציר are the same festival may be questioned. The festivals have different names and occur at different times in the agricultural cycle. As Gesundheit observes,

> The text does not make the substance of the festival sufficiently explicit, but the qualification "from when the sickle is first put to the cornstalks shall you count seven weeks" (v. 9) clearly indicates that שָׁבֻעֹת is not in fact an inaugural harvest festival; it takes place at the end of the grain harvest rather than the beginning. This contradicts Exod 23:16, which describes the festival as "the Harvest Festival: the first-fruits of your produce that you sow in the field".[23]

Such observations find further substantiation in the fact that there are no verbal overlaps between Deut 16:9 – 12 and Exod 23:16. In other words, the instructions about חג שבעות in Deut 16 are not a reworking of the instructions about חג הקציר

20 Andrew D. H. Mayes, *Deuteronomy*, NCB (Grand Rapids, MI: Eerdmans, 1981), 260 – 61.
21 "The growing seasons and harvest times observed by Dalman...seem to match a seven-week interval between the two harvest festivals perfectly. In the valleys and on the coastal plain the barley harvest would normally commence at the beginning of May. The barley harvest is followed by the wheat harvest around the middle of May, about the same time as the start of the barley harvest in the mountainous regions. The wheat harvest in the mountainous regions will in turn commence at the beginning of June...The wheat harvest in the mountainous regions will, therefore, be complete before the end of June. The period from the beginning of the barley harvest in the valleys or the coastal plain at the beginning of May until the conclusion of the wheat harvest in the mountainous regions before the end of June more or less covers the seven-week interval which separates Pesach-Massot from Shabuot" (Wagenaar, *Origin and Transformation*, 33 – 34). The suggestion is not universally accepted, see Richard D. Nelson, *Deuteronomy: A Commentary*, OTL (Louisville, KY: Westminster John Knox Press, 2002), 209.
22 For this idea and an argument that the name *Sukkot* also reflects a centralized cultic polity see Georg Braulik, "Commemoration of Passion and Feast of Joy: Popular Liturgy according to the Festival Calendar of the Book of Deuteronomy (Deut 16:1 – 17)", in *The Theology of Deuteronomy: Collected Essays of Georg Braulik, O.S.B.*, BIBAL Collected Essays 2 (N. Richland Hills, TX: BIBAL Press, 1994), 78 – 79. In my view Braulik's arguments are not fully convincing.
23 Gesundheit, *Three Times a Year*, 152.

in Exod 23.[24] For earlier scholarship the equation of the two festivals was a given, since Exod 34:22 qualified חג שבעות as "the firstfruits of the wheat harvest" (בכורי קציר חטים). However, the older critical position that the festival law in Exod 34 was of great antiquity has been shown to be untenable, and thus the grounds for identifying the two festivals are entirely eroded. It is possible that *Shavu'ot* was another traditional harvest festival and the reference to "the weeks appointed for harvest" (שבעות חקות קציר) in Jer 5:24 raises the possibility that this is a traditional designation, rather than a coinage necessitated by Deuteronomic innovation.

There are further differences between the Deuteronomy's festival calendar and that found in the Covenant Code. In addition to being celebrated at the central sanctuary, *Shavu'ot* and *Sukkot* have been assimilated to the Deuteronomic ideal of celebrating the bounty of the land in the company of indentured servants, the resident alien, and the needy widow and orphans. In contrast the harvest feasts in Exod 23 only required the presence of adult males. Secondly, both festivals also reflect the Deuteronomic association of joy with the gift of the land. The festival calendar maps a transition from mourning to joy that replicates Israel's historical experience of moving from Egypt to Promised Land.[25] Thirdly, Deut 16 makes no mention of firstfruits. Whilst Exod 23 requires the offering of "the firstfruits of your deeds" (בכורי מעשיך), Deut 16:10 speaks instead of "the freewill offering of your hand" (נדבת ידך). This voluntary offering is in addition to the tithe prescribed in Deut 14:22–29. It is the tithe that is probably to be associated with firstfruits in Deuteronomy,[26] and thus we have further evidence that the Deuteronomic Feast of Weeks is not a festival of firstfruits and is distinct from the חג הקציר of Exod 23.

---

24 There is some merit to McConville's claim that "there is very little in Dt 16.9 – 17 which provides solid evidence for the historical relationship between these laws on Weeks and Booths... and other codes" (McConville, *Law*, 110).

25 Nathan MacDonald, *Not Bread Alone: The Uses of Food in the Old Testament* (Oxford: Oxford University Press, 2008), 79 – 83. For the theme of joy in the Deuteronomic feasts see Georg Braulik, "The Joy of the Feast: The Conception of the Cult in Deuteronomy. The Oldest Biblical Festival Theory", in *The Theology of Deuteronomy: Collected Essays of Georg Braulik, O.S.B.*, BIBAL Collected Essays 2 (N. Richland Hills, TX: BIBAL Press, 1994), 27 – 65; Braulik, "Commemoration of Passion".

26 Mayes, *Deuteronomy*, 244 – 45.

Ritual Innovation and the Feast of Weeks in Leviticus 23

The festival calendar in Lev 23 is far more extensive than the three festival lists in Exod 23:14–17 and Deut 16:1–17. The calendar opens with the weekly Sabbath (v. 3). It is followed by *Pesaḥ-Maṣṣot* (vv. 4–7), a firstfruits offering (vv. 9–14), a further firstfruits offering seven weeks later (vv. 15–20), the blast of trumpets (vv. 23–25), *Yom Kippur* (vv. 26–32) and *Sukkot* (vv. 33–36). The calendar follows a regular pattern: (a) a date formula; (b) the name of the festival; (c) designation of the occasion as a holy convocation; (d) a prohibition of work; and (e) the offering of a sacrifice. The beginning of *Sukkot* offers a compact example:

> On the fifteenth day of this seventh month the festival of *Sukkot* lasting seven days to Yhwh. The first day is a holy convocation. You shall do no work. Seven days you will present a food offering to Yhwh (Lev 23:34–35).

The instructions about the days for offering firstfirsts deviate from this pattern. No fixed date in the calender is given and the days are not named. The day for offering the first sheaf is not named a holy convocation, nor is work prohibited (vv. 9–14). The day for offering the two loaves is named a holy convocation and work is prohibited, but these instructions only occur after the sacrifices are mentioned (vv. 15–21).

It would appear that the festival calendar is a harmonization of two festival traditions. The first tradition had a semi-annual format with feasts in the first and seventh months. In the first month, *Pesaḥ-Maṣṣot* was celebrated, and in the seventh month, the blast of trumpets, *Yom Kippur* and *Sukkot*. A semi-annual format is also attested in Ezek 45.18–25. The second tradition, which we have already encountered in Exod 23 and Deut 16, structured the calendar according to the three pilgrimage festivals: *Pesaḥ-Maṣṣot*, *Shavuʿot* and *Sukkot*. Wagenaar argued that the second tradition was added by a redactor, but Nihan has made a convincing case for the conflation of the two calendars as the work of H.[27]

One important divergence between the two calendar traditions concerns precise dating. In the semi-annual calendar, the dates of the festivals occur on the same day in the calendar every year. Precise dates are not prescribed for the

---

27 See Wagenaar, *Origin*, 74–100 and Christophe Nihan, *From Priestly Torah to Pentateuch*, FAT II/25 (Tübingen: Mohr Siebeck, 2007), 496–511.

three pilgrimage festivals in Exod 23 or Deut 16.[28] *Shavu'ot* in Deut 16 is a case in point; the date of the celebration is determined by the beginning of the grain harvest. The conflation of festival calendars in Lev 23 does not resolve the date for the firstfruit offerings, but transforms it onto a different level of ambiguity. According to Lev 23:15 the grain offering is to be presented "on the day after the Sabbath (השבת) from the day you bring the sheaf of the elevation offering". But which "Sabbath" is in view? The only previous mention of the Sabbath is found in v. 3, which refers to the weekly Sabbath. Is this "the Sabbath", or should "the Sabbath" be related to the festival that precedes the offering of the firstfruits in the calendar, *Pesaḥ-Maṣṣot?* The issue turns on how to relate H's language of "Sabbath" to the language of "holy convocations" that is found in the semi-annual festival tradition. According to v. 3 the Sabbath is a "holy convocation" in which no work is to be done. But is the reverse the case? Is every "holy convocation" in which no work is to be done a Sabbath? If so, then the "holy convocations" at the beginning and end of *Maṣṣot* should be understood as "Sabbaths". Even if this is the case, however, there is a further ambiguity, because it is not certain which of these "holy convocations" should be identified as "the Sabbath" of v. 15. Thus, in his conflation of the festival calendars, the H writer has left considerable ambiguity about how to determine the date of the offering of firstfruits.[29]

The challenge of conflating different calendars also explains the existence of two distinct firstfruit offerings. As we have already seen, the feast of harvest (חג הקציר) in Exod 23 and the feast of weeks (חג שבעות) in Deut 16 are not to be equated since they occur at different points in the harvest. Leviticus 23 links the two occasions, but maintains their distinction through the fifty-day period that separates them. There is the day of the waving of the sheaf (23:9–14) in which "a sheaf of the first (grain) of harvest" (את־עמר ראשית קצירכם) is offered to YHWH. Its relation to the feast of harvest in Exod 23:16 is signalled by the use of the word "harvest" (קציר) in Lev 23:10. Seven weeks later a "new (grain) offering" (מנחה חדשה) is presented to YHWH (23:15–22). This is brought in the form of two loaves and is further described as "firstfruits" (בכורים). This is clearly the same occasion as envisaged in Deut 16:9–12 as the clear verbal parallel indicates: "You shall count for yourself seven weeks" (שבעה שבעת תספר לך; Deut 16:9); "You shall count for yourselves...seven Sabbaths" (וספרתם לכם...שבע שבתות; Lev 23:15). The appearance of "Sabbaths" (שבתות) in Lev 23 is most com-

---

28 This is true even of *Pesaḥ-Maṣṣot*. Wagenaar has made a compelling case that חדש האביב should be understood as "the season of (fresh) ears" rather than "the month (named) Abib" (Wagenaar, *Origin*, 25–32).

29 For further discussion of this ambiguity see Milgrom, *Leviticus 23–27*, 2056–2063.

pellingly explained as an assimilation of Deut 16's language to one of H's characteristic themes.[30]

The brief account of the feast of harvest in Exod 23:16 does not prescribe what offering is to be made; it merely defines harvest as "the firstfruits of your deeds of what you sow in the field" (בכורי מעשיך אשר תזרע בשדה). It would appear that this has been equated with the requirement in Deut 26:1–11 that the Israelites offer the firstfruits of their harvest (ראשית כל־פרי האדמה). In the narrative presentation of Deuteronomy the offering of firstfruits is a foundation ceremony made during the first year in the land, rather than a recurring obligation.[31] The H writer has incorporated this offering into the festival calendar and made it into an annual requirement. At the start of every grain harvest a sheaf of grain is to be offered at the central sanctuary. The indebtedness of Lev 23 to Deut 26 is apparent in a number of different ways. Most conspicuously, the opening formula that introduces the raising of the sheaf (כי־תבוא אל־הארץ אשר יהוה אלהיך נתן לך) has been taken up from Deut 26:1 with only minor alterations.[32] This formula contrasts with those that introduce the other festivals in Lev 23 where the date of the feast and its name are given. Secondly, in both rituals the priest has a role in presenting the offering. This is especially significant because the only occasions that the priest appears in Lev 23 are in relation to the firstfruits offerings (vv. 10,11,20). According to Deut 26 the priest is "to lay" (הניח) the basket of firstfruits before YHWH (Deut 26:4,10). Whilst the Holiness author selects a word with clearer cultic connotations, he further signals his indebtedness to Deut 26 by chosing the phonological similar verb הניף "to elevate". Thirdly, both Lev 23 and Deut 26 speak of the offering as a ראשית. This expression is not found in Exod 23:16, nor is it found in P[g] or anywhere else in H.[33]

The account of the offering of the new grain in vv. 15–21, as we have seen, is indebted to the prescriptions for *Shavu'ot* in Deut 16:9–11. Significant changes have been introduced in Lev 23's revision; the most important of which is that

---

30 The alternative possibility – that Deut 16 took the expression from Lev 23 – stumbles on explaining why the term "Sabbath" had to be excised.

31 Nelson, *Deuteronomy*, 307.

32 The relationship to Deut 26:1 is rightly emphasized by Weyde. He observes that the clause "has a similar force to that in Lev 23:10 only in Deut 26:1" (Karl William Weyde, *The Appointed Festivals of YHWH*, FAT II/4 [Tübingen: Mohr Siebeck, 2004], 70).

33 The appearance of ראשית in Lev 2:12 is probably secondary as indicated by the general subject matter and the change in address (Rolf Rendtorff, *Leviticus 1,1–10,20*, BKAT 3/1 [Neukirchen-Vluyn: Neukirchener, 2004], 84). Similarly, the use of ראשית in Num 15:20,21 and 18:12 is post-redactional (Reinhard Achenbach, *Die Vollendung der Tora: Studien zur Redaktionsgeschichte des Numeribuches im Kontext von Hexateuch und Pentateuch*, BZABR 3 [Wiesbaden: Harrassowitz, 2003]).

the occasion is no longer a "pilgrimage festival" (חג), but a "day" (יום). This is often taken to be a downgrading of firstfruits as part of the conflation to a semi-annual structure around the festivals of *Pesaḥ-Maṣṣot* and *Sukkot*.[34] The Israelite farmer is not required to bring his firstfruit offering to YHWH at the central sanctuary, but an offering is made on behalf of all Israel. The prominence of another "day", *Yom Kippur*, in Lev 23 tells against this assumption. The intention might be not so much to downgrade firstfruits, but to make the raising of the sheaf and the offering of the new grain into a single ritual event with two parallel "days". On both days (יום) an offering of the field is elevated (הניף) by the priest. The accompanying offerings were probably also meant to parallel one another, if as seems likely vv. 18–20 are the result of a later harmonization with Num 28:27– 30.[35] Originally we may have had an offering of two loaves made from two-tenths of an ephah each accompanied by two lambs as burnt offerings.[36] In comparison to its beginning, the completion of the harvest would then be marked by a doubling of the offering as well as the offering of prepared loaves rather than unprocessed grain. Thus, the abundance of the final harvest is represented in a cultic manner.

As much as Lev 23 is indebted to Deut 16, we should not overlook the subtle contribution of Exod 23:16. The offering of the "new grain" is described using the term בכורים (Lev 23:17,20). As we have already observed Deut 16 does not associate *Shavu'ot* with firstfruits, and the idea has been transferred to it from Exod 23:16. In this way the Holiness writer finds an additional means to distinguish – and simultaneously hold together – the two days of firstfruits: the elevation

---

34 For the argument that the calendar in Lev 23 maps the traditional Israelite calendar to a semi-annual pattern which reflected Babylonian influence, see detailed discussion in Wagenaar, *Origin and Transformation*; Weyde, *Appointed Festivals*; Jacob Milgrom, *Leviticus 23 – 27*, 1947 – 2080; Nihan, *Priestly Torah*, 496 – 511. The Israelite Feast of Weeks does not correlate to the semi-annual pattern falling as it does between the first and seventh month. In this respect it is striking that the date to celebrate the raising of the Sheaf and Firstfruits is lacking. It has often been argued that the Babylonian calendar is mediated via Ezek 45:18 – 25.

35 Verses 18 – 20 are usually judged to be overloaded, for discussion of the issue and possible solutions see Nihan, *Priestly Torah*, 506 – 7. It may be wondered why scribal harmonization with the list of sacrifices in Num 28 – 29 only occurs here in Lev 23, and not elsewhere. The reason is not difficult to discern. Firstfruits is the only ritual paralleled in Num 28 – 29 where Lev 23 prescribes an offering. The tension between two lambs for a burnt offering required in Lev 23 and the more extensive sacrificial list in Num 28 called for some form of resolution.

36 Karl Elliger, *Leviticus*, HAT 1,4 (Tübingen: Mohr Siebeck, 1966), 308.

of the sheaf is a ראשית-offering and the elevation of the loaves fifty days later is a בכורים-offering.[37]

Ritual Innovation and the Renewal of the Covenant in Exodus 34

The brief reference to the Feast of Weeks in Exodus 34 provides only limited evidence for cultic innovation. The succinct version of the festival calendar has sometimes been viewed, together with other features, as evidence for an early date of composition.[38] Recent scholarship, however, has shown that Exod 34:11–26 is one of the latest legal texts in the Pentateuch dependent on other legal codes.[39] The dependence of Exod 34 on Exod 23 and Deut 16 has been repeatedly observed in this recent work and can be seen in the specific case of *Shavuʿot*. The brief account of the feast in Exod 34:22 has a similar form to Exod

---

37 A similar bifurcation of firstfruits is also found in Num 18:12–13. In v. 12 the ראשית of the oil, wine and grain are given to the priests, whilst v. 13 also provides them with the בכורים of the land. (For discussion see N. MacDonald, *Priestly Rule: Polemic and Biblical Interpretation in Ezekiel 44*, BZAW, 476 [Berlin: de Gruyter, 2015], 98–100). In a late addition to the Covenant Code both terms occur together in a tautologous expression (ראשית בכורי אדמתך; Exod 23:19).
38 Although Wellhausen's identification of *das Privilegrecht Jahwes* as the Yahwistic Decalogue proved to be extremely influential, there were always those who viewed it as one of the latest legal texts in the Pentateuch, e.g. Bernardus D. Eerdmans, *Das Buch Exodus* (Gießen: Töpelmann, 1910), 85–92.
39 See, e.g., Shimon Bar-On [=Gesundheit], "The Festival Calendars in Exodus XXIII 14–19 and XXXIV 18–26", *VT* 48 (1998): 161–195; David Carr, "Method in Determination of Direction of Dependence: An Empirical Test of Criteria Applied to Exodus 34,11–26 and Its Parallels", in *Gottes Volk am Sinai: Untersuchungen zu Ex 32–34 und Dtn 9–10*, ed. Matthias Köckert and Erhard Blum, Veröffentlichungen der Wissenschaftlichen Gesellschaft für Theologie 18 (Gütersloh: Gütersloher Verlagshaus, 2001), 107–140; Hans-Christoph Schmitt, "Das sogenannte jahwistische Privilegrecht in Ex 34,10–28 als Komposition der spätdeuteronomistischen Endredaktion des Pentateuchs", in *Abschied vom Jahwisten: Die Komposition des Hexateuchs in der jüngsten Diskussion*, ed. Jan Christian Gertz, Konrad Schmid, and Markus Witte, BZAW 315 (Berlin: de Gruyter, 2002), 157–71; Erhard Blum, "Das sogenannte 'Privilegrecht' in Exodus 34,11–26: Ein Fixpunkt der Komposition des Exodusbuches? ", in *Studies in the Book of Exodus: Redaction – Reception – Interpretation*, ed. Marc Vervenne, BETL 126 (Leuven: Peeters, 1996), 347–66; Bernard M. Levinson, "The Revelation of Redaction: Exodus 34:10–26 as a Challenge to the Standard Documentary Hypothesis", paper presented at The Pentateuch: International Perspectives on Current Research Conference, Zurich, 11 January 2010).

23:16,[40] but the title of the festival, "the Feast of Weeks" (חג שבעת), has been lifted from Deut 16. The influence of the Holiness Code is rather more difficult to discern, but is probably present as can be seen in two ways. First, the incorporation of the Covenant Code's regulations for a seven-day rest (23:10 – 12) into the middle of the festival calendar of Exod 34 and immediately prior to *Shavu'ot* probably points to the influence of Lev 23.[41] Second, whilst the Covenant Code has a vague reference to "the firstfruits of your deeds" (בכורי מעשיך), Exod 34:22 provides a more precise specification that during the feast of weeks "the firstfruits of the wheat harvest" (בכורי קציר חטים) are to be offered. Besides an interest in clarifying the Covenant Code's imprecise reference, the specificity of Exod 34 could be due to the presence in Lev 23 of two firstfruits events separated by seven weeks. The explicit association of the second celebration with the later wheat harvest allows the raising of the sheaf to be associated with the first harvesting of grain which occurs much earlier.[42] In later literature and through a process of dissimilation, the raising of the sheaf will be understood as the firstfruits of the barley harvest.

Ritual Innovation and the Firstfruits Festivals in the Temple Scroll

Not only does the Temple Scroll (11QT) provide a number of clear examples of ritual innovation, but it has a distinct advantage over the instances of ritual innovation that we have been examining in the Pentateuch. As we have seen the complex compositional history of the Pentateuch introduces a number of difficulties that must be negotiated in seeking to establish cases of ritual innovation. The Temple Scroll, on the other hand, is justifiably taken to be dependent on Pentateuchal texts. Numerous examples of ritual innovation can be found in

---

40 In both cases the name of the festival is given (וחג הקציר cf. וחג שבעת), followed by the required offering (בכורי מעשיך אשר תזרע בשדה) cf. בכורי קציר חטים). In Exod 23:16 the verb תשמר is presupposed from the Feast of Unleavened Bread in v. 15. In Exod 34:22 תעשה לך has to be interjected after the festival names because of the numerous additions between the two feasts (vv. 19 – 21)

41 Cf. Corinna Körting, *Der Schall des Schofar: Israels Feste im Herbst*, BZAW 285 (Berlin: de Gruyter, 1999), 30; Bar-On [=Gesundheit], "The Festival Calendars", 170. In addition, the prohibition of idolatry in Exod 34:17 is taken not from the Covenant Code, but from Lev 19:4. Schmitt rightly observes that the prohibition of אלהי מסכה is directly relevant to the incident of the Golden Calf (cf. Exod 32:4,8) (Schmitt, "Das sogenannte jahwistische Privilegrecht", 165).

42 Cf. Bar-On [=Gesundheit], "The Festival Calendars", 173; Gesundheit, *Three Times*, 152 – 54.

the Temple Scroll.[43] Perhaps the most conspicuous example of ritual innovation is the Temple Scroll's multiplication of firstfruits festivals. Three festivals of first-fruits are prescribed: the festival of new wheat, the festival of new wine and the festival of new oil.[44] Each festival is separated by fifty days. The stipulations show considerable indebtedness to extant biblical texts such that Swanson has argued that "there is very little which cannot be traced to a biblical source".[45] Despite this dependence upon the Pentateuch, the firstfruit festivals of new wine and new oil are not prescribed in the Bible. As we have seen various Pentateuchal festival calendars refer to a celebration at the harvesting of the grain, variously described as the "festival of harvest" (חג הקציר; Exod 23:16) and the "feast of weeks" (וחג שבעת; Exod 34:22; Deut 16:10), whilst Lev 23 de-scribes two events associated with firstfruits, though neither is identified as a חג.

---

43 The *millulim* ceremony fills a lacuna in the Pentateuch by prescribing an annual ordination ceremony (11QT 15:3 – 17:5). The unique ordination of Aaron and his sons (Exod 29; Lev 8 – 9) is loosened of its narrative particularities and transformed to suit it to an annual occurrence. The Temple Scroll also stipulates an annual festival for the wood offering (11QT 23:02 – 25:2). The inspiration would appear to be Neh 10:35 (cf. 13:31), which envisages the sanctuary needing a regular supply of wood delivered on set occasions throughout the year by various families ac-cording to lot. Various sacrificial regulations from Lev 1 and 3 are also incorporated.
44 Doubts should be raised about whether the raising of the sheaf is in fact a firstfruits festival or a "feast of new barley" as is often suggested (Dwight D. Swanson, *The Temple Scroll and the Bible: The Methodology of 11QT*, STDJ 14 [Leiden: Brill, 1995], 18 – 31; Milgrom, *Leviticus 23 – 27*, 2071 – 2076). First, the raising of the sheaf is not identified as firstfruits in the extant texts of the Temple Scroll (11QT 18:1 – 10), nor is the sheaf identified as a barley sheaf. Since the scroll is damaged the possibility cannot be excluded that a section of lost text identifies the el-evation of the sheaf with the barley harvest. There appears to be a reference to a festival of bar-ley in 4Q325 3 and 4Q326 4. The fragmentary nature of these texts means we do not know whether the festival was a festival of firstfruits. Second, although the Feast of Weeks is described as "the firstfruits of the grain of wheat" (הבכורים לדגן החטים; 11QT 43:6), the emphasis appears to be on "grain" rather than "wheat". Thus, reference is made to "the new grain offering" (מנחה חדשה; 18:13; 19:10; cf. 4Q409 1:2), "the new bread" (לחם חדש; 11QT 19:7), "cakes of new leav-ened bread" ([חלות] לחם חמץ חדש; 18:14), "the bread of the firstfruits" (לחם הבכורים; 19:12) and "the firstfruits of the grain" (הבכורים לדגן; 43:3). Third, the Temple Scroll appears to follow Lev 23:9 – 22 in viewing the raising of the sheaf and the Feast of Weeks as closely correlated. In par-ticular, some of the offerings prescribed for the Feast of Weeks in Num 28:26 – 31 are offered on the day when the sheaf is raised. Fourth, 11QT 43:3 – 12 mentions only three festivals of first-fruits. The first of which is for the "firstfruits of the grain" or "the firstfruits of the grain of wheat" (cf. 4Q251 frag. 5). These four observations suggest that we should speak about a "feast of new grain", rather than a "feast of new barley" and "feast of new wheat". In addition, our arguments about the significance of Num 18:12 and Num 15:1 – 12 for the composer of this section of the Temple Scroll would also point towards three firstfruit feasts, rather than four.
45 Swanson, *The Temple Scroll and the Bible*, 227.

Besides Lev 23, biblical inspiration to further multiply the firstfruits festival was probably provided by Num 18:12 where it is stipulated that the firstfruits of the oil, wine and grain was to be given to YHWH, and as such become part of the priestly compensation.[46] Since the traditional festival calendar provided a context in which the firstfruit of grain was to be offered, it is apparent why the need would be felt to create festivals at which the oil and wine were to be offered. This was especially the case in the later Second Temple Period, when *Sukkot* had taken on a number of other associations besides celebrating the harvesting of the vine.[47] The composer of this section of the Temple Scroll was also informed by the list of supplementary offerings in Num 15:1–12. The association of these instructions with the festival of firstfruits stems from the distinctive introductory formula in v. 2: "when you enter the land I am giving you as a home" (כי תבאו אל־ארץ מושבתיכם אשר אני נתן לכם). A number of other occurrences of this or a similar formula in the Pentateuch introduce firstfruits legislation, most especially the elevation of the sheaf and firstfruits festival in Lev 23 (כי־תבאו אל־הארץ אשר אני נתן לכם; v. 10) and the offering of the basket of firstfruits in Deut 26 (כי־תבוא אל־הארץ אשר יהוה אלהיך נתן לך נחלה; v. 1).[48] For the composer of this section of the Temple Scroll further confirmation of this association was probably provided by the fact that the supplementary offerings consisted of the three harvest crops: a *grain* offering of flour mixed with *oil* and a drink offering of *wine*. In the Scroll's prescriptions the instructions about the three types of supplementary offerings are distributed amongst the three firstfruits festivals: sheep or goat (festival of new grain), rams (festival of new wine), bovines (festival of new oil). In the festival of new wine and new oil the relevant component of the supplementary offering receives ritual emphasis. This does not occur in the festival of new grain for a ritual focusing on the loaves offered to YHWH already exists in Lev 23:15–21.[49]

---

46 Note the allusion to Num 18:12 in the context of the festivals of the firstfruits in 11QT 43:3–4.

47 See Jeffrey L. Rubenstein, *The History of Sukkot in the Second Temple and Rabbinic Periods*, BJS 302 (Atlanta: Scholars Press, 1995); Håkan Ulfgard, *The Story of Sukkot: The Setting, Shaping, and Sequel of the Biblical Feast of Tabernacles*, BGBE 34 (Tübingen: Mohr Siebeck, 1998); Weyde, *Appointed Festivals*, 145–236.

48 See וכי־תבאו אל־הארץ (Lev 19:23) which introduces the requirement to offer the first cropping of a fruit tree to YHWH; בבאכם אל־הארץ אשר אני מביא אתכם שמה (Num 15:18) introduces the offering of the first ground meal. For other occurrences see Lev 14:34; 25:2; Num 34:2; Deut 6:10; 7:1; 11:29; 17:14; 18:9.

49 In the festivals associated with new grain, the supplementary offerings for a sheep or goat accompany the purification sacrifice offered on the day of the raising of the sheaf (11QT 18:5–6). In the festival of new wine twelve rams are offered accompanied by their supplemen-

To incorporate the additional festivals into the religious year the festival calendar in Lev 23 provided the important inspiration. As we have seen this calendar describes two occasions, the raising of the sheaf and the offering of the new grain, separated by a period of fifty days. This provides a pattern for the Temple Scroll. Thus, the feast of new wine takes place fifty days after *Shavu'ot*, and the feast of new oil a further fifty days later. Maintaining a scriptural pattern appears to be more important than the practicalities of the agricultural season for the new feasts do not coincide with the reality of harvests in Palestine.[50]

The dependence of the Temple Scroll on the Pentateuch at most points is apparent as we examine the individual festivals.[51] The raising of the sheaf follows Lev 23:12–14, but has been preceded by the sin offering prescribed in Num 28:30 for *Shavu'ot* (11QT 18:1–10). In accordance with the stipulations of Lev 23 *Shavu'ot* is celebrated fifty days later. The Temple Scroll follows Lev 23:15–21, but elements of the feast are altered in order to ensure that all Israel are represented. Thus, each of the tribal leaders offers the bread to YHWH and twelve lambs are offered (11QT 18:10–19:9). Fifty days later a festival of new wine is celebrated. The prescriptions for this feast in the Temple Scroll are considerably more extensive, perhaps because it has no precedent or because it had a significant role for the composer of this text and his audience. The prescriptions for the Feast of Weeks provide a template for the overall festival, but various distinctive elements are introduced. At the beginning of the ceremony wine is offered on the altar, together with twelve rams and their remaining accompanying sacrifices. For the yearling lambs and the grain offerings that are to be offered the Temple Scroll goes into detail about the appropriate sacrificial procedures drawing on Lev 2 and 3, as well as outlining the priestly emolument with the aid of Num 18 and Lev 7. The prescriptions for the festival of new wine end with a communal drinking of the new wine (11 QT 19:11–21:10). A further fifty days later the festival of new oil is to be kept. Again the stipulations are fairly extensive and *Shavu'ot* in Lev 23 provides the pattern for the new festival. As with the wine, the first-fruits of the oil are offered on the altar. It was perhaps then used for lighting. The purification sacrifices and burnt sacrifices are then described, and the

---

tary offerings. The offering of wine is described first (11QT 19:14–15) with the rest of the offering, including the rams, appended as though they were the supplementary offerings (11QT 19:15–20:03)! In the festival of the new oil each of the tribes pour oil over the altar (11QT 21:15–16). The subsequent ritual is difficult to reconstruct with confidence because of the fragmentary nature of the Temple Scroll at this point, but the flour and oil of the supplementary offerings that accompany the bull are mentioned (11QT 22:01–05).

50 Eli Borukhov, "The Oil Festival: A Comment", *RevQ* 22 (2006): 475–78.
51 For detailed discussion see Swanson, *The Temple Scroll and the Bible*, 17–116.

priestly emolument is set out. For these prescriptions the writer again utilizes Num 18 and Lev 3. The festival ends with a festive meal and the people anointing themselves with oil. Like the communal drinking of wine, this part of the festival has no scriptural precedent (11QT 21:12–23:01).

Shavu'ot and Ritual Innovation

In this essay I have traced the history of the Israelite feast of weeks or *Shavu'ot* from its earliest appearance in the book of Deuteronomy (Deut 16:9–12) through the Holiness Code (Lev 23:9–22) and the covenant renewal after the Golden Calf incident (Exod 34:22) to the Temple Scroll (11QT 18:1–23:01). I also examined its partial precursor in the Covenant Code (Exod 23:18). Such an examination has allowed us to trace repeated transformation of the festival over a period of roughly six centuries from approximately the eighth or seventh century to the second century BCE. Four stages of development can be distinguished, not including the feast of harvest in Exod 23. Each of these stages modifies the previous stages and these changes can be examined exegetically. In the development of the ritual certain other closely related ritual texts are also utilized. The most important of these are Num. 15:1–12, 28:26–31 and Deut 26:1–11.

The development that we have traced shows that the relationship to precursor texts altered significantly during the latter half of the first millennium BCE. Each of the four stages we have examined modified an existing text or texts which appear to have been regarded as authoritative in some way. The earliest instance is found in Deut 16. This shows considerable freedom in its utilization of the Covenant Code's instructions on the festival calendar. Although there is some evidence of verbal appropriation especially in vv. 3–4 and 16–17, a number of verses show almost no verbal overlap with the earlier festival calendar, including the instructions for *Shavu'ot*. Many of the changes are determined by the agenda of cultic centralization that has been identified as so important to the earliest composition of Deuteronomy. This has no obvious textual impulse, but is usually attributed to political developments in the seventh century BCE.[52] At the opposite end of this history of development we have the innovations in the Temple Scroll. The multiplication of firstfruits festivals appears to be exegetically driven by a particular reading of Num 18:12 and Num 15. The indebtedness of the Temple Scroll to authoritative scriptural texts is apparent throughout the descrip-

---

52 For an alternative proposal in the early Persian period see Kratz, *Composition*, 130–32; Juha Pakkala, "The Date of the Oldest Edition of Deuteronomy", *ZAW* 121 (2009): 388–401.

tion of the firstfruits festivals, for the composer of this section of the Temple Scroll draws upon diverse Pentateuchal texts to generate novel rituals. Swanson argues that the resonances with scriptural texts were not intended merely to give the legislation a "biblical feel", but are conscious allusions for particular and discernible exegetical reasons. Though overstated, his claim that "there is very little which cannot be traced to a biblical source" highlights the stark differences from the textual utilization exhibited in Deut 16.[53]

Leviticus 23 and Exod 34 lie between Deut 16 and the Temple Scroll historically, but already show a number of exegetical tendencies similar to the Temple Scroll. Leviticus 23 demonstrates significant evidence of harmonizing instincts, not only in conflating the semi-annual Babylonian calendar and the three pilgrim festival calendar, but also in integrating the offering of the firstfruits in Deut 26:1–11 into the festival calendar. Though it offers less evidence for ritual innovation, Exodus 34 shows a similar concern for harmonization, integrating textual material from the Covenant Code, Deuteronomy and the Holiness Code. Whilst Lev 23 and Exod 34 show a harmonizing hermeneutic that is also found in the Temple Scroll, the Temple Scroll's multiplication of firstfruits festivals deploys an exegetical logic that goes significantly beyond harmonization.

The central role that hermeneutical and exegetical reasoning plays in the instances of ritual change that we have examined raises the question of the relationship between ritual instructions and ritual practice in ancient Israel and Second Temple Judah. Can it really be the case that novel rituals were generated textually? Such a possibility seems only conceivable in a highly textualized culture, though this is arguably what Judaism was becoming during the late first millennium BCE. But if this was so, how did such exegetical texts relate to actual festive practice? The evidence for exegetical reasoning suggests that it might be better to think of these texts in the first instance as exercises in scribal speculation and theorizing more than reflections of actual practice; an analogous situation existed in biblical and near Eastern law. Even if this were so, it is hard to imagine that speculations within the priestly-scribal groups that controlled temple ritual in the Second Temple period would not have had some impact on actual temple practice. Consequently, we should probably imagine a complex interrelationship between scribal speculation and ritual practice. Scribal speculation, particularly in texts claiming religious authority, results in changes to practice, and practice can give rise to scribal speculation. The best window we might have on this interaction would be in the later cases of ritual innovation that we examined. Thus, prior to the composition of the Temple Scroll, there was pre-

---

53 Swanson, *The Temple Scroll and the Bible*, 227.

sumably some occasion or occasions when the firstfruits of oil and wine were offered (cf. 2 Chron 31:5), and Judg 21:19–21 has been pointed to as evidence for an early festival for the harvesting of the wine.[54] If so, the Temple Scroll's prescriptions provided an exegetical justification, whilst also formalizing the time of offering. If we turn to consider the reception of the Temple Scroll's festival calendars, we should recall the practical difficulties in accommodating the Temple Scroll's calendar to agricultural realities.[55] Nevertheless, there is some evidence that such a calendar might have been followed by some in the late Second Temple period. Philo reports that the *Therapeutae* celebrate a feast every fifty days (*Cont.* 65) and some post-Second Temple texts refer to other firstfruits festivals.[56] If similarly multifaceted interactions between scribal exegesis and ritual practice are to be imagined for the earlier textual stages that we have examined then the process of ritual innovation was far more complex than even our analysis of the different textual stages of development has been able to uncover.

Since ritual innovation was such a constant feature during the first millennium BCE we might ask how such innovation was viewed. There is evidence for a negative appraisal of ritual innovation in Leviticus and 1 Kings. Increasingly it appears divine authorization from Sinai was perceived to be necessary for ritual practices to be deemed orthodox. There is, of course, a paradox here that ritual innovation is introduced precisely by attributing the altered rituals to Moses or, in the case of the Temple Scroll, to God himself. As Bell observes, although not the case with all invented rituals, some invented rituals can seek to conceal the fact of their own development.[57] Attribution to an authoritative figure is a clear way of achieving that, as is the reworking of authoritative texts. What we can perceive as ritual innovation in the Feast of Weeks may even have been hidden from those doing the innovation. This is especially the case with Exod 34 and Lev 23 where a harmonistic hermeneutic is employed. As in the modern world so also in the ancient, harmonistic exegesis can be one of the most innovative forms of exegesis, but this fact is often concealed from those interpreting the text. In other cases the innovations might have been apparent to authors and the first recipients of the text. The radical reconfiguration of Israel's worship around a single

---

54 Milgrom, *Leviticus 23–27*, 2075.

55 Milgrom rightly raises the question of whether the Temple Scrolls were theoretical or not (*Leviticus 23–27*, 2074–2075).

56 Targ. Ps.-Jon. on Exod 22:28 refers to ביכורי פירך וביכורי חמר. In addition, a fragment of Sa'adiah Gaon's *Kitāb al-Tamyīz* mentions firstfruits of barley, wheat, wine and oil (Yigal Yadin, *The Temple Scroll. Volume 1: Introduction* [Jerusalem: Israel Exploration Society, 1983], 119–22; Joseph M. Baumgarten, *Studies in Qumran Law*, SJLA 24 [Leiden: Brill, 1977], 136).

57 Bell, *Ritual*, 224–25.

sanctuary in Deuteronomy, of which the ritual calendar in Deut 16 was a part, would likely be such a case.

The question of how these innovations would have been perceived has a contribution to make to the difficult question of whether or not the textual corpora in which the festival calendars occur were designed to replace their textual precursors. Such a case has been made for the Deuteronomic code, the Holiness Code and the Temple Scroll.[58] These judgements are rightly to be made on the basis of patterns of alterations across the entire textual corpus and the rhetorical presentation of the corpus in relation to its textual precursor(s). Where such an approach has been followed, the volume of material means that it has usually only been possible to consider one text in relation to its precursor(s). By contrast, our examination of the Feast of Weeks focuses on the textual prescriptions for a single festival – eventually a complex of festivals. Whilst this introduces obvious limitations, it does allow a perspective on how the relationships to textual precursors changed during the second half of the first millennium. It seems reasonable to conclude that replacement was a more conceivable strategy at an earlier stage. The harmonizing instincts of Lev 23 and Exod 34 suggest they were understood as supplements to communally recognized authoritative texts. The Temple Scroll's many-sided dependence on earlier texts including its attention to precise textual details and its indebtedness to particular formulations points to the high authoritative status of the texts the Temple Scroll utilizes. In addition, the Temple Scroll provides far more details for the Feast of New Wine and New Oil than the Raising of the Sheaf and the Feast of New Grain. For the latter feasts the Temple Scroll does little more than harmonize the prescriptions for the Feast of Weeks in Lev 23 and Num 28 in light of Num 15. By attributing the instructions to God on Sinai, the Temple Scroll implies that Moses' instructions to the people in Leviticus are deficient in lacking the two additional firstfruits feasts. The instructions in the Temple Scroll and in the Pentateuch could have been seen as variants consistent with original delivery by God and repetition by Moses to the people. Thus, the Temple Scroll's instructions could have been intended as an authoritative commentary with significant omissions restored (!), rather than as a functional replacement of the Pentateuch.

---

58 Levinson, *Deuteronomy and the Hermeneutics of Legal Innovation*; Jeffrey Stackert, *Rewriting the Torah: Literary Revision in Deuteronomy and the Holiness Legislation*, FAT 52 (Tübingen: Mohr Siebeck, 2007); Simone Paganini, *"Nicht darfst du zu diesen Wörtern etwas hinzufügen": Die Rezeption des Deuteronomiums in der Tempelrolle. Sprache, Autoren und* Hermeneutik, BZABR 11 (Wiesbaden: Harrassowitz, 2009).

The reworking of authoritative ritual texts is a particular example of what Bernard Levinson described as the hermeneutics of legal innovation.[59] In his seminal book Levinson highlights how the authors of Deuteronomy sought to subvert and replace the Covenant Code. As I have suggested the innovations in Lev 23, Exod 34 and the Temple Scroll may be intended not so much to subvert and replace, but augment. This is particularly the case with new rituals. This hermeneutic of ritual innovation, as we may call it, presents new rituals as though in essential continuity with earlier rituals despite significant innovations. Existing rituals are necessary to provide a density of traditional ritual actions upon which the writers of the Holiness Code and the Temple Scroll can improvise. This improvisation is central to the new ritual's effectiveness, for the new ritual is intended not to displace its ritual precursors, but to take its place alongside them as part of an enlarged ritual system that imparts meaning to the ritual practitioners' world. The new ritual must draw on previous materials so as to be sufficiently continuous with them to belong to the sytem, but distinctive enough to justify its own existence.

This way of creating new festivals by creative improvisation on existing rituals can be contrasted to another form of ritual innovation that is quite different. In the same period that we have been examining a number of festivals and fast days were introduced into the Jewish calendar. Zechariah 8:19 briefly mentions four fast days that have usually been associated with events around the fall of Jerusalem, although certainty about these associations is difficult.[60] Later in the Second Temple period the book of Esther describes the legendary origins of Purim. These days in the annual calendar are introduced without seeking authoritative precedent in a developing scriptural corpus. This is not to say that certain practices familiar from other rituals – such as fasting and feasting – were not utilized, but there is no need to present them as developing existing rituals. The rituals commemorate a historical occasion that is *sui generis* and its presence in the Jewish calendar requires no further justification and no textual manipulation of the type that we have otherwise been reviewing. The ritual's dependence on an event means that not only is there no need to hide its origins, but that it would be counterproductive to do so. In sum we could say that there are two different ways to introduce new festivals into the Jewish calendar. Such a distinction should be viewed as a heuristic distinction rather than an ab-

---

59 Levinson, *Deuteronomy.*

60 See the warnings in Peter R. Ackroyd, *Exile and Restoration: A Study of Hebrew Thought of the Sixth Century B.C.* (Philadelphia: Westminster Press, 1968), 207 n. 122.

solute one, for the example of Hanukkah shows that both approaches to ritual innovation can be present at the same time.

My examination of the transformations of *Shavuʿot* also throws open a window onto what some have called the "canonical process" or scripturalization in Old Testament texts. Each stage of development that we have examined orientates itself to an authoritative precursor – even as early as *Urdeuteronomium* in the seventh century BCE – but the way that orientation takes place changes drastically over the period. Leviticus 23 and Exodus 34 exhibit a need to harmonize Pentateuchal laws, but Lev 23 in particular still retains considerable freedom in expression. The Temple Scroll also has strong harmonistic tendencies, but in addition it creates new festivals due to a sense of exegetical necessity. My examination tends to suggest that such scripturalization should not be viewed as an external act of closure – as the language of canon and canonization is often taken to suggest – but a growing development deeply embedded in the literature. The boundaries of authoritative literature are certainly not fixed, but the existing material increasingly determines the developments it can make. This does not mean that what appears to us as surprising innovations cannot be made. The Temple Scroll shows that novel developments of ritual texts can occur alongside a commitment to the traditional text. Indeed, it is arguably this commitment to the traditional text that results in such surprising innovations. It is commitment to the authoritative text that increasingly provides the community's fixed point, rather than one particular enactment of the ritual events prescribed in it.

Conclusion

Although our first instinct may be to regard it as counter-intuitive, ritual innovation is clearly evidenced in biblical texts. We may go further and say that it has a long history, some of which we are fortunate enough to be able to trace through extant biblical texts. Our dependence upon textual material and the evidence that revision of existing festivals and the creation of new festivals was exegetically inspired raises challenging questions about the relation between ritual instructions and ritual practice in ancient Israel. I have tentatively sought to address some of these questions. Is it the case that novel rituals were generated textually? How did such exegetical texts relate to actual festive practice? How did the scribes understand their textual manipulation to relate to the ritual traditions with which they were familiar? However we chose to answer these questions, it is clear that recognizing the existence of ritual innovation in biblical texts poses a challenge to cherished dichotomies: innovation versus faithfulness, text versus reality, ritual versus scripture.

Jeffrey Stackert
How the Priestly Sabbaths Work: Innovation in Pentateuchal Priestly Ritual[1]

The two major pentateuchal Priestly strata, the Priestly Source (P) and the Holiness Writings (H), each exhibit a special interest in the Sabbath, its conceptualization, and its imagined function. At the same time, P and H advance markedly different understandings of the Sabbath. In this study, I will address these distinctive perspectives and clarify the divergent views of the Sabbath in P and H. I will argue that the purpose of P's Sabbath is agricultural blessing, and Sabbath observance in P serves as a reminder (אות) *for the deity* to enact that blessing. As such, it functions much like circumcision in P and, also like circumcision, is directly related to P's promises to the patriarchs. For its part, H reimagines Sabbath observance as a reminder not for the deity but *for the Israelites*. H's Sabbath sign prompts Israel to reverence Yahweh, whose commands Israel must observe to achieve their holiness. The agricultural blessing associated with the Sabbath does not *result* from the rite in H but instead *facilitates* its observance.

I will also consider the implications of H's re-imagination of P's Sabbath. Because of the specific innovations that H introduces, it cannot be viewed in this case as simply supplementing P's Sabbath ideology without contradicting it. I will show instead that H's revisions and innovations are part of a concerted effort to expand P's Sabbath work prohibition. The result is a conceptualization of the Sabbath that stands in stark contrast to that of P. Finally, I will show that, through its careful interpolations, H in this instance substantially mutes the P substratum that it augments. Even so, once these strata are disentangled, two distinctive shapings of the Sabbath emerge, each well integrated into and thus reflective of the distinctive religious vision of its composition.

1 Earlier, abbreviated versions of this paper were presented in 2013 at the International Meeting of the Society of Biblical Literature in St Andrews and at Brandeis University. I am grateful for the invitations to present on each of these occasions and for the helpful questions and feedback I received in each venue. My arguments here were also helped significantly by conversations with my colleague, Simeon Chavel, and from the comments and critiques that I received on a written draft from my student, Liane Marquis. I warmly thank them both. I am responsible, of course, for all remaining errors here.

1. The Priestly Source

Before turning to my analysis of the Sabbath in pentateuchal Priestly literature, it is necessary to outline my approach to pentateuchal Priestly texts more generally. I begin from and build upon the well-argued position that the H stratum of the Priestly source, found both in the so-called "Holiness Code" in Lev 17–27 and in various texts in Exodus, Leviticus 1–16, and Numbers, postdates and supplements a prior P document.[2] In my view, the P text that H supplements is a continuous and independent, literary document that can be characterized, using modern categories, as a problem-oriented historical novel with mythic ambitions.[3] Its historical fiction offers a political allegory for its contemporary context, which it seeks to influence.[4]

More specifically, P's aim is to enumerate and rationalize a set of rules that, if assiduously followed, will effect the requisite circumstances for Yahweh's hab-

---

2 See esp. Israel Knohl, *The Sanctuary of Silence: The Priestly Torah and the Holiness School*, trans. Jackie Feldman and Peretz Rodman (Minneapolis: Fortress, 1995); Baruch J. Schwartz, *The Holiness Legislation: Studies in the Priestly Code* (Jerusalem: Magnes, 1999), esp. 17–24 (in Hebrew); Christophe Nihan, *From Priestly Torah to Pentateuch: A Study of the Composition of the Book of Leviticus*, FAT II/25 (Tübingen: Mohr Siebeck, 2007).
3 On the nature of P as an originally independent literary source, see, *inter alia*, Klaus Koch, "P – Kein Redaktor!: Erinnerung an zwei Eckdaten der Quellenscheidung", *VT* 37 (1987): 446–67; Baruch J. Schwartz, "The Priestly Account of the Theophany and the Lawgiving at Sinai", in *Texts, Temples, and Traditions: A Tribute to Menahem Haran*, ed. Michael V. Fox *et al.* (Winona Lake, IN: Eisenbrauns, 1996), 103–34; Joel S. Baden, "Identifying the Original Stratum of P: Theoretical and Practical Considerations", in *The Strata of the Priestly Writings: Contemporary Debate and Future Directions*, ed. Sarah Shectman and Joel S. Baden, ATANT 95 (Zurich: Theologischer Verlag, 2009), 13–29.
On the historical novel genre, including its imagined realism, literariness, and fiction, see esp. Jerome de Groot, *The Historical Novel*, The New Critical Idiom (New York: Routledge, 2010). For discussion of the close relationship between history and myth, see Bruce Lincoln, *Discourse and the Construction of Society: Comparative Studies of Myth, Ritual, and Classification* (New York: Oxford University Press, 1989), 23–26. As Lincoln notes, myth moves beyond history by being not just a credible narrative; it also seeks to be an authoritative one.
4 For a discussion of political allegory in the Hebrew Bible, see Joel Rosenberg, *King and Kin: Political Allegory in the Hebrew Bible*, ISBL (Bloomington: Indiana University Press, 1986), 1–46. For its employment in P, see esp. Simeon Chavel, *Oracular Law and Priestly Historiography in the Torah*, FAT II/71 (Tübingen: Mohr Siebeck, 2014). Chavel argues, "The author [P] does not care about Israel's origins except to the degree that they condition in some way the structure and behavior of the society in the author's own times. To this end, it seems correct to suppose that the author constructs a transparent portrayal, one that he feels he can safely assume the audience will perceive, consider with respect to its own conditions, and apply without straining" (175–76).

itation among the Israelites. This habitation, by virtue of the deity's realization and maintenance of it, confers tangible benefits upon Israel. To this end, P begins by depicting the historical origins of the world in Yahweh's creation.[5] It then describes the intolerable violence (חמס, Gen 6:11) on earth that prompts both Yahweh's decision to inhabit the world and the Flood that destroys nearly all of its creatures.[6] P then narrates the process of Yahweh's transition from the heavens to the earth. This process includes the formal selection of Abram and his descendants as Yahweh's people, the establishment of the deity's earthly habitation, the revelation of the rules that attend this sanctuary, and the eventual settlement of Yahweh's sanctuary amidst the Israelites in Canaan. In this historicized narrative, P offers a distinctive account of the origins of Israel and its religion, an account that seeks to establish credibility for its ritual, legal, and geographical claims in its present.

For its part, H revises and supplements P's historical account, with a primary focus upon legal innovation. Though H also draws from the Elohistic and Deuteronomic Torah sources, there is no doubt that P is its main intellectual font. Thus, even as H recasts P in certain respects, it must be emphasized that H's continuity with P far outweighs its divergence from it.[7]

---

5 There have been several recent attempts to attribute the Priestly creation account, in part or in whole, to H rather than P. See, e. g., Yairah Amit, "Creation and the Calendar of Holiness", in *Tehillah le-Moshe: Biblical and Judaic Studies in Honor of Moshe Greenberg,* ed. Mordechai Cogan, Barry L. Eichler, and Jeffrey H. Tigay (Winona Lake, IN: Eisenbrauns, 1997), 13*–29* (esp. 22*–26*) (in Hebrew); Edwin Firmage, "Genesis 1 and the Priestly Agenda", *JSOT* 82 (1999): 94–114; Jacob Milgrom, "H$_R$ in Leviticus and Elsewhere in the Torah", in *The Book of Leviticus: Composition and Reception,* ed. Rolf Rendtorff and Robert A. Kugler, VTSup 93 (Leiden: Brill, 2003), 24–40 (at 33–37); Bill T. Arnold, "Genesis 1 As Holiness Preamble", in *Let Us Go Up to Zion: Essays in Honour of H. G. M. Williamson on the Occasion of his Sixty-Fifth Birthday,* ed. Iain Provan and Mark J. Boda, VTSup 153 (Leiden: Brill, 2012), 331–43. These studies struggle to understand P as a narrative composition. The present study demonstrates the fundamental role that the Priestly creation account plays in P's narrative and thus the untenability of attributing it to H.
6 See Jeremy Schipper and Jeffrey Stackert, "Blemishes, Camouflage, and Sanctuary Service: The Priestly Deity and His Attendants", *HBAI* 2 (2013): 458–78 (esp. 469, 475–76), which builds upon Baruch J. Schwartz, "The Flood Narratives in the Torah and the Question of Where History Begins", in *Shai le-Sara Japhet: Studies in the Bible, Its Exegesis and Its Language,* ed. M. Bar Asher *et al.* (Jerusalem: Bialik Institute, 2007), 139–54 (esp. 150–53) (in Hebrew).
7 Jeffrey Stackert, *Rewriting the Torah: Literary Revision in Deuteronomy and the Holiness Legislation,* FAT 52 (Tübingen: Mohr Siebeck, 2007); Jeffrey Stackert, "The Holiness Legislation and Its Pentateuchal Sources: Revision, Supplementation, and Replacement", in *The Strata of the Priestly Writings: Contemporary Debate and Future Directions,* ed. Sarah Shectman and Joel S. Baden, ATANT 95 (Zurich: Theologischer Verlag, 2009), 187–204.

Pentateuchal Priestly texts, like other biblical texts, employ a royal conceit in their characterization of the deity. As I will show, this royal depiction of the deity is especially relevant for understanding the Priestly Sabbath. Yahweh's royal status is first reflected in his creation of the world and his delegation of its administration to humanity. It similarly informs H's later claim that Yahweh is the owner of the land of Canaan (Lev 25:23). P's concern to portray Yahweh as the divine monarch also informs the plan and appurtenances of the sanctuary, including its cherubic throne and footstool, the ark, as well as the lavish materials used to construct it and the details of the cultic rites performed in it. It also stands behind the strictures placed upon priestly officiation in H: like a human king, Yahweh requires his attendants, the priests, to be unblemished (Lev 21:16 – 24; cf. Dan 1:3 – 4).[8]

One concrete manifestation of Yahweh's royal status in both P and H is his desire to dwell in uninterrupted and splendid repose. In P's creation account, for example, though the deity declares the various parts of his created world "good" (טוב) – an indication of his fondness for them as well as their proper function – and even declares the whole "very good" (טוב מאד), he prefers to remain at maximum remove from it. The same preference for minimal disruption characterizes Yahweh after he inhabits the sanctuary, where he insists upon strict physical separation from the Israelites, and purity and holiness in his immediate environs.

---

8 For discussion of the deity's royal depiction in pentateuchal Priestly literature, see, e. g., Menaham Haran, *Temples and Temple Service in Ancient Israel: An Inquiry into Biblical Cult Phenomena and the Historical Setting of the Priestly School* (Winona Lake, IN: Eisenbrauns, 1985), 251 – 57; Knohl, *Sanctuary of Silence*, 187 – 89; Erhard S. Gerstenberger, *Leviticus: A Commentary*, trans. D. W. Stott, OTL (Louisville: Westminster/John Knox, 1996), 316 – 18; Jan Joosten, *People and Land in the Holiness Code: An Exegetical Study of the Ideational Framework of the Law in Leviticus 17 – 26*, VTSup 67 (Leiden: Brill, 1996), 169 – 92; Moshe Weinfeld, *Social Justice in Ancient Israel and in the Ancient Near East*, 2nd ed. (Jerusalem: Magnes; Minneapolis: Fortress, 2000), 179 – 214 (esp. 207 – 14); Bernard F. Batto, "The Divine Sovereign: The Image of God in the Priestly Creation Account", in *David and Zion: Biblical Studies in Honor of J. J. M. Roberts*, ed. Bernard F. Batto and Kathryn L. Roberts (Winona Lake, IN: Eisenbrauns, 2004), 143 – 86; Christophe Nihan, "Du premier et du second temple: Rôles et fonction du sanctuaire d'Israël selon l'écrit sacerdotal", in *Le Roi Salomon: un héritage en question. Hommage à Jaques Vermeylen*, ed. Claude Lichtert and Dany Nocquet, Le livre et le rouleau 33 (Brussels: Lessius, 2008), 165 – 203; Mark S. Smith, *The Priestly Vision of Genesis 1* (Minneapolis: Fortress, 2010), 11 – 37; Schipper and Stackert, "Blemishes, Camouflage, and Sanctuary Service."
For explicit biblical characterizations of Yahweh as king, see e. g., 1 Sam 8:7; 12:12; Isa 43:15; 44:6; 52:7; Jer 8:19; 10:10; Mic 2:13; 4:7; Zeph 3:15; Zech 14:9,17; Mal 1:14; Pss 10:16; 20:10; 24:8,10; 29:10; 47:3; 84:4; 89:9; 93:1; 95:3; 96:10; 97:1; 98:6; 99:1; 146:10. For discussion, see esp. Marc Zvi Brettler, *God is King: Understanding an Israelite Metaphor*, JSOTSup 76 (Sheffield: JSOT Press, 1989).

Yahweh's predilection for repose combines with his enjoyment of his created beings to produce something of a paradox: though Yahweh likes humans, he prefers not to interact with them. Yahweh is thus dispositionally, if benignly, inattentive to humans in pentateuchal Priestly texts, a situation that obtains regardless of his imagined presence on earth or separation from it. Yahweh's "affectionate disregard" (to borrow an expression from Annie Dillard[9]) manifests in P and H in a variety of ways. For example, in P's account of the Flood, Yahweh only becomes attentive to the ruin in the world once the bloody violence there is entirely out of control (Gen 6:12b). Similarly, in P's depiction of the Israelites' plea to the deity for relief from Egyptian bondage (Exod 2:23aβ–25), it is only a great, collective outcry that can catch the deity's ear, prompting him to look upon the Israelites' suffering and act on their behalf. The implication is that a lesser outcry might go unnoticed. The rainbow sign after the Flood is similarly large and conspicuous; if it were not so sizeable, Yahweh might fail to notice it. Yahweh's inattentiveness also explains his need for reminders in the first place. As the rainbow demonstrates – and as I will argue in the case of P's Sabbath sign as well – the Priestly Yahweh is both aware of his attention deficit and motivated to overcome it. He thus designs a series of memory aids for himself and provides incentives for the Israelites to produce them.

2. The Sabbath in P

Several Priestly texts treat the Sabbath. In both P and H, the characterization of the Sabbath as a sign (אות) in Exod 31:13 and 17 reveals its conceptualization and rationalizes the ritual practice related to it. Exod 31:12–17 are thus the central text for understanding pentateuchal Priestly Sabbath ideology. These verses comprise an original P narrative stratum overlayed by an H supplement. Verses 12–13aα,15*,16–17* belong to P (unmarked below). With the exception of וינפש ("and refreshed himself", double underscored below) in v. 17, which is the contribution of the pentateuchal compiler or a post-compilational interpolater, the rest of the text belongs to H (single underscored):[10]

---

9 Annie Dillard, *Pilgrim at Tinker Creek*, Modern Classics (New York: Harper Perennial, 2007), 169. For an analysis of Dillard's portrayal of God in *Pilgrim at Tinker Creek*, see B. Jill Carroll, *The Savage Side: Reclaiming Violent Models of God* (Lanham, MD: Rowman & Littlefield, 2001), 15–38. Note that P's depiction of the deity here resembles in part the depiction of Enlil in *Atrahasis*.

10 For a detailed explanation of the stratification here, see Jeffrey Stackert, "Compositional Strata in the Priestly Sabbath Law: Exodus 31:12–17 and 35:1–3", *JHS* 11 (2011): 1–20,

[12] ויאמר יהוה אל משה לאמר [13] ואתה דבר אל בני ישראל לאמר <u>אך את שבתתי תשמרו כי אות הוא ביני</u>
<u>וביניכם לדרתיכם לדעת כי אני יהוה מקדשכם</u> [14] <u>ושמרתם את השבת כי קדש הוא לכם מחלליה מות יומת</u>
<u>כי כל העשה בה מלאכה ונכרתה הנפש ההוא מקרב עמיה</u> [15] ששת ימים יעשה מלאכה וביום השביעי שבת
<u>שבתון קדש</u> ליהוה כל העשה מלאכה ביום השבת <u>מות</u> יומת [16] ושמרו בני ישראל את השבת לעשות את
השבת לדרתם ברית עולם [17] ביני ובין בני ישראל אות הוא לעלם כי ששת ימים עשה יהוה את השמים ואת
הארץ וביום השביעי שבת <u>וינפש</u>

[12] Yahweh said to Moses, [13] "As for you, speak to the Israelites, 'Surely my Sabbaths you
shall observe, for it is a sign between you and me in perpetuity that you may know that
I, Yahweh, sanctify you. [14] You shall keep the Sabbath, for it is holy to you. The one who
defiles it shall surely be put to death. Indeed, anyone who does work on it – that person
shall be cut off from the midst of his people. [15] On six days work may be done, but on
the seventh day is a complete cessation, holy to Yahweh. Anyone who does work on the
cessation day shall surely be put to death. [16] The Israelites shall ever keep the cessation,
performing the cessation as a perpetual requirement. [17] It is a perpetual sign between
the Israelites and me that in six days Yahweh made the heavens and the earth, but on
the seventh day he ceased and refreshed himself.'"

Exodus 35:1–3 comprise the corresponding narrative of Moses's report of this law
to the Israelites. These verses are similarly composed of P and H strata:

[1] ויקהל משה את כל עדת בני ישראל ויאמר אלהם אלה הדברים אשר צוה יהוה לעשת אתם [2] ששת ימים
תעשה מלאכה וביום השביעי <u>יהיה לכם קדש</u> שבת <u>שבתון</u> ליהוה כל העשה בו מלאכה יומת [3] <u>לא תבערו</u>
אש בכל משבתיכם ביום השבת

[1] Moses gathered the whole assembly of the Israelites and said to them, "These are the
words that Yahweh has commanded to do. [2] On six days work shall be done, but on the
seventh day shall be holy occasion for you, a complete cessation of Yahweh. Anyone
who does work on it shall be put to death. [3] You shall not kindle a fire in any of your habitations on the Sabbath day."

---

doi:10.5508/jhs.2011.v11.a15. For alternative compositional analyses of this unit, see Gerhard
von Rad, *Die Priesterschrift im Hexateuch: Literarisch untersucht und theologisch gewertet*, BWAT
(Stuttgart: Kohlhammer, 1934), 62–63; Gnana Robinson, *The Origin and Development of the Old
Testament Sabbath: A Comprehensive Exegetical Approach*, BET 21 (Frankfurt am Main: Lang,
1988), 231–36; Klaus Grünwaldt, *Exil und Identität: Beschneidung, Passa und Sabbat in der
Priesterschrift*, BBB 85 (Frankfurt am Main: Anton Hain, 1992), 171; Matthias Köckert, *Leben
in Gottes Gegenwart: Studien zum Verständnis des Gesetzes im Alten Testament*, FAT 43 (Tübingen: Mohr Siebeck, 2004), 96–102; Saul M. Olyan, "Exodus 31:12–17: The Sabbath According
to H, or the Sabbath According to P and H?", *JBL* 124 (2005): 201–209 (with a catalogue of
alternative proposals at 203 n 9). For the most recent assessment of the various proposals,
see Christophe Nihan, "Das Sabbatgesetz Exodus 31,12–17, die Priesterschrift und das Heilig-
keitsgesetz: Eine Auseinandersetzung mit neueren Interpretationen", in *Wege der Freiheit: Zur
Entstehung und Theologie des Exodusbuches; Die Beiträge eines Symposions zum 70. Geburtstag
von Rainer Albertz*, ed. Reinhard Achenbach, Ruth Ebach, and Jakob Wöhrle, ATANT 104 (Zurich: Theologischer Verlag Zurich, 2014), 131–49.

As delimited here, the P text narrates the deity's introduction to the Israelites of the seventh day as the cessation day (השבת) and his instruction that the Israelites must abstain from work on it. Work cessation is required on every seventh day going forward (ברית עולם, "a perpetual requirement"), and the penalty for working on the cessation day is death. Finally, observance of the Sabbath is a sign that is associated with the deity's cessation on the seventh day of creation (Gen 2:1–3).

H's contributions to this law, including its characterization of the Sabbath as a sign in v. 13, are relatively straightforward, and I will treat them below. By contrast, even when H's interpolations are stripped away, P's Sabbath law is less transparent. Its characterization of the Sabbath sign in v. 17 is especially opaque. At issue are both the nature of this sign and its relation to the seventh day of the Priestly creation. As I will show, these two issues are fundamentally linked.

2.1 The Sabbath as Sign

To understand the nature of P's Sabbath sign requires both an analysis of the grammar of Exod 31:17 and a consideration of other signs in P. At issue grammatically is the syntax of the כי in v. 17b and its attendant semantic function:

ביני ובין בני ישראל אות הוא לעלם <u>כי</u> ששת ימים עשה יהוה את השמים ואת הארץ
וביום השביעי שבת וינפש

It is a perpetual sign between the Israelites and me *kî* in six days Yahweh made the heavens and the earth, but on the seventh day he ceased and refreshed himself.

Is the כי particle here a causal conjunction, or is it a syndetic complementizer?[11] If the כי introduces a causal clause ("for"), v. 17b may be read as rationalizing Sabbath observance as a form of *imitatio dei*, but the purpose/content of the

---

11 For discussion of linguistic complementation in biblical Hebrew, including specific discussion of כי, see Talmy Givón, *Verb Complements and Relative Clauses: A Diachronic Case Study in Biblical Hebrew*, Afroasiatic Linguistics 1.4, Monographic Journals of the Near East (Malibu: Undena, 1974); Barry Louis Bandstra, "The Syntax of Particle 'ky' in Biblical Hebrew and Ugaritic" (PhD diss., Yale University, 1982), 97–98, 116–18; Cynthia L. Miller, *The Representation of Speech in Biblical Hebrew Narrative: A Linguistic Analysis*, HSM 55 (Winona Lake, IN: Eisenbrauns, 2003), 95; Bracha Nir, "Complementizer", in *Encyclopedia of Hebrew Language and Linguistics*, ed. Geoffrey Khan, (Brill Online, 2013). http://referenceworks.brillonline.com/entries/encyclopedia-of-hebrew-language-and-linguistics/complementizer-EHLL_COM_00000792.

sign in v. 17a remains undefined.[12] If the כי is a complementizer ("that"), the sign points specifically to the deity's actions on the seventh day of creation.

Exod 20:11a, which exhibits verbatim overlap with Exod 31:17b, has guided most exegetes' interpretations of the latter text:[13]

כי ששת ימים עשה יהוה את השמים ואת הארץ את הים ואת כל אשר בם וינח ביום השביעי

For in six days Yahweh made the heavens and the earth, the sea and all that is in them. Then he rested on the seventh day (Exod 20:11a).

Yet the similarity between Exod 20:11a and 31:17b, at least with regard to the כי clause, is misleading. In 20:11a, the כי clause is unambiguously causal, but it is not preceded by אות. This difference is determinative for understanding the syntax of each verse and the corresponding semantics of כי.[14] Thus, notwithstanding

---

12 In such a case, the sign is most readily understood as consistent with the description of the Sabbath in v. 13 as a sign for the Israelites. For attempts to read vv. 13 and 17 as consistent with each other, see, e. g., S. van den Eynde, "Keeping God's Sabbath: אות and ברית", in *Studies in the Book of Exodus: Redaction–Reception–Interpretation*, ed. Marc Vervenne, BETL 126 (Leuven: Leuven University Press, 1996), 501–11 (at 510). See also the discussion below.

13 See explicitly in, e. g., Samuel Rolles Driver, *The Book of Exodus*, Cambridge Bible for Schools and Colleges (Cambridge: Cambridge University Press, 1911), 345; Matitiahu Tsevat, "The Basic Meaning of the Biblical Sabbath", *VT* 22 (1972): 447–59 (at 448–49); Köckert, *Leben in Gottes Gegenwart*, 101; Alexandra Grund, *Die Entstehung des Sabbats: Seine Bedeutung für Israels Zeitkonzept und Erinnerungskultur*, FAT 75 (Tübingen: Mohr Siebeck, 2011), 282. For modern renderings of the כי in Exod 31:17 as a causal particle, see Niels-Erik A. Andreasen, *The Old Testament Sabbath: A Tradition-Historical Investigation*, SBLDS 7 (Missoula, MT: Society of Biblical Literature, 1972), 200–201 (notwithstanding his translation); Michael V. Fox, "The Sign of the Covenant: Circumcision in the Light of the Priestly *'ôt* Etiologies", *RB* 81 (1974): 557–96 (at 577, with explicit argumentation); Grünwaldt, *Exil und Identität*, 170; van den Eynde, "Keeping God's Sabbath", 503, 508; Olyan, "Exodus 31:12–17", 209; William H. C. Propp, *Exodus 19–40: A New Translation and Commentary*, AB 2A (New York: Doubleday, 2006), 494; Smith, *Priestly Vision*, 105; Grund, *Die Entstehung des Sabbats*, 273–74; KJV; ASV; NASB; NJPS; NIV; NKJV. For כי rendered as a complementizer, see, e. g., Cornelis Houtman, *Exodus*, trans. Sierd Woudstra, HCOT, 4 vols. (Leuven: Peeters, 2000), 3: 587–89; Olyan, "Exodus 31:12–17", 204; RSV; NRSV; ESV.

14 Note too that, notwithstanding the claims of many scholars, Exod 20:11 should not be ascribed to P. It is instead an interpolation, most likely from the pentateuchal compiler. See Baruch J. Schwartz, "The Sabbath in the Torah Sources" (paper presented at the annual meeting of the SBL, San Diego, CA, 19 November 2007); Jeffrey Stackert, "The Sabbath of the Land in the Holiness Legislation: Combining Priestly and Non-Priestly Perspectives", *CBQ* 73 (2011): 239–50 (at 241 n. 4); Stackert, "Compositional Strata", 8 n. 26. The compiler's reuse of the כי clause from Exod 31:17 may constitute the earliest recorded interpretation of this כי as causal. It is also significant that the understanding of the divine blessing of the seventh day in Exod 20:11 differs from what I will argue below is P's view.

the verbatim parallel between Exod 20:11a and 31:17b, other כי (...) אות constructions in biblical Hebrew provide a firmer basis for evaluating Exod 31:17b than does Exod 20:11a.

Comparable instances of כי (...) אות formulations appear in Exod 3:12; 13:16; 2Kgs 20:8–9//Isa 38:22;[15] and Jer 44:29:

ויאמר כי אהיה עמך וזה לך <u>האות כי</u> אנכי שלחתיך בהוציאך את העם ממצרים תעבדון את האלהים על ההר
הזה

He said, "I will be with you, and this shall be <u>the sign that</u> I have sent you: when you bring the people out from Egypt, you will serve God on this mountain." (Exod 3:12)

והיה ל<u>אות</u> על ידכה ולטוטפת בין עיניך <u>כי</u> בחזק יד הוציאנו יהוה ממצרים

It shall be <u>a sign</u> on your hand and a marker between your eyes <u>that</u> with a strong hand Yahweh brought us out from Egypt. (Exod 13:16)

[8] ויאמר חזקיהו אל ישעיהו מה <u>אות כי</u> ירפא יהוה לי ועליתי ביום השלישי בית יהוה [9] ויאמר ישעיהו זה לך <u>האות</u>
מאת יהוה <u>כי</u> יעשה יהוה את הדבר אשר דבר הלך הצל עשר מעלות אם ישוב עשר מעלות

[8] Hezekiah said to Isaiah, "What is <u>the sign that</u> Yahweh will heal me and that I may go up to the temple of Yahweh on the third day?" [9] Isaiah said, "This will be Yahweh's <u>sign</u> for you <u>that</u> Yahweh will do what he said: shall the shadow advance ten steps or retreat ten steps?" (2Kgs 20:8–9)

וזאת לכם <u>האות</u> נאם יהוה <u>כי</u> פקד אני עליכם במקום הזה למען תדעו כי קום יקומו דברי עליכם לרעה

This shall be <u>the sign</u> for you, says Yahweh, <u>that</u> I am going to visit you in this place, in order that you will know that my threats of harm shall be established against you! (Jer 44:29)

In each of these instances, the כי functions as a complementizer and closely resembles the כי that follows a verb of cognition, perception, or mental state.[16] Such similarity between the כי that follows these verbs and the כי in כי (...) אות constructions is unsurprising, for all of the signs in the כי (...) אות constructions cited here function as proofs or mnemonic aids. They are thus closely associated

---

15 Compare the use of אשר rather than כי in Isa 38:7 (//2 Kgs 20:9). As Givón demonstrates, the use of אשר as a complementizer is a development that occurs in late biblical and post-biblical Hebrew (*Verb Complements and Relative Clauses*, 10–22).

16 See James Muilenberg, "The Linguistic and Rhetorical Usages of the Particle כי in the Old Testament", *HUCA* 32 (1961): 135–60 (at 144); Joüon §157d–f (with explicit relation of the two constructions); Bandstra, "The Syntax of Particle 'ky' in Biblical Hebrew and Ugaritic", 97–99, 103–10; Miller, *Representation of Speech*, 98; Carl Martin Follingstad, *Deictic Viewpoint in Biblical Hebrew Text: A Syntagmatic and Paradigmatic Analysis of the Particle* ki (Dallas: SIL International, 2001), 446–55.

with perception and knowledge.[17] This philological data strongly suggests that the כי in Exod 31:17 should be rendered as a complementizer, with the result that the seventh day of creation is that to which the Sabbath sign points.[18]

How and for whom does this sign function? In an insightful article from 1974, Michael V. Fox showed that the Priestly source includes several mnemonic cognition signs (אותות).[19] Paradigmatic examples include the rainbow after the Flood (Gen 9:12,13,17) and the blood on the doorposts at Passover (Exod 12:13).[20] In each of these cases, the sign functions as a memory aid for Yahweh, prompting him to recall and thus act upon a commitment that he made previously. Thus, when Yahweh sees the rainbow in the sky, he will recall his commitment (ברית) to never again destroy all flesh with a flood. Likewise, when Yahweh sees the blood around the door of the Israelites' homes, he will protect them from the destruction of the firstborn in Egypt.[21] Though the purpose of the sign of circumcision is less overtly described in the text, Fox makes a convincing argument that it too functions in P as a memory aid for the deity. When the Israelites have sexual intercourse, Yahweh will observe the male's circumcised penis, and this circumcision will remind him to bless the Israelites' sexual unions with fertility (Gen 17:16,20).[22]

---

17 Similar examples of nouns of cognition/perception that appear with the complementizer כי are עדה (Gen 21:30, but contrast Josh 24:27), זכרון (Isa 57:8 and possibly Exod 17:14), and מופת (Zech 3:8).

18 In light of the consistent function of כי in אות (...) כי constructions, Propp's suggestion that the meaning of כי in Exod 31:17 is ambiguous should be rejected (*Exodus 19–40*, 494). The correct interpretation of כי as a complementizer in Exod 31:17 is found already in LXX (ὅτι). That ὅτι should be read as a complementizer is clear by contrasting LXX's causal reading of כי in Exod 13:16. Note too that LXX renders כי as a complementizer with ὅτι in the undisputed cases of Exod 3:12; 2 Kgs 20:8–9; Isa 38:22; and Jer 44:29. It also correctly renders the complementizer אשר with ὅτι in Isa 38:7. Contrast John William Wevers's evaluation of LXX Exod 31:17: "This is quite different from MT, where the covenant refers to the demands made upon the people to observe; in Exod [=LXX] it is something that points to God's rest after the six days of creation" (*Notes on the Greek Text of Exodus*, SBLSCS 30 [Atlanta: Scholars Press, 1990], 515).

19 Fox, "Sign of the Covenant".

20 The full list of signs in P includes Gen 1:14; *9:12–13, 17*; *17:11*; Exod 7:3; *12:13*; *31:17*; Num 2:2 (mnemonic cognition signs in italics). Note that Fox does not distinguish between P and H as I do. My identification of P's signs thus does not precisely match his.

21 The meaning of לכם, "for you", in אתם שם אשר הבתים על לאת לכם הדם והיה, "The blood shall be a sign for you upon the houses where you are", in Exod 12:13aα is determined contextually by Exod 12:13aβ: עלכם ופסחתי הדם את וראיתי, "I will see the blood, and I will protect you." In other words, the sign will be *for* Yahweh to see and *for the benefit of* the Israelites.

22 Fox, "Sign of the Covenant", 594–95. For further development, see Schipper and Stackert, "Blemishes, Camouflage, and Sanctuary Service", 463–64, 474–77. David A. Bernat counters Fox's argument by arguing that circumcision signifies the individual's commitment to heed Yah-

Like the Priestly circumcision sign, the Sabbath sign in Exod 31:17 is not extensively elaborated. Taking Exod 31:12–17 as a unity (albeit on dubious, formal grounds),[23] Fox interprets v. 17 on the basis of v. 13: the Sabbath sign in each case is mnemonic for the Israelites, reminding them that Yahweh is the one who sanctifies them.[24] As a part of this interpretation, Fox rejects the possibility that the כי in v. 17 is a complementizer ("that"). He claims that such a rendering problematically identifies the Sabbath as a proof sign, to which he objects, "Why would knowledge of that fact [viz., that Yahweh created in six days and ceased on the seventh] be an end in itself?"

---

weh's precepts rather than a cognition sign for Yahweh (*Sign of the Covenant: Circumcision in the Priestly Tradition*, AIL 3 [Atlanta: Society of Biblical Literature, 2009], 36–40, 50–52). Nonetheless, as Bernat acknowledges, according to P's historical myth, Yahweh establishes circumcision as a sign *prior to* the giving of precepts at Sinai. This sequence creates an anachronism in Bernat's reconstruction. It should also be noted that circumcision applies in P both to Isaac and his descendants as well as to Ishmael and his descendants (Gen 17:18–26), making it unlikely that circumcision is related to heeding Yahweh's precepts. As I will show, Bernat's argument is closer to H's view than P's. See now also Barat Ellman, *Memory and Covenant: The Role of Israel's and God's Memory in Sustaining the Deuteronomic and Priestly Covenant* (Minneapolis: Fortress, 2013), 161–69. Ellman argues that circumcision is protective in P, akin to the rainbow and the Passover application of blood. In so doing, however, she conflates P's view with that of J (Exod 4:24–26). For a recent discussion of the history of Jewish and Christian interpretation of circumcision, see Nina E. Livesey, *Circumcision as a Malleable Symbol*, WUNT II/295 (Tübingen: Mohr Siebeck, 2010).

23 Fox follows and builds upon the formal analysis of Burke O. Long, *The Problem of Etiological Narrative in the Old Testament*, BZAW 108 (Berlin: Töpelmann, 1968), 69–78. He identifies a sequence of a) identification of the sign, b) purpose of the sign, and c) function of the sign in the P sign etiologies, sometimes with a recapitulation of elements following the a-b-c sequence (Fox, "Sign of the Covenant", 569–70, 576). Others have identified a larger chiastic structure in Exod 31:12–17. See, e. g., Meir Paran, *Forms of the Priestly Style in the Pentateuch: Patterns, Linguistic Usages, Syntactic Structures* (Jerusalem: Magnes, 1989), 167–69 (in Hebrew). Among recent studies, Timmer follows the formal arguments of Fox and also makes theologically-motivated, anti-critical arguments in favour of the unity of Exod 31:12–17 (*Creation, Tabernacle, and Sabbath: The Sabbath Frame of Exodus 31:12–17; 35:1–3 in Exegetical and Theological Perspective*, FRLANT 227 [Göttingen: Vandenhoeck & Ruprecht, 2009], 43–44, 53 and *passim*). Other treatments of Exod 31:12–17 as a unity include Knohl, *Sanctuary of Silence*, 14–19; Jacob Milgrom, *Leviticus 17–22*, AB 3A (New York: Doubleday, 2000), 1341–44; Milgrom, "H$_R$ in Leviticus", 29; Nihan, *From Priestly Torah*, 567–68; Grund, *Die Entstehung des Sabbats*, 275. See also Nihan's more recent treatment of this unit ("Sabbatgesetz"). In it he he turns away from his previous assignment of the unit to H and instead identifies it as a post-Priestly supplement (albeit one that builds upon H).

24 Fox, "Sign of the Covenant", 576–77. Regarding the compositional history of Exod 31:12–17, Fox suggests that it is possible that P took up earlier traditions in this unit, but he argues specifically that vv. 13 and 17 should not be ascribed to different hands.

In rejecting this view, Fox challenges a long tradition of interpreting the sign as a proof while rendering the כי as a complementizer. Abraham ibn Ezra already stated, "In my view, however, the meaning of 'it is a sign' is 'that six days he worked.' The one who does work on the Sabbath denies the work of creation."[25] In other words, Sabbath observance reminds the Israelites that Yahweh created the world, an act that demonstrated his sovereignty. Cornelis Houtman similarly argues that the Sabbath sign in v. 17 reminds the Israelites of Yahweh's creation. He avers, "Inherent in the latter is an important message: those belonging to Yahweh are to pattern the rhythm of their work after Yahweh's". He thus translates v. 17, *"for all time it is a sign between me and the Israelites. (It helps you to bear in mind) that Yahweh made the heaven and the earth in six days and rested on the seventh day and caught his breath."*[26]

These interpretations (and others like them) differ markedly from each other,[27] but they agree on one point: that the Sabbath sign is *for the Israelites*. It is this claim that requires re-evaluation, and it is with such reconsideration that a new interpretive solution emerges.[28] Immediately suggesting an alternative reading – that the sign is for the deity, *not* for the Israelites – are the other mnemonic cognition signs in P. As noted already, P's rainbow, circumcision, and Passover blood signs are all oriented toward the deity. In each case, Yahweh establishes the sign as a reminder *for himself.*[29] But if the same is the case for the

---

25 "ולפי דעתי כי פי׳ אות היא כי ששת ימים עשה. והנה העושה מלאכה בשבת מכחיש הוא במעשה בראשית" (*Torah Commentaries of Rabbi Abraham ibn Ezra*, ed. Asher Weiser, 3 vols [Jerusalem: Mosad Harav Kook, 1976], 2: 203).

26 Houtman, *Exodus*, 3: 587–89 (italics original).

27 Several aspects of the interpretations of Fox, ibn Ezra, and Houtman are problematic. For example, Fox's reading of causal כי in v. 17 is grammatically unlikely, as demonstrated already. Fox also dubiously harmonizes v. 17 with v. 13. For its part, ibn Ezra's reading suffers contextually. Neither Exod 31:12–17 nor any other P text expresses concern for acknowledgment or denial of the work of creation. This interpretation thus amounts to a *non sequitur*. Houtman's interpretation also suffers contextually, for it fails to recognize P's consistent employment of mnemonic cognition signs for the deity and, in so doing, tends to conflate vv. 13 and 17.

28 It should be noted that another interpretation is sometimes suggested, viz., that the sign is directed outwardly to other peoples/nations, making it an identity sign. See, e.g., Martin Noth, *Exodus: A Commentary*, trans. J. S. Bowden, OTL (Philadelphia: Westminster, 1962), 241; Grünwaldt, *Exil und Identität*, 179–80, 184. For decisive critique of this view, see Fox, "Sign of the Covenant", 576; van den Eynde, "Keeping God's Sabbath", 507.

29 H. Holzinger notes that the seeming orientation of the sign toward the Israelites rather than the deity is a departure from P's norm (*Exodus*, KHC 2 [Tübingen: Mohr, 1900], 147). Brevard S. Childs argues that the sign is a reminder both for the Israelites and for Yahweh. His reading appears to be problematically based on the reciprocity expressed by ביני ובין בני ישראל in Exod 31:13 and 17. Moreover, the connection he makes between covenant and creation in P is not sustain-

Sabbath, why should the deity seek a reminder of the seventh day of creation? What should he recall, and how does it relate to Israelite Sabbath observance? P describes the seventh day of creation in Gen 2:1–3:

¹ ויכלו השמים והארץ וכל צבאם ² ויכל אלהים ביום השביעי מלאכתו אשר עשה וישבת ביום השביעי מכל מלאכתו אשר עשה ³ ויברך אלהים את יום השביעי ויקדש אתו כי בו שבת מכל מלאכתו אשר ברא אלהים לעשות

¹ The heavens and the earth and their entire host were finished. ² On the seventh day God finished his work that he had done. He ceased on the seventh day from all of his work that he did. ³ God blessed the seventh day and set it apart, for on it he ceased from all the work of creation that he had done.

Beyond the deity's cessation on the seventh day, v. 3 reports that God also blessed the seventh day and set it apart from the previous days on which he worked. Though Exod 31:17's reference to the seventh day only cites the deity's cessation, this allusion is best understood as a *pars pro toto* reference to the entirety of God's actions that day, including his acts of blessing (בר״ך) and separation (קד״ש). These latter actions are properly understood in relation to each other.[30] That is, it is first by ceasing from his work on the seventh day that the deity sets it apart from the previous six days, but the distinctiveness of the seventh day also adheres specifically in the blessing it receives, for none of the other days is so treated.

What is the significance of the seventh day blessing? Divine blessings in P are blessings of fertility. Within P's creation account, the verb בר״ך appears twice prior to the description of the seventh day, each time with reference to fertility:

ויברך אתם אלהים לאמר פרו ורבו ומלאו את המים בימים והעוף ירב בארץ

God blessed them, saying, "Be fruitful and multiply and fill the waters in the seas, and let the birds multiply on the earth". (Gen 1:22)

---

able (*Exodus: A Critical, Theological Commentary*, OTL [Philadelphia: Westminster, 1974], 416, 522).

30 The meaning of קד״ש in Gen 2:3 must be determined within the larger context of P. Timmer correctly notes that, since the cult has not yet been established in Gen 2:3, קד״ש here cannot carry the cultic connotation that it will after the establishment of the sanctuary (*Creation, Tabernacle, and Sabbath*, 73). Yet such a cultic sense is unnecessary semantically. On the semantics of קד״ש in the Hebrew Bible generally and P in particular, see Baruch J. Schwartz, "Israel's Holiness: The Torah Traditions", in *Purity and Holiness: The Heritage of Leviticus*, ed. Marcel J. H. M. Poorthuis and Joshua Schwartz, Jewish and Christian Perspectives Series 2 (Leiden: Brill, 2000), 47–59.

ויברך אתם אלהים ויאמר להם אלהים פרו ורבו ומלאו את הארץ וכבשה

God blessed them and said to them, "Be fruitful and multiply and fill the earth and subdue it". (Gen 1:28a)

A survey of other divine blessings in P attests that fertility is consistently the benefit enjoyed by the recipient of the blessing (Gen 9:1; 17:16,20; 28:3; 35:9,11; 48:3 – 4).[31]

As Christopher Wright Mitchell observes, P's divine blessings do not impart fertility in cases where fertility would not otherwise exist.[32] P instead assumes that sexual activity will result in procreation – both for those who are blessed by the deity and for those who are not.[33] This is part of the goodness of creation in P: the deity deems good that which functions correctly, and such correct function includes reproductive capabilities.[34] By providing an extra measure of fertility, Yahweh's blessing allows its recipient to surpass this norm or to deviate from it, a point underscored by the special circumstances that attend each of P's divine blessings. Both at creation and following the Flood, the earth is uninhabited; the deity thus enables a superabundant proliferation to quickly populate it (Gen 1:22,28//5:2; 9:1; cf. 8:17). A special circumstance obtains, too, when Yahweh blesses Sarah in Gen 17:16. As a human, she should be able to bear children, but both she and Abraham are far past the age of childbearing (17:17). Moreover, typical human fertility does not entail birthing a multitude of nations (cf. 17:2–5). Yahweh thus blesses Sarah, enabling fertility in a case of infertility – and to abundance.[35] The subsequent articulations of this divine blessing, announced ei-

---

31 On blessing in the Hebrew Bible, including its relation to fertility, see Josef Scharbert, "ברך", *TDOT* 2: 279–308; Kent Harold Richards, "Bless/Blessing", *ABD* 1: 753–55; Christopher Wright Mitchell, *The Meaning of BRK "To Bless" in the Old Testament*, SBLDS 95 (Atlanta: Scholars Press, 1987); J. K. Aitken, *The Semantics of Blessing and Cursing in Ancient Hebrew*, ANES 23 (Leuven: Peeters, 2007).
32 Mitchell, *Meaning of BRK*, 63.
33 Within P's creation account, this point is underscored by the omission of any blessing on the land animals (Gen 1:24–25), in contrast to the water creatures and birds (1:20–22). Though not blessed by the deity, land animals are still capable of reproduction. For discussion, see, e.g., Hermann Gunkel, *Genesis*, trans. Mark E. Biddle, Mercer Library of Biblical Studies (Macon: Mercer University Press, 1997), 112; Claus Westermann, *Genesis 1–11*, trans. John J. Scullion, CC (Minneapolis: Fortress, 1994), 141–42.
34 BDB 374a; Westermann, *Genesis 1–11*, 113; I. Höver-Johag, "טוב", *TDOT* 5: 297–317 (esp. 304); Schipper and Stackert, "Blemishes, Camouflage, and Sanctuary Service", 468–70.
35 It appears that P presumes a kind of steady state theory of population growth and magnitude: population grows at a conventional rate and, after reaching its threshold, is self-sustaining. More rapid population growth or growth beyond the threshold can be achieved only through divine blessing. On population growth in P, see, e.g., Konrad Schmid, "The Quest for 'God': Mon-

ther to Jacob (Gen 28:3; 35:9 – 11) or recounted by him (Gen 48:3 – 4), represent the maintenance of the special selection and endowment of Abraham and his descendants.[36]

The blessing of the seventh day closely resembles the other divine blessings in P: it too concerns fertility, and it too addresses a special circumstance. The fertility that it bolsters, however, is not related to offspring. As noted already, P associates a *different* ritual practice with progeny, namely, circumcision.[37] The Sabbath is instead oriented toward agricultural fertility. H's sabbatical year law makes explicit the connection between Sabbath and the blessing of agricultural fertility. In Lev 25:20 – 21, Yahweh addresses the question of how Sabbath year observance will impact food production and access:

וכי תאמרו מה נאכל בשנה השביעת הן לא נזרע ולא נאסף את תבואתנו ²¹ וצויתי את ברכתי לכם בשנה ²⁰
השׁשׁית ועשׂת את התבואה לשׁלש השׁנים

[20] "And should you say, 'What will we eat in the seventh year if we do not sow nor harvest our produce?' [21] I will command my blessing for you in the sixth year, and it will produce a three-year harvest."

Though it is not explicitly described as a blessing, a similar instance of supernatural abundance and preservation of food appears in the Priestly account of the manna in Exod 16*. In this narrative, the manna that Yahweh provides is to be collected and consumed daily but not retained from one day to the next (vv. 16 – 20). The Israelites need not worry about what they will eat on the Sabbath when they cannot collect the manna, for what they gather on the sixth day miraculously doubles itself (v. 22). Moreover, unlike the manna gathered on other days (v. 20), the sixth day abundance will not spoil when stored from one day to the next (vv. 23 – 24).[38]

---

otheistic Arguments in the Priestly Texts of the Hebrew Bible", in *Reconsidering the Concept of Revolutionary Monotheism*, ed. Beate Pongratz-Leisten (Winona Lake, IN: Eisenbrauns, 2011), 271 – 89 (at 280 – 82).

36 The priests' blessing in Num 6:23 – 27 likely functions similarly. Within the Priestly fiction, it is a reaffirmation of the blessings first articulated to Abraham that contributes to the maintenance of the deity's presence in the midst of Israel.

37 To greater or lesser degrees, most recognize connections between circumcision and Sabbath. See, e. g., Fox, "Sign of the Covenant"; Grünwaldt, *Exil und Identität*, 183 – 85; Köckert, *Leben in Gottes Gegenwart*, 99.

38 For explicit correlation of the wilderness manna account and landed agricultural practice and for the connection between Lev 25:20 – 22 and Exod 16:21 – 25, see Simha (Simeon) Chavel, "The Legal Literature of the Hebrew Bible", in *The Literature of the Hebrew Bible: Introductions and Studies*, ed. Zipora Talshir, 2 vols. (Jerusalem: Yad Ben-Zvi Press, 2011), 1: 227 – 72 (at

In P, the agricultural blessing on the seventh day, the day on which the deity *did not work*, is a substitute for the labour that would otherwise engender productivity on that day. It is this special circumstance – work cessation – that Yahweh addresses with his blessing.[39] As in the case of procreation, P imagines for agriculture a norm that may be surpassed through direct divine intervention. Crops naturally grow each day, including on the seventh day, but Israel's mimicry of Yahweh's cessation will remind the deity of his seventh-day blessing, prompting him to effect a similar fertility boost, in this case not for the whole world but instead for Israel alone. The Sabbath will thus be a time of superfruitfulness for the Israelites. They need not fear taking off the seventh day from their labours: ceasing on the seventh day will actually result in a *greater* harvest than they would have if they were to labour on seven days rather than six.

To understand the Sabbath as such a sign requires consideration of the setting in which P imagines Sabbath practice. According to P, the beginning of Sabbath observance (Exod 35:1–2) is nearly contemporaneous with the construction and indwelling of Yahweh's sanctuary (Exod 35:4–40:34). Thus, when the Israelites practice Sabbath cessation, they do so in *close proximity* to the deity: Yahweh is dwelling in his repose in the sanctuary, and the Israelites are situated around it (Num 2:2). For six days every week, they go about their business in full hubbub while Yahweh enjoys the inconspicuous ministrations of his servants, the priests. Yet P also assumes that Yahweh can see through the sanctuary's fabric walls to the surrounding encampment of Israel. This ability to see through opaque surfaces is confirmed in P's conceptualization of circumcision, described already. If Yahweh is to observe the Israelite male's circumcised penis during intercourse, he must be able to see through tent, roof, and bedclothes. H extends the application of this divine "x-ray vision" in its conceptualization of the blemishes that disqualify a priest from altar service (Lev 21:16–24). Among these disqualifying blemishes is a crushed testicle (מרוח אשך, v. 20), a defect that the deity is able to observe even when it is concealed by the priest's sacred vestments (Exod 28:1–43).[40]

In the case of the seventh day Sabbath, P imagines that Yahweh observes the cessation of work around him, and this stoppage prompts him to remember his

251 n. 38; in Hebrew); Chavel, *Oracular Law and Priestly Historiography*, 175. See below for further discussion.

39 It is possible that the special circumstance of the seventh day in Gen 2:1–3 also includes the lack of mature growth and crop production necessary to feed the specially-fecund humans and animals discussed above.

40 Schipper and Stackert, "Blemishes, Camouflage, and Sanctuary Service", 470–74.

own seventh day cessation and blessing. The effectiveness of this work stoppage as a memory aid is difficult to imagine because such communal cessation is rare in the contemporary world. It is perhaps most akin to what happens on Saturday in the predominantly Orthodox Jewish communities of Petach Tikva or Jerusalem or, for that matter, Teaneck, New Jersey. The contrast between the tumult of the first six days of the week and the cessation of the seventh in such places is marked and thus conspicuous. P imagines its Sabbath as similarly arresting: the Israelites' work stoppage captures Yahweh's attention and, in so doing, reminds him to act with blessing.

2.2 The Sabbath as ברית

With the Sabbath as sign so clarified, it is possible to address the relationship between this rite and the idea of covenant, an issue raised by Exod 31:16:

ושמרו בני ישראל את השבת לעשות את השבת לדרתם ברית עולם

The Israelites shall ever keep the cessation, performing the cessation as a perpetual re-quirement.

This verse has prompted significant deliberation of the Sabbath's possible connection to a prior covenant in P or even outside of P.[41] Yet Exod 31:16 refers to no foregoing covenant in P or any other text. As in several other instances in pentateuchal Priestly literature, the term ברית in Exod 31:16 has the limited sense of "obligation/requirement" and, as such, refers simply to the Israelites' *future* obligation to observe Sabbath cessation (cf. Gen 17:10,13; Lev 2:13; 26:15,25).[42] This means that neither this obligation nor its corresponding sign

---

41 See, e.g., Robinson, *Origin and Development of the Old Testament Sabbath*, 261–62; Childs, *Exodus*, 416; Nihan, *From Priestly Torah*, 567–68; Timmer, *Creation, Tabernacle, and Sabbath*, 53–57; Baden, *Promise to the Patriarchs*, 194.

42 Cf. Grünwaldt, *Exil und Identität*, 183. On Priestly "covenants" (ברּיתות), including the specific, limited meaning "obligation/requirement", see Ernst Kutsch, *Verheissung und Gesetz: Untersuchungen zum sogenannten Bund im Alten Testament*, BZAW 131 (Berlin: de Gruyter, 1973) (see esp. the summary on p. 27); James Barr, "Some Semantic Notes on the Covenant", in *Beiträge zur alttestamentlichen Theologie: Festschrift für Walther Zimmerli zum 70. Geburtstag*, ed. H. Donner, R. Hanhart, and R. Smend (Göttingen: Vandenhoeck & Ruprecht, 1977), 23–38; Walter Gross, *Zukunft für Israel: Alttestamentliche Bundeskonzepte und die aktuelle Debatte um den Neuen Bund*, SBS 176 (Stuttgart: Katholisches Bibelwerk, 1998), 45–70; Christophe Nihan, "The Priestly Covenant, Its Reinterpretations, and the Composition of 'P'", in *The Strata of the Priestly Writings: Contemporary Debate and Future Directions*, ed. Sarah Shectman and Joel

is perpetual (בְּרִית עוֹלָם, אוֹת הוּא לְעֹלָם) by virtue of its hearkening back to the Sabbath's origin in creation, as has sometimes been claimed.[43] Israelite Sabbath observance in P is *not* an imitation of the deity's Sabbath observance following creation. In fact, P's historical myth precludes this possibility. In the P narrative, cultic observance is specifically tied to the deity's presence among the Israelites, and even the *idea* of the cult (to say nothing of its institution) is only hatched once Yahweh realizes that his initial arrangement – with people on earth and himself in heaven – is untenable.[44]

In P, then, Yahweh does not observe the Sabbath *and never did*. The Sabbath is established not at creation but precisely when it is commanded – when the Israelites are at Sinai.[45] Its observance *resembles* Yahweh's cessation on the seventh day of creation, and it is this observance that is commanded in perpetuity to remind the deity to bless Israel. In this sense, בְּרִית עוֹלָם in v. 16 and אוֹת הוּא לְעֹלָם in v. 17 corre-

S. Baden, ATANT 95 (Zurich: Theologischer Verlag Zurich, 2009), 87–134 (at 102); Jeffrey Stackert, "Distinguishing Innerbiblical Exegesis from Pentateuchal Redaction: Leviticus 26 as a Test Case", in *The Pentateuch: International Perspectives on Current Research*, ed. Thomas B. Dozeman, Konrad Schmid, and Baruch J. Schwartz, FAT 78 (Tübingen: Mohr Siebeck, 2011), 369–86.

43 From a variety of perspectives and with varying details, see the claims to the origin of P's Sabbath at creation in Andreasen, *Old Testament Sabbath*, 182–86; Fox, "Sign of the Covenant", 577–78; Grünwaldt, *Exil und Identität*, 184; Knohl, *Sanctuary of Silence*, 163; Schwartz, "Sabbath in the Torah Sources"; Smith, *Priestly Vision*, 104–105; Arnold, "Genesis 1", 335. The establishment of Sabbath at creation is also a regular claim in the history of pre-modern interpretation. My arguments here also modify Stackert, "Sabbath of the Land", 239–41.

44 The initial indication in P of Yahweh's intent to maintain a sustained involvement on earth is in Gen 9:5, where the deity promises to intervene himself when any animal or human sheds human blood. The delay between the Flood and Yahweh's selection of Abram seems to accommodate the need to repopulate the earth. If Yahweh chose Noah immediately after the Flood, all humanity would belong to Israel. However, such a scenario does not accord with P's contemporary situation, where Israel is distinguishable from many other people groups who do not worship Yahweh.

For the same reasons of plot and narration, it is not possible to characterize the created world as a sort of divine sanctuary in P, even though P uses similar language to describe the creation of the world and the construction of Yahweh's sanctuary. For the latter claim, see, e.g., Moshe Weinfeld, "Sabbath, Temple and the Enthronment of the Lord – the Problem of the Sitz im Leben of Genesis 1:1–2:3", in *Mélanges bibliques et orientaux en l'honneur de M. Henri Cazelles*, ed. A. Caquot and M. Delcor, AOAT 212 (Kevelaer: Butzon & Bercker; Neukirchen-Vluyn: Neukirchener, 1981), 501–12; Smith, *Priestly Vision*, 75–76, 107–8; Jared C. Calaway, *The Sabbath and the Sanctuary: Access to God in the Letter to the Hebrews and its Priestly Context*, WUNT II/349 (Tübingen: Mohr Siebeck, 2013), 32–42. The parallels often adduced between Gen 1–2 and Exod 39–40 (see Calaway, *Sabbath and Sanctuary*, 41, for a nice summary) are best understood simply as reflecting a literary pattern, not a theological message.

45 Though with different inferences, see Timmer, *Creation, Tabernacle, and Sabbath*, 37, 45.

spond precisely: the mnemonic will be effective for as long as the Israelites properly enact the cessation, which they are to do in perpetuity *from this point on.*

To the extent that Yahweh's seventh-day cessation foreshadows the eventual establishment of the Sabbath and the larger cult of which it is a part, it is necessary to distinguish between P's *narrator* and its *characters*. By virtue of his historical vantage point, the narrator of Gen 2:1–3, like the author of P, is fully aware of the cult whose founding he will eventually describe. By contrast, P's characters, *including the deity*, are not omniscient. Their knowledge is instead limited historically, which is to say, in relation to P's plot. It is this limitation that enables P's characters to experience real, dynamic development. It also informs the relationship between Gen 2:1–3 and Sabbath. Both the narrator and the reader (if only by virtue of his cultural knowledge) stand in an elevated position vis-à-vis the character Yahweh. That is, they know of the Sabbath that Yahweh has not yet imagined and thus also recognize its foreshadowing in Gen 2:1–3. Yet the narrator prioritizes his emplotment: Gen 2:1–3 thus include no Sabbath command or even a reference to the Sabbath as a rite.[46] In this sense, the seventh day cessation in Gen 2:1–3 is similar to the אותת ומועדים ("set times") in Gen 1:14: while these set times *will be* exploited in the cult once it is founded, they are not, at the level of the narrative, established *for the cult.*[47] The sequence of events in P's fiction entails its historical and theological claim: the cult is shaped according to the patterns and norms of the created world, including its calendrical framework.[48] These patterns and norms, which reflect the deity's character and preferences, are agreeable to Yahweh from the

---

46 For the insertion of the Sabbath command into the creation account (and its origin even prior to creation), see already Jub. 2. On the historical reorientation of pentateuchal laws in Jubilees through their insertion into Genesis narratives, see Gary A. Anderson, "The Status of the Torah Before Sinai: The Retelling of the Bible in the Damascus Covenant and the Book of Jubilees", *DSD* 1 (1994): 1–29; Florentino Garcia-Martinez, "The Heavenly Tablets in the Book of Jubilees", in *Studies in the Book of Jubilees*, ed. M. Albani, J. Frey, and A. Lange, TSAJ 65 (Tübingen: Mohr Siebeck, 1997), 243–60; James C. VanderKam, "The Origins and Purpose of the Book of Jubilees", in *Studies in the Book of Jubilees*, ed. M. Albani, J. Frey, and A. Lange, TSAJ 65 (Tübingen: Mohr Siebeck, 1997), 3–24; Michael Segal, *The Book of Jubilees: Rewritten Bible, Redaction, Ideology and Theology*, JSJSup 117 (Leiden: Brill, 2007), 43–94, 273–316. For a chart of legal passages in Jubilees, see Segal, *Book of Jubilees*, 24.
47 See, e.g., Baden, *Promise to the Patriarchs*, 107; Erhard Blum, *Studien zur Komposition des Pentateuch*, BZAW 189 (Berlin: de Gruyter, 1990), 312.
48 On P's narrative as the historical and theological infrastructure upon which its laws are built, see Chavel, "Legal Literature", esp. 249–50.

beginning. They thus need no alteration when he later decides to initiate the cult.[49]

Yet even if the term ברית in Exod 31:16 does not reference anything beyond the requirement to observe the Sabbath, P nonetheless fully integrates this rite with its promise to the patriarchs. In fact, P's promise is explicitly achieved *ritually*. Circumcision and Sabbath observance align with the two features of the patriarchal promise: circumcision reminds the deity to bless the Israelites with numerous progeny (Gen 17:4–6), and Sabbath observance prompts Yahweh to bolster the productivity of the land he has allotted to them (Gen 17:8). These exceptional grants of progeny and land fully accord with P's royal characterization of its deity and the nature of his blessings. Israel's role as host to the majestic divine sovereign is the special circumstance that requires divine blessing. Without a prodigious population and corresponding agricultural bounty, it would be impossible for Israel to resource the lavish sanctuary of Yahweh in its midst.[50]

3. The Sabbath in H

Both through its repeated engagement of the Sabbath topic and its revisionary treatment of P's Sabbath legislation, H demonstrates its special concern for the Sabbath. Because of its primary literary orientation toward P, H's baseline is P's Sabbath, as described above. The starting point for understanding H's alternative view of the Sabbath is its characterization of the Sabbath as a sign. In Exod 31:13b, H directs the Sabbath's signification not *toward the deity* but instead *toward the Israelites*:

כי אות הוא ביני וביניכם לדרתיכם לדעת כי אני יהוה מקדשכם

For it is a sign between you and me in perpetuity that you may know that I, Yahweh, sanctify you.

---

49 Cf. Smith, *Priestly Vision*, 114. Addressing the foreshadowing of the cult in P's creation account, Smith distinguishes between the descriptive and the prescriptive. Yet terming P's foreshadowing "prescriptive" risks undervaluing P's plot development and, with it, its larger etiological and theological claims. For example, in his discussion of the prescriptive in P's creation account, Smith problematically universalizes P: Sabbath and festivals are for the Israelites alone in P, not for all humanity, as he claims.

50 Note too that the time needed to allow Israel's population to grow to sufficient size to support Yahweh's sanctuary provides the explanation in P for Israel's long sojourn in Egypt (Exod 1:7; 12:37–38, 40–41). On the (imagined) physical size of the deity and his sanctuary, see Mark S. Smith, "Like Deities, Like Temples (Like People)", in *Temple and Worship in Biblical Israel*, ed. John Day, LHBOTS 422 (London: T&T Clark, 2005), 3–27.

In H's view, Israelite Sabbath observance is a ritual acknowledgment of the deity. To the extent that the Israelites benefit as a result of Sabbath cessation, they do so by virtue of the credit accrued from the act itself: Sabbath observance reminds Israel that Yahweh sanctifies them. As Baruch J. Schwartz explains, this sanctity is a communicable effervescence that exudes from the deity who is in Israel's midst. It is in this way that holiness is transmitted to the Israelites. Yet it is also necessary that Israel be properly receptive to this holiness. To be so receptive is, according to H, to engage in specific behaviours. Thus, when H famously presents the deity's insistence upon Israel's holiness – "You shall be holy, for I, Yahweh your god, am holy" (קדשים תהיו כי קדוש אני יהוה אלהיכם, Lev 19:2b) – it does so as the introduction to a litany of commands, including instructions to observe the Sabbath (vv. 3,30). The deity concludes these laws in v. 37 with a charge: "You shall observe all my statutes and all my judgments, and you shall do them. I am Yahweh" (ושמרתם את כל חקתי ואת כל משפטי ועשיתם אתם אני יהוה). H's miscellany of laws in Lev 19:3–36, introduced and concluded by vv. 2 and 37, thus represents an expanded formulation of the command in Lev 20:7–8:

והתקדשתם והייתם קדשים כי אני יהוה אלהיכם ⁸ ושמרתם את חקתי ועשיתם אתם אני יהוה מקדשכם ⁷

⁷ You shall sanctify yourselves and be holy, for I, Yahweh your god, am holy. ⁸ Thus you shall observe my statues and do them: I am Yahweh, who sanctifies you.

In Schwartz's words, "The message is clear: the indiscriminate and scrupulous compliance with every sort of law and statute is the means by which Israel is to fulfil the command 'sanctify yourself; be holy'."[51] P, by contrast, does not envisage even the possibility of Israelite lay holiness.[52] Accordingly, P's Sabbath is not related at all to the sanctification of lay Israelites.

H's view of the Sabbath as a sign directed toward the Israelites rather than toward the deity corresponds closely with its view of the ציצת ("fringe") in Num 15:38–39:[53]

51 Schwartz, "Israel's Holiness", 54–57 (quote from 56); Schwartz, *Holiness Legislation*, 267–68. See also Knohl, *Sanctuary of Silence*, 180–86.
52 Knohl, *Sanctuary of Silence*, 189–92; David P. Wright, "Holiness in Leviticus and Beyond: Differing Perspectives", *Int* 53 (1999): 351–64 (at 352–55).
53 On the association of this unit with H, see already August Klostermann, "Beiträge zur Entstehungsgeschichte des Pentateuchs", *Zeitschrift für die gesamte Lutherische Theologie und Kirche* 38 (1877): 401–45 (at 409); Julius Wellhausen, *Die Composition des Hexateuch und der historischen Bücher des Alten Testaments*, 4th ed. (Berlin: Walter de Gruyter, 1963), 175; Abraham Kuenen, *An Historico-Critical Inquiry into the Origin and Composition of the Hexateuch (Penta-*

38 דבר אל בני ישראל ואמרת אלהם ועשו להם ציצת על כנפי בגדיהם לדרתם ונתנו על ציצת הכנף פתיל תכלת

39 והיה לכם לציצת וראיתם אתו וזכרתם את כל מצות יהוה ועשיתם אתם ולא תתרו אחרי לבבכם ואחרי עיניכם אשר אתם זנים אחריהם

[38] Speak to the Israelites and said to them that they should ever make a fringe for themselves on the edges of their garments. They shall place on the fringe a blue cord. [39] It shall be your fringe: you shall see it and remember to do all the commandments of Yahweh. You shall thereby not turn away, following your heart or eyes, after which you might go astray.

It has long been posited that v. 39 should not begin והיה לכם לציצת, "it shall be your fringe", but והיה לכם לאות, "It (the blue cord) shall be <u>a sign</u> for you…".[54] H's view of the Sabbath sign adds weight to this emendation by providing another example in H of the performance of a ritual as a reminder to the Israelites to keep the divine commandments.

Yet the parallel between the Sabbath and fringes also extends beyond their shared rationale. These rituals also correspond in their respective temporal orientations. H's Sabbath and fringe rites marshal recurring intervals of time to underscore the regularity of the Israelites' legal responsibilities. As such, these routinized practices – daily dress and weekly cessation – orient the entirety of Israelite life toward the deity's commands.[55]

In line with this reorientation of the Sabbath sign, H reimagines the function and timing of the agricultural blessing associated with Sabbath observance. As observed already, like P, both Exod 16:21–25 and Lev 25 explicitly associate agricultural blessing with the Sabbath. Yet these texts' understanding of the function and timing of this blessing, while in agreement with each other, diverge from P's view. Leviticus 25 is undisputedly H. Thus, even as this text introduces the

---

teuch and Book of Joshua), trans. Philip H. Wicksteed (London: Macmillan, 1886), 54 n. 12, 96 n. 38; Bruno Baentsch, *Exodus, Leviticus, Numeri*, HKAT I,2 (Göttingen: Vandenhoeck and Ruprecht, 1903), 533. More recently, see Knohl, *Sanctuary of Silence*, 186.

54 See, e. g., Henricus Oort, ed., *Textus Hebraici emendationes quibus in Vetere Testamento Neerlandice vertendo usi sunt A. Kuenen, I. Hooykaas, W. H. Kosters, H. Oort* (Leiden: Brill, 1900), 15; Arnold B. Ehrlich, *Randglossen zur hebräischen Bibel: textkritisches, sprachliches und sachliches*, 7 vols. (Leipzig: Hinrichs, 1908–1913), 2: 168; Fox, "Sign of the Covenant", 578–79; Chavel, *Oracular Law and Priestly Historiography*, 194 n. 17.

55 See Simeon Chavel's similar arguments for the Sabbath in Num 15:32–36 as representative of the full range of divine commands in relation to the fringes command in vv. 37–41 ("Numbers 15, 32–36: A Microcosm of the Living Priesthood and Its Literary Production", in *The Strata of the Priestly Writings: Contemporary Debate and Future Directions*, ed. Sarah Shectman and Joel S. Baden, ATANT 95 [Zurich: Theologischer Verlag Zurich, 2009], 45–55 [at 50–51]). On the regularity of the Sabbath, cf. Tsevat, "Basic Meaning", 455–58 (without specific reference to H).

innovative notion of a Sabbath year, its underlying view of Sabbath and its literary style align with the H Sabbath day material in Exod 31*. The compositional origin of the Priestly portion of Exod 16, by contrast, remains in dispute. I will thus discuss Lev 25 before turning to Exod 16*.

In Lev 25, neither the Sabbath year nor any ritual act associated with it prompts Yahweh to enact a specific blessing. As vv. 18–19 state explicitly, no benefit accrues to Israel due to the land's observance of the Sabbath year beyond the general one that attends all obedience to the deity:

¹⁸ ועשיתם את חקתי ואת משפטי תשמרו ועשיתם אתם וישבתם על הארץ לבטח ¹⁹ ונתנה הארץ פריה ואכלתם
לשבע וישבתם לבטח עליה

¹⁸ You shall keep my statutes, and you shall observe my laws and perform their requirements, that you may dwell upon the land in security. ¹⁹ The land will then give its harvest, and you will eat until filled, and you will dwell upon it in security.

It might be countered that special advantages, such as Jubilee benefits, land-fallowing benefits, and the sixth year bumper crop, are in fact related to Sabbath year observance. Yet the text does not substantiate such claims. In the case of the Jubilee, while the Sabbath year count does provide the framework for its enactment (Lev 25:8–12), the Jubilee itself – the fiftieth year – and the benefits associated with it are independent of the Sabbath year.[56] Claims to a link between Sabbath blessing and land fallowing face an even greater challenge. If the Sabbath year legislation simply provides an ideological basis for a pragmatic agricultural practice, it stands at odds with that practice by claiming that the least fertile year, the sixth year, produces the most abundant harvest. The Sabbath year thus cannot be straightforwardly correlated with land fallowing or any benefits that it produces.[57] Neither does the sixth-year crop itself align with P's notion of Sabbath blessing. H characterizes the bumper crop not as a positive blessing that Yahweh would enact in response to the cessation but as a *special accommodation* that he provides to make possible the seventh-year ritual's performance. In other words, while the bumper crop is a blessing, it is not the *purpose or result* of the rite. It instead *facilitates* Sabbath observance.

---

56 For recent attempts to reconstruct the system for Jubilee calculation, see Robert Kawashima, "The Jubilee, Every 49 or 50 Years?", *VT* 53 (2003): 117–20; John S. Bergsma, "Once Again, the Jubilee, Every 49 or 50 Years?", *VT* 55 (2005): 121–25.
57 Stackert, *Rewriting the Torah*, 138–39 n. 65. For an attempt to reconstruct patterns of crop rotation in relation to the Sabbath year, see Jacob Milgrom, *Leviticus 23–27*, AB 3B (New York: Doubleday, 2001), 2248–51.

This understanding of blessing as a facilitator for Sabbath observance motivates H's reorientation of the Sabbath blessing's timing. According to the schema developed in Lev 25, it is not in the *seventh* year – the Sabbath year – that the blessing is enacted. It is instead in the *sixth* year. Recall Lev 25:21:

וצויתי את ברכתי לכם בשנה הששית ועשת את התבואה לשלש השנים

I will command my blessing for you in the sixth year, and it will produce a three-year harvest.

This view stands in contrast to the blessing described for the seventh day in Gen 2:3a:

ויברך אלהים את יום השביעי ויקדש אתו

God blessed the seventh day and set it apart.

In P, it is the *seventh* member of the series of seven that receives the blessing, and, as argued above in relation to the sign in Exod 31:17, *in response to* Sabbath observance. In H, by contrast, the blessing is enacted in relation to the *sixth* member, i.e., *prior to* the cessation, and its effect persists through the seventh.

Turning to Exod 16, Joel S. Baden has recently assigned the entirety of the Priestly portion of this chapter, which he identifies as vv. 1–3,6–25, and 31–36, to P.[58] Others, however, identify at least part of the Priestly material in this chapter as H or H-like,[59] while still others, including Israel Knohl, assign the entire Priestly portion to H.[60] Recommending the assignment of at least part of the

---

58 Baden follows Chavel in this source division ("Numbers 15, 32 – 36", 48 n. 13). Baden also suggests that the Priestly text in Exod 16 is physically displaced from its original position in the once-independent P work, a claim that he argues on the basis of this text's anachronisms in relation to the larger P history when Exod 16* is situated, as it is in its canonical position, prior to the Israelites' arrival at Sinai, their reception of the Sabbath command, and their construction of the sanctuary. In Baden's view, the Priestly account in Exod 16* was originally positioned after the Israelites' sentence to forty years of wilderness wandering (Num 14:28 – 35) (Joel S. Baden, "The Original Place of the Priestly Manna Story in Exodus 16", *ZAW* 122 [2010]: 491 – 504). See now also Chavel, *Oracular Law and Priestly Historiography*, 20 n. 51, which augments Baden's argument. In a subsequent article, Baden has offered an even more precise placement, arguing that this unit was originally situated between Num 15:16 and 17. In this position, the Priestly manna account introduces the law of the first-baked offering in Num 15:17 – 21 and serves as a focal point in the structure and logic of Num 15 as a whole (Joel S. Baden, "The Structure and Substance of Numbers 15", *VT* 63 [2013]: 351 – 67 [at 354 – 57]).
59 See, e.g., Nihan, *From Priestly Torah*, 568 n. 666.
60 Knohl, *Sanctuary of Silence*, 17 – 18, 62. Milgrom assigns material in Exod 16 to P, but he does not offer a source division of the chapter ("H$_R$ in Leviticus", 38 – 39).

Priestly story in Exod 16 to P is Josh 5:12, which reports that the manna ceased upon the Israelites' entry into Canaan. This statement, which presumes a preceding manna account, accords well with P's larger narrative structure and historical claims; it also shows no signs of H influence. In addition, Josh 5:12 corresponds closely with Exod 16:35, which is likewise free of H markers.

There are also several other issues that call into question Knohl's analysis of Exod 16 and especially his ascription of the entire Priestly portion of this chapter to H. First, Knohl fails to separate the Priestly and non-Priestly material in this chapter even as he claims that the chapter is composed of an early JE stratum that has been overwritten by H. As Baden demonstrates, however, two entirely independent and complete narratives can be separated from each other – one Priestly, the other non-Priestly (in this case, J).[61] A second issue is Knohl's reliance upon stylistic criteria for identifying the stratum to which the Priestly material belongs. To assign the Priestly material in Exod 16 to H, Knohl points especially to the language וידעתם כי אני יהוה אלהיכם ("and you shall know that I am Yahweh your god") in v. 12 and, in v. 23, שבתון שבת קדש ליהוה ("a Sabbath of complete rest, holy to Yahweh"). Yet stylistic criteria such as these are problematic for any source division in the Torah and are particularly unreliable as the primary basis for differentiating H from P. As Knohl and others have demonstrated well, H draws extensively from P for content, ideology, and style. Thus distinguishing H's special stylistic contribution from its stylistic inheritance without consideration of additional factors is inherently fraught.[62]

Yet there is ideologically distinct content in Exod 16 that suggests that at least part of it belongs to H. As discussed already, the miraculous double ration on the sixth day in Exod 16:22–25 and its preservation through the seventh day cessation corresponds closely with H's Sabbath blessing in Lev 25:20–22, where the multiplied harvest immediately prior to the Sabbatical period persists through its duration (and beyond). As such, it stands in opposition to P's view of Sabbath blessing (Gen 2:3). Exod 16:22–25 state,

²² ויהי ביום השׁשׁי לקטו לחם משׁנה שׁני העמר לאחד ויבאו כל נשׂיאי העדה ויגידו למשׁה ²³ ויאמר אלהם הוא אשׁר דבר יהוה שׁבתון שׁבת קדשׁ ליהוה מחר את אשׁר תאפו אפו ואת אשׁר תבשׁלו בשׁלו ואת כל העדף הניחו

---

61 Note, however, that there is a sequential problem in vv. 6–12 that Baden does not address. Verses 11–12 are the most natural continuation of vv. 1–3, and there are further problems of sequence in vv. 6–10. Thus, Baden's claim that there is uninterrupted continuity from v. 3 to v. 6 and then through v. 25 ("Original Place", 492) requires re-evaluation. I am grateful to my student, Liane Marquis, with whom I have discussed these issues extensively and whose observations have influenced my views.
62 See Baden, "Identifying the Original Stratum"; Stackert, "Compositional Strata", 10–11; Stackert, "Holiness Legislation and Its Pentateuchal Sources."

לכם למשמרת עד הבקר ²⁴ ויניחו אתו עד הבקר כאשר צוה משה ולא הבאיש ורמה לא היתה בו ²⁵ ויאמר משה אכלהו היום כי שבת היום ליהוה היום לא תמצאהו בשדה

²² On the sixth day, they gathered double the amount of food – two omers for each person – and all of the community leaders came and reported to Moses. ²³ He said to them, "This is what Yahweh meant: tomorrow is a Sabbath of complete cessation, set apart for Yahweh. Bake what there is to bake, and boil what there is to boil, and whatever remains (after you eat) set aside for safekeeping until the morning." ²⁴ They set it aside until morning, just as Moses commanded, and it did not spoil, and worms did not get into it. ²⁵ Moses said, "Eat it today, for today is a Sabbath of Yahweh. You will not find anything in the field today."

This emphasis upon sixth-day abundance and seventh-day preservation also accords well with H's focus on Sabbath as reminder to Israel to reverence Yahweh: agricultural abundance is the *facilitator* of Sabbath observance rather than the *result* of it. In light of the marked theological divergence from P in Exod 16:22–25 and its concord with H, the Priestly portion of this chapter is best understood as an original P narrative with a secondary H stratum.[63] Exod 16:22–25 also confirm that H's views of the Sabbath day and Sabbath year are conceptually consistent.

The mutually exclusive conceptualizations of the Sabbath in P and H are summarized in the following chart:

Sabbath Feature	P	H
Timing of blessing	Seventh day	Sixth day
Nature of blessing	Purpose/result of observance	Facilitator of observance
Purpose of sign	Reminder to bless	Reminder to obey
Orientation of sign	Toward the deity	Toward Israel

---

63 Note that this analysis aligns in part with Knohl's identification of H material in v. 23 (see above). Chavel argues that the Sabbath material in the Priestly portion of this chapter (in his view, vv. 16–25) is an insertion into an earlier Priestly account ("Numbers 15, 32–36", 48 n. 13). Nihan identifies a late insertion in vv. 22–28 that exhibits "the influence of H" (*From Priestly Torah*, 568 n. 666). In so doing, however, he relies primarily on style (specifically, in vv. 23 and 28). He also harmonizes the Priestly material in this chapter and in Exod 31:12–17 with non-Priestly material both from Exod 16 (J) and other parts of the Torah (both E and D). On the latter point, see also Stackert, "Distinguishing Innerbiblical Exegesis from Pentateuchal Redaction", 374–84.

4. Ritual Innovation: From P to H

To this point, I have alluded only briefly to reasons for H's re-imagination of P's Sabbath. Yet H does include several details that highlight the concerns that drive its Sabbatical innovations. Primary among these concerns is the extent of the Sabbath cessation. Knohl argues that P requires no Sabbath cessation and that H seeks to rehabilitate the Sabbath cessation rite that P "neglected".[64] Yet as I have argued, P does include a Sabbath work prohibition (Exod 31:15*). The question is thus not whether P or H does or does not require Sabbath cessation; it is instead, what work do P and H, respectively, prohibit? Taken together, P's conceptualization of the Sabbath and H's re-imagination of it demonstrate that P and H disagree on this fundamental issue.

The fundamental tie between Sabbath cessation and agricultural production in P hints already at its understanding of Sabbath cessation. It is occupational labour and, in particular, *agricultural labour* that P envisions and prohibits in its Sabbath law. P does not, however, command the Israelites to refrain from food preparation.[65] The meanings of מלאכה, "work", and כל העשה מלאכה, "anyone who does work", in Exod 31:15 can thus be clarified: they refer to the occupational work of agricultural production and labourers, not to food preparation/preparers and the efforts that attend it.

H's supplements to P's Sabbath law and to P's narrative of Moses's report of this law to Israel argue against P's view. Most conspicuous is H's prohibition against lighting a fire in Exod 35:3: לא תבערו אש בכל משבתיכם ביום השבת, "You shall not kindle a fire in any of your habitations on the Sabbath day." This prohibition – like the woodgatherer incident in Num 15:32–36 to which it is closely related – targets food preparation on the Sabbath.[66] No wood may be collected and no fire may be kindled because, according to H, food preparation – and not just occupational labour – is prohibited on the Sabbath. H expresses its views on the preparation of food for the Sabbath in Exod 16:23:

---

64 Knohl, *Sanctuary of Silence*, 14–19, 196.

65 Note that I have assigned all of the Sabbath material in the Priestly stratum of Exod 16 to H. What remains in the P stratum of this text allows the Israelites to gather manna on the seventh day. The H stratum in this text appears to know the same Sabbath tradition as that attested in the J account in this chapter (vv. 4–5, 26–30). It is unclear, however, whether H knows this J text specifically.

66 On the association of Num 15:32–36 with H, see, e. g., Wellhausen, *Composition*, 175; Kuenen, *Hexateuch*, 96 n. 38; Knohl, *Sanctuary of Silence*, 18, 53, 90; Chavel, "Numbers 15, 32–36", 45.

ויאמר אלהם הוא אשר דבר יהוה שבתון שבת קדש ליהוה מחר את אשר תאפו אפו ואת אשר תבשלו בשלו
ואת כל העדף הניחו לכם למשמרת עד הבקר

He said to them, "This is what Yahweh meant: tomorrow is a Sabbath of complete cessation, set apart for Yahweh. Bake what there is to bake, and boil what there is to boil, and whatever remains (after you eat) set aside for safekeeping until the morning."

The sixth day's miraculous double portion resources a doubled food preparation, the second part of which serves the Sabbath day.

H's interpolation of the word שבתון in Exod 31:15a and 35:2 similarly signals its strengthened Sabbath work prohibition. The term שבתון is unique to H in biblical Hebrew. When employed alongside שבת (normally in construct), it signals complete work cessation, including both vocational and domestic labour.[67] Exodus 16:23, just cited, demonstrates the extent of this cessation: it includes even food preparation on the Sabbath day. H's reiteration of its Sabbath command in Lev 23:3 likewise attests the meaning of total cessation for שבת שבתון:

ששת ימים תעשה מלאכה וביום השביעי שבת שבתון מקרא קדש כל מלאכה לא תעשו שבת הוא ליהוה בכל
מושבתיכם

On six days, work may be done, but on the seventh day is a Sabbath of complete cessation, a proclaimed sanctum. You shall do no work: it is Yahweh's Sabbath in all of your habitations.

This verse pairs the designation שבת שבתון with a prohibition against כל מלאכה, "all work". As Jacob Milgrom and David P. Wright have shown, H employs the expression כל מלאכה in its prohibitions against all work, including domestic labour. When H means to ban heavy or occupational labour but to allow domestic activities, it employs the qualified expression כל מלאכת עבדה.[68] H's locution שבת

---

67 שבתון appears in Exod 16:23; 31:15; 35:2; Lev 16:31; 23:3,24,32,39 (*bis*); 25:4,5. For its identification as a stereotypically H locution and for discussion of its meaning, see, e.g., Jacob Milgrom, *Studies in Levitical Terminology, I: The Encroacher and the Levite; the Term 'Aboda*, Near Eastern Studies 14 (Berkeley: University of California Press, 1970), 80–81 n. 297; Jacob Milgrom, *Leviticus 1–16*, AB 3 (New York: Doubleday, 1991), 1057–58; Milgrom, *Leviticus 23–27*, 1959; Knohl, *Sanctuary of Silence*, 17, 35; Nihan, *From Priestly Torah*, 567; Timmer, *Creation, Tabernacle, and Sabbath*, 47–51. Note, however, that Milgrom's argument regarding the expression of the superlative in the construct chain is problematic, for such constructions normally take the plural in the position of *nomen rectum*. Moreover, as Milgrom notes, the use of שבתון alone does not necessarily signify complete cessation.
68 Milgrom, *Studies in Levitical Terminology*, 80–81; David P. Wright and Jacob Milgrom, "מלאכה", *TDOT* 8: 325–31 (at 328–29); Milgrom, *Leviticus 23–27*, 1777–78. כל מלאכת עבדה appears in Exod 36:1; Lev 23:7,8,21,25,35,36; Num 28:18,25,26; 29:1,12,35. For the identification of Num 28–29 as post-H and drawing upon H, see Christophe Nihan, "Israel's

שבתון thus connotes total labour cessation and stands as a positive expression of its prohibition against all labour on the Sabbath.

H's selective interpolation of שבתון in Exod 31:15a and 35:2 also preserves the diachronic development of the Sabbath work prohibition in pentateuchal Priestly thought. H does not insert שבתון alongside every instance of שבת that it finds in P (e. g., Exod 31:15b, 16); nor does it always employ שבתון in tandem with שבת in its own compositions (e. g., Exod 31:13,14; 35:3). H instead inserts שבתון in Exod 31:15a because this verse contains P's basic Sabbath law. That is, because this line defines Sabbath procedure in P, it requires the elaboration שבתון. The same situation obtains in Exod 35:2: H inserts שבתון into Moses's report of the Sabbath command because it is the initial description of the rite for Israel and outlines for them the procedure for its performance. Subsequent usages of שבת are thus inflected by this norm.

H's reorientation of the Sabbath sign toward the Israelites and their holiness coordinates closely with its strengthened work prohibition. As discussed already, one of H's major theological interests is to introduce a robust notion of lay holiness into Priestly religion, and it conceptualizes this lay holiness as a cooperative achievement of Yahweh and Israel that requires of Israel fastidious obedience to Yahweh's commandments. H's work prohibition makes a greater demand upon the Israelites than P's prohibition does. As such, it serves as a more powerful reminder to obey the rest of the deity's rules than P's less stringent work prohibition would.

H's conceptualization of the Sabbath sign as a mnemonic for the Israelites also acknowledges for this rite what theorists contend is a major purpose for all ritual activities, namely, their shaping effect on the identity and outlook of their practitioners. In her theorization of ritual, Catherine Bell emphasizes the effect of ritual actions (or, in her terminology, "ritualization") upon those who perform them. Building on Pierre Bourdieu's notion of "practical mastery",[69] she coins the term "ritual mastery" to describe this effect: ritual practitioners, through their embodied acts, successfully take upon themselves the hierarchies and structures that order their ritually constructed worlds. The schemes of clas-

---

Festival Calendars in Leviticus 23 and Numbers 28–29 and the Formation of Priestly Literature", in *The Books of Leviticus and Numbers*, ed. Thomas Römer, BETL 215 (Leuven: Peeters, 2008), 177–231. On the term מקרא קודש and the Sabbath as a מקרא קודש, see Baruch J. Schwartz, "*Miqra' Qodesh* and the Structure of Leviticus 23", in *Purity, Holiness, and Identity in Judaism and Christianity: Essays in Memory of Susan Haber*, ed. Carl S. Ehrlich, Anders Runesson, and Eileen Schuller, WUNT 305 (Tübingen: Mohr Siebeck, 2013), 11–24.

69 Pierre Bourdieu, *Outline of a Theory of Practice*, trans. Richard Nice, Cambridge Studies in Social and Cultural Anthropology (Cambridge: Cambridge University Press, 1977), esp. 87–95.

sification and differentiation of these worlds, Bell states, "come to be embedded in the very perceptions and dispositions of the body [of the ritual practitioner] and hence are known only in practice as the way things are done".[70] Ritual practitioners thus experience and cultivate for themselves a misrecognition of the constructed order of their world and the ritual practices that constitute it. Yet in so doing, they are not only effectively habituated, which might carry a (primarily) negative connotation. Ritual also affords its practitioners an empowering sense of coherence, an experience that Bell terms "redemptive hegemony".[71]

Applying such theorization to the Priestly Sabbaths, immediately notable is H's rejection of the externalization of the effects of Sabbath observance in P, namely, P's bold claim that this ritual impacts and benefits the deity rather than the Israelites. By reorienting the Sabbath sign, H acknowledges the reflexivity of this ritual act and its special role in shaping Israelite religious identity. In other words, H consciously deploys Sabbath observance in service of a goal much like Bell's ritual mastery. In so doing, it also diminishes (though hardly eliminates) the strategic misrecognition that is so prominent in P's conceptualization of Sabbath observance.

H's reorientation of the Sabbath sign also sets the stage for the break between ritual time and space that eventually occurred in Jewish Sabbath practice. As I have argued, P's Sabbath ideology is fundamentally linked to its ideology of sacred space and divine presence: the divine blessing enacted in response to Sabbath observance serves the purpose of resourcing Yahweh's sanctuary in Israel's midst. Without such a marriage of ritual time and place, P's Sabbath loses its rationale. Yet a connection between ritual time and space is not a necessary one. As Jonathan Z. Smith notes, ritual temporalities, themselves constituted by ritual actions, can survive the displacement of rites.[72] Though H presumes like P that Israelite Sabbath observance will take place in close proximity to Yahweh's sanctuary,[73] its conceptualization of Sabbath is not so spatially determined – or

---

70 Bell, *Ritual Theory, Ritual Practice* (New York: Oxford University Press, 1992), 98–108 (quote from p. 107). See also Jonathan Z. Smith, "The Bare Facts of Ritual", in *Imagining Religion: From Babylon to Jonestown* (Chicago: University of Chicago Press, 1982), 53–65; Michael Stausberg, "Reflexivity", in *Theorizing Rituals*, ed. Jens Kreinath, Jan Snoek, and Michael Stausberg, Numen Book Series: Studies in the History of Religions 114.1–2, 2 vols. (Leiden: Brill, 2006), 1: 627–46.
71 Bell, *Ritual Theory, Ritual Practice*, 114–17.
72 Jonathan Z. Smith, *To Take Place: Toward Theory in Ritual* (Chicago: University of Chicago Press, 1987), 92–95.
73 See the explicit correlation of Sabbath and sanctuary in Lev 26:2. See also Schwartz, "Israel's Holiness", 57.

at least not overtly so. As H presents it, the Sabbath can serve as an effective reminder to the Israelites to obey Yahweh's laws regardless of their location or the deity's. In this way, H's Sabbath can also be aligned more readily with notions of Sabbath in non-Priestly Torah texts (Exod 16:4–5,26–30; 20:8–11; 23:12; 34:21; Deut 5:12–15), and harmonistic readings of them in relation to each other, than can P's Sabbath.[74]

Turning attention to the mechanics of H's revision, H is able to accomplish its reorientation of P's Sabbath sign without excessive disruption. This is at least partially due to the fact that P's Sabbath, both conceptually and textually, is well suited to H's aims. A comparison between P's circumcision and Sabbath signs exemplifies the conceptual suitability of the latter for H's holiness agenda. As noted above, like its tassels sign (Num 15:37–41), H's Sabbath sign capitalizes on its periodic recurrence to underscore consistent obedience to Yahweh's laws. Sabbath observance is also explicitly performative, and each Israelite's performance is observable by other Israelites. Circumcision, by contrast, does not display these features. Its temporal orientation is toward a single event on the eighth day of life (Gen 17:12), not a recurrent one. Moreover, the one circumcised is not the *agent* but the *patient* in relation to the act; circumcision thus would not naturally point to regular performance of commands. Finally, while circumcision is visible to the deity, it is shrouded from other Israelites. It would thus hardly serve as an observable prompt to Israel to obey Yahweh's laws.

P's Sabbath sign is also situated textually in such a way that H can accomplish its revision to it with minimal disruption. As argued already, H is able to preserve the entirety of P's Sabbath texts. Moreover, in reorienting P's Sabbath sign, H makes no interpolations or revisions at all to P's specific description of the sign (Exod 31:17). Its strongly articulated definition of the sign in Exod 31:13 is a sufficient guide for the interpretation of v. 17; as such, it aligns v. 17 with v. 13. The substantial success of H's harmonization – and of its revision of Exod 31:12–17 overall – is attested in the history of this text's interpretation.[75]

Finally, H's re-imagination of P's Sabbath contributes to other Sabbath innovations that it introduces, most notably, its Sabbath year law and the personifi-

---

74 On the reception of Priestly Sabbath traditions in early Judaism and Christianity in relation to questions of sacred space and time, see esp. Calaway, *Sabbath and Sanctuary*.

75 Alexandra Grund's comment is representative: "Da sich der Text also sprachlich, strukturell und konzeptionell ohne weiteres einheitlich verstehen lässt, wird er im Folgenden als Einheit gedeutet" (*Die Entstehung des Sabbats*, 275).

cation of the land therein.[76] In P's Sabbath directives, the agents who must enact cessation are Israelite humans (e. g., Exod 31:15). According to Lev 25, however, the agent observing Sabbath is *the land of Israel*. H reinforces and expands this innovation in the following chapter, where Yahweh states that the land must "repay" (using the verb רצ"י) the Sabbath years that it has failed to observe (Lev 26:34–35,43).[77] According to the argument here, in P's view, the land actively produces on the seventh day, even if the Israelites do not cultivate or harvest on it. By making the land the agent that ceases from work during the Sabbatical year, H disrupts the role that P imagines for it: instead of "working" on the Sabbath, the land must now abstain from its "labour".

The seeds of H's personification of the land as Sabbath observer appear already in its conceptualization of the Sabbath day. Translated from its wilderness setting to a settled one, the double ration in Exod 16:22–25 permits the land to cease from its productivity on the seventh day alongside the Israelites. Put differently, the land observes the Sabbath like the Israelites do. Thus, even though H does not assert such Sabbath observance by the land in Exod 16, its connection of superabundance to the sixth day rather than the seventh makes possible its subsequent conceptualization of the land as practitioner of Sabbath cessation; what is left to do in Lev 25 is to reimagine the cycle of sevens as years rather than days.

Conclusion

To sum up, I have offered here a description of the Sabbath in both P and H and have explained the process and implications of H's revision of P. P imagines the Sabbath day as a ritual practice that prompts Yahweh to renew his agricultural blessing, a blessing first enacted on the seventh day of creation. Sabbath observance provides for Israel a special fertility advantage akin to that effected for them by circumcision. Each of these blessings is coordinated with P's promise to the

---

76 On the personification of the land in H, see Josef Plöger, "אדמה", *TDOT* 1: 88–98; Norman C. Habel, *The Land is Mine: Six Biblical Land Ideologies*, OBT (Minneapolis: Augsburg Fortress, 1995), esp. 84–88; 101–104; Joosten, *People and Land*, 152–54; Stackert, "Sabbath of the Land", 246–48.
77 On H's view of "repaying" Sabbaths, see Gary A. Anderson, "From Israel's Burden to Israel's Debt: Towards a Theology of Sin in Biblical and Early Second Temple Sources", in *Reworking the Bible: Apocryphal and Related Texts at Qumran*, ed. Esther C. Chazon, Devorah Dimant, and Ruth A. Clements, STDJ 58 (Leiden: Brill, 2005), 1–30 (esp. 19–24).

patriarchs and serves P's larger goal of situating and resourcing the deity in Israel's midst.

For its part, H adopts and adapts P's Sabbath and in so doing, innovates a Sabbath ideology that cannot be reconciled with P's view. H accepts the link that P asserts between the Sabbath and fertility blessing, but it reorients that blessing, applying it to the sixth day (and, in its Sabbath year law, the sixth year) rather than the seventh. This redirection of blessing is part of a larger reconceptualization of the Sabbath's purpose. In H, Sabbath practice is not a reminder *to Yahweh* to enact a special blessing for Israel. It is instead a reminder *to Israel* to reverence Yahweh, who sanctifies them. In other words, by virtue of its regularity, Sabbath observance – like the donning of tassels in H – prompts Israel to follow carefully all of the other divine rules as well. Such obedience to law, according to H, leads to Israel's sanctification. Finally, H's reconceptualization of the Sabbath allows it to introduce additional ritual innovations, most notably its institution of the Sabbath year. By shifting the blessing to the sixth member of the seven member temporal sequence, the land is freed from its responsibility to produce on the Sabbath. H is then free to reimagine the agent that observes Sabbath cessation as the land rather than the Israelites.

Roy E. Gane
Innovation in the Suspected Adulteress Ritual (Num 5:11–31)

1. Introduction

Through investigation of innovation in the ritual legislation regarding the suspected adulteress in Num 5:11–31, this essay sheds light on several debated issues. These include the purpose and logic of the procedure, whether or not it is magic, whether or not it is a trial by ordeal, whether it benefits an innocent woman or not, and the authorship of the literary unit, which provides our only access to the ritual.

Numbers 5:11–31 addresses a husband's jealousy (קנ"א) regarding his wife. For some unspecified reason, he suspects her of going astray (שט"ה) to commit adultery. No humans have witnessed this crime (v. 13), so if she is guilty, she and her paramour cannot be condemned to death by human agency (contrast Lev 20:10).[1] However, she would "bear her culpability" (תשא את עונה; Num 5:31), which implies that God would punish her (cf. Lev 5:1,17; 7:18; 17:16; 19:8, etc.).[2] Her husband could rest assured that justice would be done.

2. Legal-Social Problem

A husband's acceptance of justice administered by God could be the end of the story if it were not for the fact that the divine penalty for a person who bears culpability (נשא עון) can be the terminal punishment of כרת, "cutting off" from one's people (Lev 19:8; 20:17), which denies the offender an afterlife and most likely involves extirpation of his/her line of descendants (cf. 20:2–3—in addition to hu-

---

1 Such condemnation would require at least two witnesses (Num 35:30; Deut 17:6; 19:15).
2 Jacob Milgrom, "The Case of the Suspected Adulteress, Numbers 5:11–31: Redaction and Meaning", in *The Creation of Sacred Literature: Composition and Redaction of the Biblical Text*, ed. Richard E. Friedman, University of California Publications: Near Eastern Studies 22 (Berkeley: University of California Press, 1981), 69–75 (here 73–74); Tikva Frymer-Kensky, "The Strange Case of the Suspected Sotah (Numbers V 11–31)", *VT* 34 (1984): 11–26 (here 22–23), citing Walther Zimmerli, "Die Eigenart der prophetischen Rede des Ezechiel", *ZAW* 66 (1954): 1–26 (here 8–11).

manly administered capital punishment).[3] If a man's adulterous wife is divinely punished by forfeiting her line of descendants, which could happen through her infertility, he too would lose his afterlife through a line of descendants.[4]

The jealous husband's problem is that he does not know whether his wife is under divine punishment or not. His remedy would be to divorce her (cf. Deut 24:1) and remarry, or retain her but take another wife to ensure that he would have progeny. However, if his wife is innocent, she would be punished by divorce or by becoming an unloved wife in a bigamous household. If her husband already had children by her or one or more other wives when he began to suspect her, his ability to have a line of descendants would not be in jeopardy. Nevertheless, he might divorce her, and if he did not, she would at least lose favour and the quality of her life would plummet, especially if he denied her conjugal rights so that she could not have any more children.[5]

3. Ritual Solution

To prevent the possibility of a tragic miscarriage of justice and unnecessary destruction of a marriage or serious damage to it, there was a need for prompt disclosure of the divine verdict in a way that would convince the husband of his wife's moral status so that he could make an informed decision regarding

---

3 Donald Wold, "The Meaning of the Biblical Penalty *Kareth*" (PhD diss., University of California, Berkeley, 1978), esp. 251 – 55; Jacob Milgrom, *Leviticus 1 – 16: A New Translation with Introduction and Commentary*, AB 3 (New York: Doubleday, 1991), 457 – 60; Baruch Schwartz, "The Bearing of Sin in the Priestly Literature", in *Pomegranates and Golden Bells: Studies in Biblical, Jewish, and Near Eastern Ritual, Law, and Literature in Honor of Jacob Milgrom*, ed. David P. Wright, David Noel Freedman, and Avi Hurvitz (Winona Lake, IN: Eisenbrauns, 1995), 3 – 21 (here 13). Childlessness of a couple guilty of an illicit union could effect such extirpation (Lev 20:20 – 21). Cf. the narrative of Gen 20, in which Abimelech, king of Gerar, took Sarah because Abraham said she was his sister (v. 2). Before Abimelech could consummate his marriage with her, God threatened him with death because she was a married woman (vv. 3 – 4) and prevented his wife and maidservants from bearing children (v. 17). In this case, divinely inflicted infertility of a man's women was only a warning to prevent him from committing adultery.
4 So why not just wait to see if she becomes pregnant? For one thing, a woman's inability to conceive may be temporary and is not necessarily evidence of adultery (Gen 11:30; 25:21; 29:31; Judg 13:2; 1Sam 1:2). Then she could go into menopause, and it would be too late for her husband to have children by her. Furthermore, even if she does get pregnant, the כרת penalty could take effect later in another way.
5 Cf. the notice in 2Sam 6:23 that Michal was childless, which comes immediately after her argument with David (vv. 20 – 22), which could be taken to imply that she was punished by David and/or God.

what to do with her. The suspected adulteress ritual in Num 5:11–31, one of the most innovative rituals in the Pentateuch, provides such divine revelation. As is well known, the dramatic ceremony links Israelite criminal and ritual law as the only sanctuary ritual that arrives at a judicial verdict from God himself by supernatural means in the absence of human witnesses.[6] Innovative elements include a grain offering (מנחה) of barley, letting someone's hair down (v. 18), reciting and writing an imprecatory oath (vv. 19–23a), and making the person drink holy water containing dust from the floor of the tabernacle and words of the oath that are erased into the water (vv. 17,23b–24,26–27). The verdict manifests itself through the presence or absence of unique divinely inflicted punishment.

Several factors confirm that the primary purpose of the ritual is to provide a jealous husband with timely evidence so that if his wife is innocent, he will not reject her. First, the ritual prescription encourages the husband to initiate the proceedings if he is jealous. He only needs to bring a grain offering of barley, the least expensive sacrifice attested anywhere in the Pentateuch, and if she is exonerated, he will bear no culpability for having acted to clear up suspicion (v. 31),[7] as he would if he had falsely accused her (contrast Exod 20:16; Deut 19:16–21; 22:13–19).

Second, the solemnity of the ritual at the sanctuary, officiated by a priest, in which the suspected wife must stand before the Lord for judgment in a liminal state with her hair hanging loosely (פר״ע)[8] and holding a grain offering (Num

---

6 Cf. Milgrom, "The Case of the Suspected Adulteress", 75, citing Nachmanides. In Exod 22:7–8 (ET vv. 8–9), God decides cases, but the means of obtaining his verdicts is not specified (cf. 18:19).

7 "The man" here must be the husband, not his wife's illicit lover, because only the husband has been mentioned (v. 12; cf. Jacob Milgrom, *Numbers: The Traditional Hebrew Text with the New JPS Translation*, JPS Torah Commentary [Philadelphia: Jewish Publication Society, 1990], 43).

8 Cf. Daniel Miller, "Another Look at the Magical Ritual for a Suspected Adulteress in Numbers 5:11–31", *Magic, Ritual, and Witchcraft* 5 (2010): 1–16 (here 11). She must have a humble appearance because she is approaching the deity for judgment, just as the Israelite high priest must wear only plain linen garments when he approaches YHWH in the holy of holies on the Day of Atonement (Lev 16:4), rather than his usual resplendent vestments (Exod 28). Compare the fact that the high priest of Marduk removes the royal insignia from the Babylonian king in preparation for bringing him before the god Bēl (Marduk) for judgment on the fifth day (Nisannu 5) of the Babylonian New Year Festival of Spring ("Temple Program for the New Year's Festival at Babylon", trans. A. Sachs [*ANET* 334, l. 415–17]). This is humbling, but not shaming. It is true that mourners and persons afflicted with scaly skin disease also let their hair hang loose (פר״ע; Lev 10:6; 13:45; 21:10), but this does not mean that a suspected wife was in disgrace any more than a mourner was in disgrace (*contra* Milgrom, *Numbers*, 40). Alice Bach is off target when she states: "The existence of the Sotah within the biblical corpus functions as a means of social con-

5:18) that invokes him as a personal being would implicitly, but powerfully, convey a message to her husband. It would tend to persuade him that the divine Supreme Court is really in session, God is taking his concern seriously, and he can expect an answer that will definitively put his question to rest.

Third, the graphic and emphatically repeated language of the conditional imprecatory oath that the priest recites to the woman (Num 5:19–22a), and to which she must assent (v. 22b), would convince the husband that the divine penalty will be adequate if she is guilty. Moreover, if she maintains her composure and is not constrained to confess guilt, her husband could at least tentatively conclude that she is confident of her immunity to the punishment because she is innocent (v. 19).

Fourth, the water-drinking ritual manifests the divine verdict by the presence of gynaecological damage if the wife is guilty, but absence of such harm and ability to conceive if she is innocent (vv. 19–22,24,27–28). If she is guilty, the divine punishment fits her sexual crime. If she is innocent, she is not under divine condemnation to childlessness, so the husband can have a line of descendants through her.

4. Logic of Innovation in the Water Drinking Ritual

The suspected adulteress ritual is actually a ritual complex that includes three individual rituals bound together: a grain offering (Num 5:15,18a,25–26a), a conditional imprecatory oath (vv. 19–22), and a water-drinking ritual (vv. 17,18b,23–24,26b–28).[9] The grain offering prescription is based on the general rule for grain offerings in Lev 2:1–3, modified by omission of oil and frankincense like the purification offering of grain in Lev 5:11–13, and with the substitution of barley for semolina to make the sacrifice even less expensive (cf. 2Kgs 7:1,16,18). Some conditional imprecatory oaths appear in biblical narratives (Josh 6:26; 1Sam

---

trol over wives who might ignite their husband's anger. The ritual shames her, even if she is found innocent" ("Good to the Last Drop: Viewing the Sotah [Numbers 5.11–31] as the Glass Half Empty and Wondering How to View It Half Full", in *Women in the Hebrew Bible: A Reader*, ed. Alice Bach [New York: Routledge, 1999], 503–22 [here 515; cf. 507]). Bach refers to the "half-disrobed woman" (505), but this is not in the biblical text; Bach is reading it in from m. Soṭah 1:5–6.

9 On definition of the "individual ritual" and "ritual complex" levels of ritual hierarchy see Roy Gane, *Ritual Dynamic Structure*, Gorgias Dissertations 14, Religion 2 (Piscataway, NJ: Gorgias: 2004), 60–61, 75–76.

14:24,28), but the one in Num 5 is unique in explicitly specifying that one who is innocent of violating its prohibition is immune to its curse (v. 19) and in requiring a person's assent to being placed under it within a juridical context.[10]

The water ritual is the most innovative component of the suspected adulteress ritual complex. This ritual, performed by the priest except for the woman's drinking, includes preparatory mixing of dust from the floor of the tabernacle into holy water (Num 5:17), writing the curse (literally "curses") just recited and then wiping the writing into the water to infuse the curse into the liquid in material form (v. 23),[11] and making the suspected wife drink the mixture (vv. 24,26b). Some scholars have recognized that the dust from the floor of the sacred area and erasure of the curse that contains the divine name enhance the sanctity of the holy water, which was likely drawn from the sacred laver.[12] So the woman imbibes a holy (קדוש) substance, with harmful results if she is morally impure (טמ״א), but no results if she is pure (טה״ר).

Despite the fact that Num 5:11–31 includes ritual speech with ritual actions, a rare phenomenon in the Pentateuch (cf. Deut 21:1–9),[13] interpreters have not

---

10 This is not an exculpatory oath, such as that which appears in Exod 22:10 (ET v. 11) or the parallel to the case of the suspected adulteress in law #131 of the Code of Hammurabi: "If her husband accuses his own wife (of adultery), although she has not been seized lying with another male, she shall swear (to her innocence by) an oath by the god, and return to her house" ("The Laws of Hammurabi", trans. Martha Roth [*COS* 2.131:344]). The oath in the Middle Assyrian fragment (VAT 9962) cited by Michael Fishbane ("Accusations of Adultery: A Study of Law and Scribal Practice in Numbers 5:11–31", *HUCA* 45 [1974]: 25–45 [here 39]), which is combined with drinking ("they will draw [water], drink, swear and be pure"), is also exculpatory.
11 The medium of writing is unspecified, which leaves open the nature of the erased material that goes into the water. In any case, the text does not indicate that the brew is harmful in terms of its material properties from a scientific point of view (William McKane, "Poison, Trial by Ordeal and the Cup of Wrath", *VT* 30 [1980]: 474–92 [here 478]; cf. Jack M. Sasson, "Numbers 5 and the 'Waters of Judgement'", *BZ* 16 [1972]: 249–51 [here 250]; *contra* Miller, "Another Look", 14–15). The water is potentially מי המרים (vv. 18,19,23,24; cf. 27), i.e., for a guilty adulteress, because of special ritual dynamics, not because the liquid is inherently toxic (cf. Dennis Pardee, "Mārîm in Numbers V", *VT* 35 [1985]: 112–15 [here 113]; Miller, "Another Look", 16). The expression מי המרים is commonly rendered as "water of bitterness" (e.g., JPS, NASB, NJB, NRSV, ESV, CEB), which could be taken to mean that it produces harmful results (e.g., Jer 2:19; 4:18; George B. Gray, *A Critical and Exegetical Commentary on Numbers*, ICC [Edinburgh: T&T Clark, 1903], 52; Miller, "Another Look", 14–15), including illness (Pardee, "Mārîm"). For other interpretations, see, e.g., Sasson, "Numbers 5", 250; Herbert C. Brichto, "The Case of the ŠŌṬÂ and a Reconsideration of Biblical 'Law'", *HUCA* 46 (1975): 55–70 (here 59); Frymer-Kensky, "Strange Case of the Suspected Sotah", 25–26.
12 Milgrom, "The Case of the Suspected Adulteress", 71; cf., Milgrom *Numbers*, 39; Frymer-Kensky, "Strange Case of the Suspected Sotah", 19.
13 Fishbane, "Accusations of Adultery", 27.

penetrated the rationale for the different effects of a holy substance on a pure or impure woman.[14] This rationale emerges from consideration of the dynamics of holiness in relation to purity and impurity within the context of sexual intercourse. First, Lev 15:18 presents the principle that both a woman and a man, presumably wife and husband, who have sex that involves an emission of semen incur permitted physical ritual impurity (טמ״א) that lasts until evening if they bathe.

Second, Lev 7:20 warns: "but a person who eats the flesh of a shared sacrifice of well-being that belongs to the Lord while he is in a state of impurity (טמ״א) will be cut off from his people".[15] This indicates that taking a holy substance into one's body while in a state of physical ritual impurity (including from sexual intercourse) results in the divinely inflicted penalty of כרת.

Third, Lev 18:20 reads literally and uneuphemistically: "You shall not put/ give your penis (שכבת) for seed to your neighbour's wife to be impure (טמ״א) by her".[16] This innovative designation of adultery in physical terms, with a man incurring impurity through his sperm (cf. 15:16 – 18) implies that such impurity has a physical ritual aspect. However, unlike the impurity in 15:18, this defilement from illicit sexual intercourse with a married woman other than one's wife is prohibited physical ritual impurity, which constitutes a moral fault because it violates a divine command regarding bodily defilement (cf. 21:1,4,11; 22:8; Num 6:7).[17] Not only that, the same act is adultery, which breaks a moral/ethical commandment (Exod 20:14; Deut 5:18) and constitutes irremediable moral impurity (cf. Lev 18:23 – 24,30; 19:31; Num 35:33 – 34).[18] One who com-

---

14 McKane comments: "The most that can be said is that the mysteriousness of the potion is essential to the procedure and that it is in virtue of its ingredients (holy water and holy dust) that it becomes poisonous when a curse is actuated" ("Poison", 476 – 77; cf. 478).

15 Translation by Roy E. Gane and William K. Gilders, "Draft Translation of Leviticus for the Common English Bible"; cf. v. 21.

16 On the rendering "penis" for שכבת, see Harry Orlinsky, "The Hebrew Root ŠKB", *JBL* 63 (1944): 19 – 44 (here 40).

17 Roy Gane, *Leviticus, Numbers*, NIV Application Commentary (Grand Rapids: Zondervan, 2004), 523; cf. Jacob Milgrom, "The Graduated Ḥaṭṭā't of Leviticus 5:1 – 13", *JAOS* 103 (1983): 249 – 54 (here 251 – 52); Milgrom, *Leviticus 1 – 16*, 310 – 13; David P. Wright, *The Disposal of Impurity: Elimination Rites in the Bible and in Hittite and Mesopotamian Literature*, SBLDS 101 (Atlanta: Scholars, 1987), 19 n. 9. For clear analysis of distinctions between the various kinds of impurities, including between permitted and prohibited impurities, see David P. Wright, "Two Types of Impurity in the Priestly Writings of the Bible", *Koroth* 9 (1988): 180 – 93; David P. Wright, "The Spectrum of Priestly Impurity", in *Priesthood and Cult in Ancient Israel*, eds. Gary A. Anderson and Saul M. Olyan, JSOTSup 125 (Sheffield: JSOT Press, 1991): 150 – 81.

18 On irremediable moral impurity, see Jacob Milgrom, *Leviticus 17 – 22: A New Translation with Introduction and Commentary*, AB 3 A (New York: Doubleday, 2000), 1326; Jonathan Kla-

mits such a serious offense is condemned to terminal punishment: death executed by the community if humans apprehend the wrongdoer (Lev 20:2,10 – 16; Deut 22:22) and/or כרת inflicted by God (Lev 18:29; Lev 20:3,5,6,17,18).[19]

Whereas the Decalogue simply uses the verb נאף to denote "adultery" (Exod 20:14; Deut 5:18), Lev 18 refers to impurity resulting from violation of this commandment to emphasize estrangement from divine moral holiness and to facilitate the concept that moral defilement of the people would cumulatively transfer to the land on which they dwell, leading to their exile from it (vv. 25,27–28). Thus, referring to moral faults with language of defilement is a powerful strategy of persuasion to encourage compliance with law by emphasizing inevitable consequences through dynamic cause and effect. Sexual sins lend themselves to this strategy because even legitimate intercourse generates physical ritual impurity, so moral impurity resulting from prohibited intercourse would be a logical extension.

The second protasis of the imprecatory oath that the priest recites to the suspected שוטה in the special case of Num 5:20 alludes to Lev 18:20 (see further below)[20] and applies its general principle that adultery causes impurity (טמ"א).[21] In the following table, similar words, including from the same root,

---

wans, *Impurity and Sin in Ancient Judaism* (Oxford: Oxford University Press, 2000), especially 21 – 31; Jay Sklar, *Sin, Impurity, Sacrifice, Atonement: The Priestly Conceptions* (Sheffield: Sheffield Phoenix Press, 2005), 139 – 53.

19 Cf. divine penalties implicitly associated with כרת in Lev 20:19—נשא עון, "bear culpability"; vv. 20 – 21—ערירי (מות), "die childless".

20 Israel Knohl (personal communication) notes that the order טמא followed by נתן + שכבת in Num 5:20 reverses the order of these elements in Lev 18:20 (טמא, שכבת + נתן), indicating the possibility that one passage refers to the other, without showing on this basis which is earlier (cf. Pancratius C. Beentjes, "Discovering a New Path of Intertextuality: Inverted Quotations and their Dynamics", in *Literary Structure and Rhetorical Strategies in the Hebrew Bible*, ed. L. J. de Regt, J. de Waard and J. P. Fokkelman [Assen: Van Gorcum, 1996]: 31 – 50, citing and critiquing on pp. 33 – 35 the work of Moshe Seidl, מקבילות בין ספר ישעיה לספר תהילים ["Resemblances between the Book of Isaiah and the Book of Psalms"], *Sinai Yarhon* 19 [1955 – 56]: 149 – 72; 229 – 40; 273 – 80; 333 – 53). Knohl maintains that Num 5:20 belongs to PT (Priestly Torah), which came first, and therefore Lev 18:20, as part of the later HS (Holiness School) material alludes to it (see Israel Knohl, *The Sanctuary of Silence: The Priestly Torah and the Holiness School* [Minneapolis: Fortress, 1995], esp. 101, 105; see further below in nn. 39, 42). I have based my opinion that the direction of allusion is the other way around on the fact that Num 5:20 makes a special application of the general principle expressed in Lev 18:20 (see below in Conclusion).

21 The first part of the oath in Num 5:19 addresses the contingency that the woman is innocent (protasis), in which case she will be immune from the harmful effects of the water (apodosis). The second part in vv. 20 – 22 vividly serves her notice that if she is guilty (protasis; v. 20), she will suffer the damaging results of the curse from the Lord (v. 21) and from the water (v. 22).

are highlighted. To expedite analysis, my English translation is literal and uneuphemistic.

Leviticus 18:20	Numbers 5:20
ואל־אשת עמיתך לא־תִתֵּן שְׁכָבְתְּךָ לזרע לְטָמְאָה־בָה:	ואת כי שטית תחת אישך וכי נִטְמֵאת וַיִּתֵּן איש בך את־שְׁכָבְתּוֹ מבלעדי אישך:
To your neighbor's wife You shall not <u>put</u> your <u>penis</u> for seed to be <u>impure</u> by her.	But you, if you have turned aside under your husband[22] and if you have made yourself <u>impure</u> and a man has <u>put</u> his <u>penis</u> in you other than your husband.

These are the only two verses in the Hebrew Bible where the noun שכבת, "penis", appears with reference to sexual intercourse between two humans.[23]

---

22 These words (cf. vv. 19,29) are usually understood to mean that the woman has turned aside (while) under (the authority of) her husband (e. g., NASB; NJB; NRSV; NKJV; ESV; Milgrom, *Numbers*, 40), i.e., married to him (JPS; NIV; CEB), following the usage of תחת, "under", in Ezek 23:5, which allegorically refers to northern Israel as a wife who is promiscuous while under God's authority. This interpretation of "under" in Num 5 would correlate with reference to the woman's unfaithfulness against her husband in vv. 12,27 by exceptional uses of words from the root מעל for violations against someone other than God. In any case, these instances of מעל link the suspected adulteress unit to the preceding law (5:6) and invite comparison to unfaithfulness (מעל) against YHWH by turning to other gods (Lev 26:40; Num 31:16; Milgrom, *Numbers*, 37).

23 The other two occurrences (Lev 18:23 and 20:15) are in contexts of bestiality. In all four instances, the noun is the direct object of the verb נתן, "give, put". In Lev 18:23; 20:15 and Num 5:20, נתן is qualified by a prepositional phrase consisting of ב + noun or pronoun indicating the person or animal "in" which one's שכבת, "penis", is put. The preposition ב here likely has a locative meaning "in/on/at" because it carries this sense with the verb שכב, "lie (down)" (e. g., Lev 14:47; Deut 24:12 – 13; 2Sam 11:13; 1Kgs 1:2), from the same root as that of שכבת. The fact that Lev 18:23 must use different terminology for bestiality received by a woman indicates that the שכבת is not simply "lying" in the general sense of "copulation", but something belonging to a male that he puts into a female. On Lev 18:20, *HALOT* interprets the preposition ל in לזרע שכבתך as replacing the genitive construction (following GKC §129e), so that the meaning of this expression is equivalent to the construct שכבת־זרע, "ejaculation of semen" ("שכבת", *HALOT*, 1488). If so, a man puts his semen in a female. This interpretation could be convincing if the expression with ל in Lev 18:20 used the same noun from the root שכב that appears in שכבת־זרע. Instead, it refers to שכבת. The expression שכבת־זרע is never the object of the verb נתן, which refers to voluntary action; semen just comes out of a man when he ejaculates (Lev 15:16,32; 22:4). All things considered, as Harry Orlinsky recognized, the שכבת that a man intentionally puts into a female is his penis (Orlinsky, 40; cf. 36 – 39 on שכבת־זרע, "outpouring [or flow] of seed",

Whereas a man explicitly becomes impure through adultery in Lev 18:20,[24] a woman who receives the שכבת of a man other than her husband explicitly makes herself impure in Num 5:20 (Niph. of טמא; cf. vv. 13,14,27–29). Like Lev 18:20, Num 5:20 employs physical language with reference to impurity that has both prohibited physical ritual and irremediable moral aspects.

The fact that an innocent wife could have sex with her husband and still be regarded as טהרה, "pure", according to Num 5:28 confirms that impurity in this context must be moral/ethical in nature.[25] The fact that moral defilement is irremediable explains why there is no statute of limitations, as there would be in a case of permitted physical ritual impurity lasting one day if it is ritually remedied (Lev 15:18).

The fourth point regarding dynamics of holiness with purity versus impurity is the major innovation of Num 5: Taking a holy substance into one's body while in a state of prohibited physical ritual impurity and irremediable moral impurity results in a prompt divinely inflicted penalty. This principle is most clearly seen in the combination of verses 17 and 22:

---

i.e., semen). Why should the biblical text use the expression נתן, "put/give" + שכבת, "penis", rather than יצא/שכב, "lie/go out" + שכבת־זרע, "(ejaculation of) semen", which also results in impurity (טמא; Lev 15:18; cf. vv. 16–17,32; 22:4; Num 5:13) and can be prohibited (Lev 19:20; Num 5:13)? In both Lev 18:20 and Num 5:20, נתן, which indicates intentionality and goes with שכבת, but not with שכבת־זרע, forms a crucial link to the following verses. Whereas Lev 18:20 prohibits an Israelite from giving (נתן) his penis to his neighbor's wife for seed = sperm (זרע), v. 21 forbids giving (נתן) one's seed = offspring (זרע) for transfer to Molech. This נתן + זרע connection between adultery and Molech worship provides a literary justification for inclusion of the law against Molech worship in the chapter, which otherwise concerns sexual offenses. The connection associates religious unfaithfulness with marital unfaithfulness and introduces the topic of Molech worship for further development at the beginning of chap. 20 (vv. 2–5). In Num 5, if a man other than the woman's husband has put (נתן) his penis in her (v. 20; protasis), YHWH will turn (ל + נתן; cf. Jer 24:9; 2Chr 7:20) her into a curse among her people when he makes (נתן) her thigh drop and her belly swell (v. 21; apodosis, first part). Thus, this negative protasis and the first part of its apodosis are inextricably connected by the verb נתן in order to make the punishments introduced by נתן fit the moral crime of receiving illicit נתן + שכבת. Rather than gaining honor through legitimate pregnancy and childbirth, the woman would experience shame and pain that would not bring a child.

24 Presumably the woman also becomes impure, but this is not stated. Lev 18:20,23 prohibit a man from putting/giving (נתן) his שכבת (in)to (אל) his neighbor's wife or in (ב) an animal לטמאה־בה, "to be(come) impure by her/it". Following the verb טמא, the preposition ב has an instrumental meaning, "by" (cf. Lev 5:3; 11:43; 15:32; 18:24,30; 19:31; 22:8). However, in cases of sexual penetration, impurity is also incurred "in" a person or animal.

25 Cf. Milgrom, *Numbers*, 37, on v. 13.

The priest will take holy water in a clay jar, and taking dust from the floor of the dwelling, the priest will place it in the water (Num 5:17; CEB).

and this cursing water will come in your insides, to swell the womb and make the thigh sag (Num 5:22).[26]

The woman's penalty is gynaecological in nature, and its outward manifestation in pain would announce the divine verdict so that others would also know that she is cursed (v. 27). The text does not specify the lapse in time before the consequences would appear,[27] but it is implied that they would occur soon enough to be perceived as resulting from the ritual.

The fact that an innocent woman can conceive (v. 28) implies that the divine penalty inflicted on a guilty woman, by contrast, involves sterility.[28] What is primarily at stake in the suspected adulteress ritual is the ability of a woman to produce heirs. Obviously this ritual legislation is primarily concerned with married women of childbearing age.[29]

The punishment exquisitely fits the crime. If the woman has received another man's penis into her body (v. 20), when she receives the water brew into her body she suffers the gynaecological harm (v. 22) that YHWH causes (v. 21). The ritual fluid punishes the sexual penetration of the wayward wife by penetrating

---

26 Richard E. Friedman, *The Bible with Sources Revealed: A New View Into the Five Books of Moses* (New York: HarperCollins, 2003), 248. Regarding the nature of these gynaecological effects, see Frymer-Kensky, who proposes that the woman suffers a prolapsed uterus ("Strange Case of the Suspected Sotah", 18–21). Brichto suggests "false pregnancy" ("Case of the ŜŌṬĀ", 66). Some interpreters have thought that the woman is probably pregnant and that the water causes miscarriage (McKane, "Poison", 474, 478; Baruch Levine, *Numbers 1–20: A New Translation with Introduction and Commentary*, AB 4 [New York: Doubleday, 1993], 198; Miller, "Another Look", 14, 16), but the biblical text contains no solid evidence of this (Frymer-Kensky, "Strange Case of the Suspected Sotah", 18–19). The JPS rendering of 5:28b regarding an innocent woman – "she shall be unharmed and able to retain seed" – implies that she is pregnant "and her pregnancy would continue. The reverse of that outcome would be the termination of pregnancy by what amounted to an induced miscarriage or abortion" (Levine, *Numbers*, 198; cf. 199). However, the *niphal* of זרע refers to being sown with seed (cf. Deut 21:4 of a wadi receiving human agricultural activity), in this case conception by a woman (with most English translations of Num 5:28), not to retaining seed (cf. Lev 11:37 – seed for sowing that is yet to be sown, not retained). Neither does this text express the belief that the woman could become pregnant as a direct result of the water trial (*contra* Frymer-Kensky, "Strange Case of the Suspected Sotah", 19).
27 Frymer-Kensky, "Strange Case of the Suspected Sotah", 21–22; m. Soṭah 3:4–5 grapples with this issue.
28 Brichto, "Case of the ŜŌṬĀ", 62.
29 Cf. m. Soṭah 4:1–3.

her and affecting the same reproductive organs that would be affected by an illicit pregnancy. The analogy is strengthened by the law's recognition that a man's penetration of her would bring into her his שכבת־זרע, "semen" (v. 13), which is fluid. So penetration of holy, cursing fluid punishes morally impure penetration of fluid.[30]

Jacob Milgrom has pointed out that a guilty שוטה is not put to death by a human court because she was not apprehended by humans, but by God, who makes the punishment more precisely fit the crime.[31] Baruch Schwartz has added that her barrenness could be regarded as a form of כרת,[32] that is, if she does not already have a child. Even if she has one or more children, her physical and social suffering in an honour-shame society would be a death-like fate for an Israelite woman.

Recently Daniel Miller has argued that the suspected adulteress procedure is originally and thoroughly Yahwistic, as shown by the sanctuary setting, priestly officiant, grain offering, and holy water containing tabernacle-floor dust and ink from the written name of YHWH. Without contradiction, according to Miller, the procedure is also a magical ritual, which a priest can practice within normative Yahwism. The priest accomplishes the operational ritual logic through accessing cosmic energy, a measure of YHWH's power that he has made available to those who know the correct ritualization, by uttering a curse incantation and then infusing the energy into holy water by writing the curse and rubbing it off into the water. When the woman drinks the magically charged potion, she literally brings the curse inside her body, where it causes deleterious effects if she has been unfaithful.[33]

Miller's evidence that the ritual is compatible with the normative religion of YHWH is compelling, and it is true that there are magical ancient Near Eastern analogues to elements of the suspected adulteress procedure.[34] However, in view of the present study, the operational ritual logic is no more magical than the effect of divinely inflicted כרת on a physically impure person who eats from a well-being offering (Lev 7:20–21). The suspected adulteress ritual invokes (rather than summons) the deity YHWH and interacts with the power of his holy presence at the sanctuary, which he directs as his instrument. The consequences for innocent

---

30 Bach observes: "Instead of her lover's semen entering her, it is the water of judgment that streams into the woman" ("Good to the Last Drop", 512).
31 Milgrom, "The Case of the Suspected Adulteress", 73–75.
32 Schwartz, "The Bearing of Sin", 13 n. 40.
33 Miller, "Another Look", 4–16. Miller provides quite a long list of references to studies that see at least some magic in the ritual (p. 5 n. 15).
34 Miller, "Another Look", 6–8, 14 n. 54; cf. Fishbane, "Accusations of Adultery", 38 n. 45.

or guilty women do not inevitably flow from ritual power because YHWH's personal knowledge and volition must be involved to differentiate/judge between cases of moral purity or impurity, categories that depend on actions in social relationships rather than physical states. Thus, the ritual is not magic that manifests supernatural empowerment in an automatic and impersonal way.[35]

Herbert C. Brichto has shown that although the water drinking trial could be regarded as an ordeal in a broad sense, it differs from trials by ordeal that are fraught with real physical danger apart from any intervention by the deity, so that the accused is treated as guilty unless proven innocent. The Israelite water test is harmless even to a guilty person without the divine element, so that the accused is innocent unless proven guilty by God.[36]

5. Conclusion

The purpose of the ritual concerning a suspected adulteress (Num 5:11–31) is to gain prompt disclosure of a divine verdict so that her husband will know whether or not he can obtain a line of descendants through her in order to have an afterlife. This unusual procedure is designed to protect innocent women from unjust rejection, divorce, and consequent inability to have children and share a line of descendants. Men did not need such protection in a patriarchal society, which explains why there is no corresponding ritual regarding a suspected adulterer.[37]

---

35 Brichto, "Case of the ŚŌṬĀ", 65. How this ritual relates to other definitions of "magic" is an interesting question, but it is beyond the scope of the present study.
36 Brichto, "Case of the ŚŌṬĀ", 64–66. Frymer-Kensky rejects classification of the test as a trial by ordeal on other grounds ("Strange Case of the Suspected Sotah", 24–25). Victor Matthews regards the procedure as an ordeal in the sense that it is a physical test that exposes the defendant to a potentially life-threatening experience and utilizes ritual procedures and an execration ("Honor and Shame in Gender-Related Legal Situations in the Hebrew Bible", in *Gender and Law in the Hebrew Bible and the Ancient Near East*, ed. Victor H. Matthews, Bernard M. Levinson, and Tikva Frymer-Kensky, JSOTSup 262 [Sheffield: Sheffield Academic, 1998], 103 n. 29, 104). On extra-biblical parallels to the drinking of a potion, see Frymer-Kensky, "Strange Case of the Suspected Sotah", 25, especially n. 19. The suspected adulteress law and ritual does not contain a close parallel to law #132 of the Code of Hammurabi, in which a man's wife accused of adultery by someone other than her husband must "submit to the divine River Ordeal for her husband" (trans. Roth, "The Laws of Hammurabi", 344) because the Israelite procedure is only initiated by a jealous husband (Frymer-Kensky, "Strange Case of the Suspected Sotah", 17, *contra* Fishbane, "Accusations of Adultery", 37–38).
37 Milgrom proposed that by taking the case out of human jurisdiction, the law could have the purpose of protecting an innocent woman from an unjust death sentence imposed by a male court ("The Case of the Suspected Adulteress", 74; Jacob Milgrom, "A Husband's Pride, A

The ritual through which the divine verdict is revealed involves introducing holy liquid into a woman's body. This functions like a litmus test, a kind of ability-to-have-pregnancy test, because purity can safely be brought into contact with holiness, but impurity cannot, as shown in Lev 7:20–21 with regard to physical ritual impurity.[38] The major innovation of Num 5 is to mandate application of this principle to a specific case of impurity that has both prohibited physical ritual and irremediable moral aspects in order to disclose a judicial decision.

The idea in Num 5 that adultery generates moral impurity comes from Lev 18:20. By building on Lev 15:18 to extend the concept of impurity from permitted physical ritual impurity contracted through marital sexual intercourse to prohibited physical ritual impurity and moral impurity incurred through adultery, Lev 18:20 paved the way for Num 5, which plugs the idea of moral impurity into the dynamic of Lev 7:20–21, where bringing (physical ritual) impurity into contact with something holy results in loss of one's afterlife (כרת). Numbers 5 takes the principle and language from the straightforward law of Lev 18:20 and applies them in a sophisticated ritual way to address an ambiguous situation that can only be resolved through divine intervention.

In view of the logical trajectory just described, Num 5:20 alludes to and therefore is a later development than Lev 18:20, which belongs to the holiness legislation (Lev 17–26). This correlates with Milgrom's observation that Numbers borrows from Leviticus, especially from the holiness portion, which leads him to conclude that "Numbers is posterior to Leviticus".[39] Critics have generally assigned Num 5:11–31 to the priestly (P) documentary source.[40] However, the

---

Mob's Prejudice", *BRev* 12 [1996]: 21). Note that Num 5 is only concerned with the relationship between husband and wife, but presumably the paramour of a convicted adulteress would bear his culpability and suffer divine punishment as she would (v. 31; cf. m. Soṭah 5:1), even if his identity remained undisclosed to humans.

38 Gane, *Leviticus, Numbers*, 525. Cf. Isaiah's fear of God's holiness because he had impure lips (Isa 6:5).

39 Milgrom, *Numbers*, xxi.

40 E.g., Sasson, "Numbers 5", 249 (although reflecting a tradition embedded in the past); Milgrom, "The Case of the Suspected Adulteress", 72; Levine, *Numbers*, 64–65; Friedman, *The Bible with Sources Revealed*, 4–5, 248–49. Israel Knohl (personal communication) observes that the suspected adulteress and Nazirite units contain the word תורה, "instruction" (Num 5:29–30 and 6:13, 21, respectively), which occurs in PT (cf. Knohl, *The Sanctuary of Silence*, 69) but not HS texts (except for the concluding summary in Lev 26:46). However, Antony F. Campbell and Mark A. O'Brien place the Num 5–6 collection of various laws among Nonsource Texts (*Sources of the Pentateuch: Texts, Introductions, Annotations* [Minneapolis: Fortress, 1993], 74 n. 89, 200), following Martin Noth, who suggested that these laws "come from a comparatively late period, even if they do contain older traditional material" (*Numbers*, OTL [Philadelphia: Westminster, 1968], 45).

oath (vv. 19–22) and holy water litmus test (vv. 17,23–24,26b–28) are based on recognition of irremediable moral impurity, which is characteristic of the holiness legislation (Lev 18, etc.).[41] This holiness concept is essential to the central dynamics attested in Num 5:11–31, which several scholars have shown to be a coherent unit, even though its literary qualities, including redundancies and introversions, are unusual for a pentateuchal law.[42] Therefore, it appears that holiness influence goes far beyond v. 21, which Israel Knohl has regarded as an HS (Holiness School) interpolation to interpret PT ("Priestly Torah") legislation in terms of direct punishment from YHWH.[43]

---

41 Milgrom, *Leviticus 17–22*, 1326.

42 Fishbane, "Accusations of Adultery", 28–35; Brichto, "Case of the *ŚŌṬĀ*", 55–64; Milgrom, "The Case of the Suspected Adulteress", 69–71; Frymer-Kensky, "Strange Case of the Suspected Sotah", 12–17. Milgrom identifies the oath as the middle and therefore most important section in an introverted literary structure ("The Case of the Suspected Adulteress", 71). It is precisely here in the oath section that v. 20 alludes to Lev 18:20.

43 Knohl maintains that the colophon (vv. 29–30) of the passage and its style, including absence of the root זנה and impersonal description of punishment in an original version of the imprecatory oath (vv. 19,20,22), testify to PT (Priestly Torah) origin. However, v. 21 interrupts the narrative with what he identifies as an HS (Holiness School) innovation, according to which YHWH directly punishes a guilty adulteress (Knohl, *The Sanctuary of Silence*, 87–88, 91). Therefore, Knohl lists Num 5:11–31 among PT sections that were adapted and edited by HS (*The Sanctuary of Silence*, 105; cf. 104). To Milgrom's idea that P added v. 21 when it incorporated an imprecatory oath with impersonal punishment (vv. 19–20,22) that was originally a non-Israelite magic spell ("The Case of the Suspected Adulteress", 71–72), Knohl responds that impersonal punishments are characteristic of PT (*The Sanctuary of Silence*, 88). Jaeyoung Jeon expands HS influence in Num 5:11–31 by attributing to HS the reworking of a water ordeal law stratum composed by the "Priestly School" and addition of a ritual-oath law ("Two Laws in the Sotah Passage [Num. v 11–31]", *VT* 57 [2007]: 181–207). Gray already identified v. 21 as an addition, but he suggested that it consists of glosses, with v. 21b explaining v. 22 to insist that damage to the woman comes from YHWH, not from the water (53). However, the facts that the woman is brought before YHWH (vv. 16,18) and the ritual complex includes a grain offering to him (vv. 15,18,25–26) also indicate his personal involvement, so v. 21 does not add this concept. If v. 21 is integral to the legislation, the interruption at the beginning of this verse ("let the priest make the woman take the oath of the curse and say to the woman", NRSV; cf. v. 19) could be understood as a rhetorical device that emphasizes the horrifying apodosis by delaying it and setting it apart from what precedes, and the chiastic repetition of the penalty in vv. 21–22 (v. 21 – thigh sag, swell womb; v. 22 – swell womb, thigh sag) could be taken to indicate that the agency of YHWH (v. 21) is represented by that of the water (v. 22). Miller argues that vv. 21 and 22 were written at the same time, as evidenced by their shared language and chiastic parallelism of ירך, "thigh" and בטן, "belly", that binds them together. This chiastic parallelism is embedded in "a further synthetic parallelism; the first half of the curse identifies the source of the power to be accessed by the priest (the what), while the second half specifies the manner in which that power will be actualized (the how)" ("Another Look", 12).

To briefly summarize, the purpose of the suspected adulteress ritual legislation (Num 5:11– 31) is to benefit a suspected but innocent woman by persuading her husband not to reject her. The logic of the procedure is that of a "litmus test" based on dynamics of holiness versus impurity. The ritual is not magic in the sense of summoning a supernatural force that empowers in an automatic or impersonal way, nor is it a trial by ordeal that carries inherent physical danger. In terms of authorship, the innovative legislation alludes to, builds on, and therefore follows a text in the holiness portion of Leviticus (18:20), whatever the implications of that may be.[44]

---

44 Exploration of implications for the literary placement of Num 5:11 – 31 within the book of Numbers and its theological contribution to the book must also await a further study.

Christian Frevel
Practicing Rituals in a Textual World: Ritual *and* Innovation in the Book of Numbers

1. Introduction

My essay addresses questions of performance and indexicality of the rituals in the book of Numbers, which are very interesting in terms of ritual performance. My focus will be on textuality *and* performance, asking about their relationship to one another, rather than playing one off against the other. Although aspects of ritual theory are in the background,[1] my primary interest is explaining certain aspects of innovation within the rituals of the book of Numbers. The underlying assumption of my essay is that the textual context of the rituals in the Pentateuch shapes and transforms them in terms of their indexicality, meaning, and performance.[2] Out of the limited number of rituals in the book of Numbers, I will address only Num 5–6, by focusing on: a) the composition of these two chapters, and b) the relation of these rituals to other texts, especially Lev 5.[3] My question will be: How does the *textuality* of the rituals relate to innovation? I will also draw some conclusions on the relation between text and ritual in the book of Numbers. Since the subtle, but significant, alteration of the book's title from "Ritual Innovation" to "Ritual *and* Innovation" has been deliberately chosen in this essay let me start with some general observations on ritual innovation.

---

1 See esp. Jens Kreinath, "Semiotics", *Theorizing Ritual: Issues, Topics, Approaches, Concepts*, ed. Jens Kreinath et. al. (Leiden: Brill, 2006), 429–70 and other essays in that volume.

2 This aspect was discussed under the descriptor "rhetoric" in James W. Watts, *Ritual and Rhetoric in Leviticus: From Sacrifice to Scripture* (Cambridge: Cambridge University Press, 2007). It was also underlined by Brian Bibb in his study on Leviticus as a complex blending of descriptive narrative and prescriptive ritual and how it "ritualizes narrative" and "narrativizes ritual". See Brian D. Bibb, *Ritual Words and Narrative Worlds in the Book of Leviticus*, LHBOTS 480 (New York: T&T Clark International, 2009).

3 Anthropological issues of these rituals were raised in a parallel paper entitled "On the Imperfection of Perfection: Remarks on Ritual Anthropology in the Book of Numbers", which will be published in the volume Christian Frevel, *Studies in the Book of Numbers*, FAT (Tübingen: Mohr Siebeck, 2016).

2. Ritual Innovation in Ritual Mastery, Performance and Textual Representation

The understanding of ritual innovation has two aspects: on the one hand, the textual process of redaction and composition, and, on the other, the ritual performance and its relation to religious history. For the first aspect, we may observe in general, that adaptation, adjustment, and alignment, or in other words "innovation", has been an explanatory approach to the *arrangement* of laws in the book of Numbers for a long period. Quoting, for instance, Heinrich Holzinger with regard to Num 5:5–10:

> Für eine Vermutung darüber, warum die Novelle nicht an Lev 5 ₂₆ angeschlossen wurde, sind keine bestimmten Anhaltspunkte ersichtlich. Am nächsten liegt die Vermutung, dass ein R^S Novellen zu den Sinaigesetzen, die vielleicht nach der Redaktion des Korpus des Esra oder erst nach dessen Vereinigung mit JED aus praktischem oder theoretischem Bedürfnis in den maßgebenden Schriftgelehrten Kreisen angewachsen waren, vielleicht aber auch schon vorher vorhanden gewesen sind und bei der Redaktionsarbeit R^jedp bei Seite gelassen worden sind, ohne Eingriff in das gegebene Gefüge der Sinaigesetzgebung einfach als Nachträge zu dieser noch vor dem Aufbruch vom Sinai unterbrachte.[4]

This assumption has evolved into something like the standard hypotheses for the compilation of Num 5 in modern research. Diether Kellermann conjectures, for instance, that since this supplement was not attached to Lev 5, the author was writing at a time when Lev 5 was already embedded in a larger context. For him the only docking place for this supplement was after Num 1–4, which was not as stable as the antecedent material.[5] We can find the same idea in Jacob Milgrom's commentary that Num 5:5–10 is a supplement to Lev 5:20–26.

---

4 Heinrich Holzinger, *Numeri*, Kurzer Hand-Commentar zum Alten Testament (Tübingen: Mohr Siebeck, 1903), 18. My own translation: "For a guess as to why the amendment was not added to Lev 5:26, no specific indications are apparent. The most probable is to assume that the R^S redactor supplemented the Sinai laws without changing the already given framework of the Sinai laws. Hence he put it just before the departure from Sinai. These materials were either of older origin and formerly rejected by the redactor of the Yahwist-Elohist-Deuteronomistic-Priestly-sources within the course of his editorial work; or they were accrued in authoritative scribal circles as a result of practical or theoretical needs. This took place in the time after the editing of the Ezra material or after the association of JED with Ezra."
5 "Da dieser Nachtrag nicht mehr an Lev 5 angeschlossen wurde, muß man annehmen, daß der Verfasser zu einer Zeit schreibt, in der Lev 5 bereits fest in einem größeren Zusammenhang eingefügt vorlag und in der nach Num 1–4 der Zustand des Textes noch die Möglichkeit bot, den Abschnitt einzufügen" (Diether Kellermann, *Die Priesterschrift von Numeri 1,1 bis 10,10: Literarkritisch und traditionsgeschichtlich untersucht*, BZAW 120 [Berlin: de Gruyter, 1970], 69).

That this law assumes and supplements the law of Lev. 5:20 – 26 bears momentous weight in determining the redaction of the Book of Numbers. The fact that the redactor could not merely attach this supplement to the main body of the law on Leviticus can only mean that, for him at least, the text of Leviticus was already fixed. Thus, if this supplement was incorporated into the Book of Numbers, the only possible conclusion is that it was assembled after the Book of Leviticus had achieved its final form.[6]

This idea was generally followed by Thomas Römer and others with the hypothesis of a "Triateuch" which ended either in Lev 9:24 or Lev 16:34. For Römer this corpus and the book of Deuteronomy had a *proto-canonical* status, so that any additional material which belonged to the legal material in these books was clustered in Numbers. "Apparently it was impossible to interpolate them in these books, which were already more or less closed to important additions".[7] Although it is true that Num 5:5 – 10 is supplementary to Lev 5, the general hypothesis, namely that the amendment was *too late* to be placed within the book of Leviticus, is not the only possible explanation. In contrast to this view, Israel Knohl has argued for different schools as the origin of both texts:

> Num 5:5 – 8 is, in my opinion, the revised version of that law [Lev 5:20 – 26]. Although this passage is usually explained as a supplement to the Law of Leviticus 5, adding the law applying to theft from someone who has no heirs, I find this explanation difficult: why, then, did the codifier add the law in another passage, when he could have appended it directly to Leviticus 5! I believe that the key to understanding this passage, its location in the text, and its innovation lies in the recognition of its H[oliness] S[chool] origin…Once we recognize that the two versions of the law were composed by two different schools who agree as to the relation between morality and cult, we may identify the essential difference between the version in Leviticus an the text in Numbers.[8]

Although I am not convinced by the assumption of a "Holiness School", the statement on composition and difference is important. In terms of composition

---

6 Jacob Milgrom, *Numbers*, JPS Torah Commentary (Philadelphia: Jewish Publication Society of America, 1990), 302 n. 5.

7 Thomas Römer, "Israel's Sojourn in the Wilderness and the Construction of the Book of Numbers", in *Reflection and Refraction: Studies in Biblical Historiography in Honour of A. Graeme Auld,* ed. Robert Rezetko, Timothy H. Lim and Brian Aucker, VTSup, 113 (Leiden: Brill, 2007), 419 – 45, (here 428, cf. 427, 438, 443) and for a discussion of this hypothesis: Christian Frevel, "Alte Stücke – späte Brücke? Zur Rolle des Buches Numeri in der jüngeren Pentateuchdiskussion", *Congress Volume Munich 2013,* ed. Christl M. Maier; Leiden: Brill, 2014), 255 – 99 (English translation in Christian Frevel, *Studies in the Book of Numbers* [Tübingen: Mohr Siebeck, 2017]).

8 Israel Knohl, *The Sanctuary of Silence: The Priestly Torah and the Holiness School* (Winona Lake, IN: Eisenbrauns, 2007), 176.

– as we will see in a moment – Num 5 is *not* an accidental hodgepodge, but comprises several cases of ritual innovation. In general, one has to emphasize that ritual innovation in texts is often, but not necessarily, "late".

This first aspect that we have been discussing identifies ritual innovation within the relation of two texts, one supplementing, correcting, commenting, adjusting, or amending the other. The range of relations is wide: the dependent text may require the presumed text and cannot be understood without it, or it may be possible to read both texts independently of the other, even if they are also obviously related to each other. The example mentioned above lies between these two poles: "The Numbers version is patently a digest of its Levitic counterpart".[9] But this aspect, particularly the reference to "breaking faith with the Lord" (למעל מעל ביהוה; Num 5:6), will be discussed further below in all its profoundity. These sorts of issues have been discussed extensively under the heading "inner biblical/scriptural interpretation".[10] The second aspect of innovation in ritual performance mentioned above is much more recent and has been inspired by ritual studies in general. It also needs to be elaborated briefly.

Within religious studies, the term or phrase "ritual innovation" is part of a more recent discussion of theorizing rituals. It is used alongside invention, adoption, adaption and transformation of ritual by, in, beneath and beyond practice. Since the traditional view took rituals as fixed repetitive patterns, which were essentially unchangeable, ritual invention and substantial innovation were simply considered as contradictions in terms. By taking the dynamics of ritual performance, the perspective of ritual agents, ritual masters and recipients and finally the dynamics of textual representation into account, the situation has changed dramatically in ritual studies.[11] Recent topics focus on adoption, adaption, transformation and invention of rituals.

We have to face ritual transfer and adoption from different religious contexts, adaptation and transformation of rituals and ritual aspects by recipients and ritual masters, and even ritual invention that results from taking ritual ele-

---

9 Jacob Milgrom, *Leviticus 1–16*, AB 3 (New York: Doubleday, 1991), 368.

10 See as an overview Andrew Teeter, *Scribal Laws: Exegetical Variation in the Textual Transmission of Biblical Law in the Late Second Temple Period*, FAT 92 (Tübingen: Mohr Siebeck, 2014); Bernhard Levinson, *Der kreative Kanon: Innerbiblische Auslegung und religionsgeschichtlicher Wandel* (Tübingen: Mohr Siebeck, 2012), 107–206, and Christian Frevel, "Vom Pathos zur Patina: Das Neue im Alten Testament und die Innovation der Tradition", *Die Theologie und "das Neue": Perspektiven zum kreativen Zusammenhang von Innovation und Tradition*, ed. Wilhelm Damberg and Matthias Sellmann (Herder: Freiburg, 2015), 29–54.

11 Nadja Miczek, *Biographie, Ritual und Medien. Zu den diskursiven Konstruktionen gegenwärtiger Religiosität* (Bielefeld: Transcript, 2013), 212.

ments and composing them anew in religious practice.[12] In these processes of invention, the ritual script of the "new" ritual is rarely completely new, but rather *adopted* from other contexts and transformed. Thus ritual innovation is a new perspective in modern ritual research. Ritual innovations, however, give rise to questions about legitimacy, authority (or better: authoritativity), authorization, ritual interpretation, the role of ritual mastery, and not at least about ritual innovation beyond ritual practice within ritual scripts or better ritual texts. Whereas ritual performance and ritual scripts are mutually dependent on each other rather than fully detached, textual fixation or, better, representation of rituals may diverge severely from ritual practice.

3. Ritual Grammar and Ritual Innovation – Some Preliminary Methodological Remarks

Taking a short detour in my argument, the addition or supplementation of a given ritual by new ritual parts or even a change in ritual immediately raises a question of method. Due to the obvious formality of ritual which has been uniformly emphasized, for instance by Catherine Bell[13] or Roy Rappaport[14], it seems natural to describe ritual action in a formalized and structured way. Thus one should be sensible to the possibility of developing an abstract meta-language for the description of rituals in a formalized way. The way for this was paved by the pioneers Edmund Ronald Leach, E. Thomas Lawson and Robert N. McCauley, following Claude Lévi-Strauss.[15] Recently this has been discussed in ritual

---

12 For the topic of invention in religious tradition see first and foremost Eric Hobsbawm, "Introduction: Inventing Traditions", in *The Invention of Tradition*, ed. Eric Hobsbawm and Terence Ranger (Cambridge: Cambridge University Press, 1983), 1–15; further, *Religious Identity and the Invention of Tradition: Papers Read at a Noster Conference, Soesterberg, January 4–6, 1999*, ed. Jan Willem van Henten and Anton Houtepen (Assen: Van Gorcum, 2001) and Michael A. Williams, Collett Cox and Martin S. Jaffee, "Religious Innovation: An Introductory Essay", in *Innovation in Religious Traditions: Essays in the Interpretation of Religious Change*, ed. Michael A. Williams, Collett Cox and Martin S. Jaffee, Religion and Society 31 (Berlin: de Gruyter, 1992), 1–18.
13 Catherine Bell, *Ritual: Perspectives and Dimensions*, 2nd ed. (Oxford: Oxford University Press, 2009), 139–44 (note that she often uses language as a paradigm).
14 Roy Rappaport, *Ritual and the Making of Humanity* (Cambridge: Cambridge University Press, 1999), 29–35.
15 See Bell, *Ritual*, 68–76; Ingwer Paul, *Rituelle Kommunikation: Sprachliche Verfahren zur Konstitution ritueller Bedeutung und zur Organisation des Rituals* (Tübingen: Gunter Narr, 1990).

studies from a structural viewpoint under the rubric "grammar of rituals".[16] The term "grammar", however, is employed much more on a metaphorical level than by taking rituals as a language.[17] That being said, one should not expect to identify the structural relations of clauses, phrases in rituals as in a language, but rather to describe some set of structural rules in a formal way as "syntax" of rituals. In addition, one may ask with Roy Rappaport, whether the surface of a ritual can be "dealt with apart from the symbolism of a ritual".[18] Therefore, heuristically (!) it may even be seen as an improvement to define the elements of ritual and their compositions without finding an overall grammar.[19] In the field of Hebrew Bible studies Naphtali Meshel has attempted to develop "The 'Grammar' of Sacrifice".[20] This is not the place to discuss this book extensively, but one may wonder, whether Meshel reached the level of ritual syntax or a parataxis of elements (see for instance his "Jugational Patterns" for several rituals). The "grammar of ritual" of Axel Michaels addresses the "question of how and to what extent ritual sequences can be transformed, left out, added, and transposed, and how, by this, the priest creates his own ritual referring to, or as agency for, a set of established formal ritual elements more or less known to his fellow priests and customers, thus using a kind of ritual language in both a stereotype and creative way".[21] This is most relevant for understanding "ritual innovation", despite the fact that the practice of biblical rituals and thus their spontaneous performative variability is missing. In addition, I doubt that the aspect of "ritual innovation" can be comprehensively described within a grammar of ritual, although it has to be conceded that the formal description can properly emphasize changes

---

16 Axel Michels, ed. *Grammars and Morphologies of Ritual Practices in Asia* (Wiesbaden: Harrassowitz, 2010); Axel Michaels, *Homo Ritualis: Hindu Ritual and Its Significance for Ritual Theory* (Oxford: Oxford University Press, 2015), 74.

17 Michaels, *Homo Ritualis*, 78.

18 Rappaport, *Ritual*, 30. Although using the term "grammar" often (e. g. Rappaport, *Ritual*, 172, 251), Roy Rappaport remains generally reluctant about the idea, when he – discussing form and structure of rituals – states: "This is not to say that ritual should be conceived as somehow analogous to grammar" (Rappaport, *Ritual*, 470). See the same reluctance in Bell, *Ritual*, 68, questioning the priority of "description" against "interpretation".

19 See also Gerald A. Klingbeil, *Bridging the Gap: Ritual and Ritual Texts in the Bible* (Winona Lake, IN: Eisenbrauns, 2007), who addresses ritual *morphology, syntax, semantic, and pragmatics* without systematizing ritual in a structuralist grammar scheme, but rather emphasizing a certain meaning of rituals in their textualization.

20 Naphtali Meshel, *The "Grammar" of Sacrifice: A Generativist Study of the Israelite Sacrificial System in the Priestly Writings with a Grammar of Σ* (Oxford: Oxford University Press, 2014).

21 Michaels, *Homo Ritualis*, 72.

between rituals on a very formal level. As a result of the above argument, I do not focus on a structuralist attempt to formalize ritual innovation in this paper.

4. Ritual Innovation and Tradition

How old are the rituals in the biblical tradition? Are they the ancient heritage of a priestly class from a mostly unchanged, conservative, traditional cult? The biblical account suggests performance began at Mt. Sinai in the desert and then continued within the cult of the Solomonic temple. The assessment of the antiquity of ritual in Exod 19–Num 10 is determined by the date of the textual tradition, which is broadly assigned by academics to the priestly literature. The range of dates for this textual material and its traditions could not be wider. Since the school of Yezekiel Kaufmann assigns a preexilic date to P, all the ritual of P should be from the First Temple cult. In Western European scholarship this dating has fewer followers than the exilic or post-exilic dating of the Priestly Code. But dating the textualization is not the same as dating the ritual tradition: "Needless to say, a postexilic date does not exclude some degree of continuity in liturgical and ritual practice, though in fact, practices alluded to in texts generally thought to be preexilic rarely, if ever, confirm the antiquity of practices described in P and are often quite different".[22] The situation is puzzling due to the lack of reliable criteria. Asking for the variables or conditions that effect the conservation of tradition, former study (especially in the Western European context apart from the Kaufmann-School) often hinted at the so-called "templeless age" (borrowing a term from Jill Middlemas[23]), that is, the time between the destruction of the First Temple and the consecration of the Second. The exiled priests (following the fate of Ezekiel in Babylon or the lists of priestly and Levite returnees in Ezra 2:1–67; Nehemiah 7:6–68) were made responsible for the preservation of the oral ritual tradition of the temple cult despite their distance from actual practice. Thus they put the rituals into writing and scripturalized them within the "Priestly Code" which was then brought into the Torah in the time of the Second Temple. The priestly Code could thus become *a ritual textbook* for the continued cult within the Second Temple. By this they produced a lot of innovation in comparison to the oral rituals of the cult of the First Temple. "Perhaps the most popular explanation for religious innovation has been to

---

22 Joseph Blenkinsopp, *Sage, Priest, Prophet: Religious and Intellectual Leadership in Ancient Israel* (Louisville: Westminster John Knox, 1995), 70.
23 Jill Anne Middlemas, *The Templeless Age* (Louisville: Westminster John Knox, 2007).

point to the role of some personal and/or social stress or crisis. Religious individuals and communities experience a crisis with which the existing religious tradition does not allow them to cope, and so they innovate".[24] Having said that, Michael A. Williams, Collett Cox, and Martin S. Jaffee address correctly the overemphasis upon the crisis paradigm: "However, we do mean to suggest that crisis has been much overused as an explanation".[25] Although one should not neglect the fact that crisis, challenge and the threat of loss are important triggers for determining or preserving a tradition, the crisis paradigm is not the only background for the textualization of rituals. This simple, but common model can already be questioned on the basis of more recent scholarly discussion about the dating of the Priestly Code and the constant reduction of this literary strand, which excluded most of the rituals from the original narrative.[26] Already Julius Wellhausen understood the priestly texts "to reflect postexilic innovations in the ritual of the Second Temple which, after being codified, would have found their way into P's account of Israel's origins to be granted a greater legitimacy".[27] However, the diametrical opposition between oral transmission and textualization is much too simple. Textualization of rituals is much more complex; it is not just the securing of existing oral rituals textually for the sake of preservation. It has often been emphasized "that texts are not rituals and rituals are not texts".[28] One obvious aspect of textualization is the authorization of tradition; another is an interest in systematization and homogenization of different aspects of ritual practice. The role of shared traditions (for instance between "Jews" and "Samaritans") has been underrated so far.

5. Ritual Innovation and Rituals in the Book of Numbers

All of these aspects are relevant, when it comes to the question of ritual innovation. But as recent ritual studies have emphasized, rituals are rarely completely new, they consist of antecedent or prior components and aspects. "Often, it is the connection to earlier, ancient ritual tradition that makes ritual innovation

---

24 Williams, Cox and Jaffee, "Religious Innovation", 7.
25 Williams, Cox and Jaffee, "Religious Innovation", 8.
26 See Christophe Nihan, *From Priestly Torah to Pentateuch: A Study in the Composition of the Book of Leviticus*, FAT II/25 (Tübingen: Mohr Siebeck, 2007), 1–19 for the history of exegesis and the certain bias therein.
27 Nihan, *Priestly Torah*, 3.
28 Watts, *Leviticus*, 63.

attractive".[29] As Angelos Chaniotis has shown, ritual recursiveness or ritual recycling was already an important factor in antiquity.[30] Thus, cultural exchange or the taking over of ritual elements from other contexts, merging existing rituals to form new ones, ritual transformation, recycling of ancient rituals and ritual innovation are also to be expected in biblical rituals. This is even more probable, if we recognize the fact that most of the biblical rituals are integrated into postexilic priestly strata. Apart from the sacrificial and festival cult, it is striking that rituals and similar texts in the Torah are found particularly in the book of Numbers: the *sôtah* of Num 5:11–31, the vow of the Nazirite in Num 6:1–21, the ritual formula of priestly blessing in Num 6:22–27, or very prominently the ritual of the red heifer in Num 19. In older commentaries all this material was considered to belong to "age old traditions" tracing back to the First Temple cult and beyond. The texts – even if they were perceived as belonging to P^s, H, or other late redactional layers – were considered to be condensed priestly knowledge based on oral tradition or constant practice, rather than the result of ritual invention or innovation. As we have already seen, this approach is unproductive, and the relation between textualization and practice is more intricate as is the relation between oral and textual practice.[31] The gap between ritual text and ritual practice becomes obvious, when one takes into account that not all elements of ritual are represented in the text.[32] On the one hand, the ritual text is not completely detached from practice. It refers to practice and is related to practice rather than based solely on practice or borrowed from practice. On the other hand, the ritual text has its own focus, intention, context, pragmatic etc. "Written texts usually encode rhetorical purposes different from the goals that motivate ritual performances".[33] Biblical rituals are not only part of literature, they *are* literature.[34] Nevertheless, we should expect the ritual script is capable of being applied in practice, rather than forming a completely fictive ritual.

---

29 Klingbeil, *Gap*, 144–45.
30 Angelos Chaniotis, "Wie (er)findet man Rituale für einen neuen Kult? Recycling von Ritualen – das Erfolgsrezept Alexanders von Abonouteichos", *Forum Ritualdynamik* 9 (2004), 16 pages (here 7), http://www.ub.uni-heidelberg.de/archiv/5103.
31 There is very much discussion on this aspect. I just mention from the "rhetoric" side: Dorothea Erbele-Küster, "Reading as an Act of Offering: Reconsidering the Genre of Leviticus 1", in *The Actuality of Sacrifice: Past and Present*, ed. Alberdina Houtman et al., Jewish and Christian Perspectives Series 28 (Leiden: Brill, 2014), 34–46.
32 See Bibb, *Words*, 95–97.
33 Watts, *Leviticus*, 63.
34 See Watts, *Ritual*, 27–29.

6. Textualized Rituals and Ritualized Texts

How are we then to relate ritual scripts to religious practice in general? Presuming that biblical ritual scripts were not identical with the performative practice at any time, I discuss briefly the three basic options: ritual texts reflect practice, establish practice, or generate practice. In other words, either all the rituals of the biblical texts were rooted in antecedent ritual practice of the First and Second Temple cult, as was assumed in earlier biblical studies; or, biblical ritual scripts established innovative ritual practice, they were produced to form new practice; or, finally – and this possibility should not be excluded *a priori* – biblical rituals reflect theoretical considerations of textual experts rather than any ritual practice. They solve problems of the *textual world*, were merely known to the very limited circles of priests, solely used within the learned study of literary traditions, and, most importantly, were *never* practiced, even if they relate to practice. What is meant by this absolute negation is that the rituals were not practiced according to the allegedly "ritual script" we find in the biblical text. If what was mentioned above about the preserving, legitimizing, authorizing and homogenizing function of biblical rituals holds true, the process of textualization may hint at an additional issue: despite the fact that several postexilic groups acknowledged the same tradition, they differed in practice and belief at particular points. For instance, we have the Judeans in Jerusalem, the Samarian Yahwists with their cult at Gerizim, the community of the Nabu-Yhw-temple in the Negev, the "Jews" of Elephantine, the exiled Babylonian communities and perhaps even the inhabitants of Transjordan as another group. The textualization of rituals may also formulate a certain cultic benchmark, by which a single "religion" under the rule of the Torah is formed. The ritual world is placed at the sanctuary in the Sinai desert (thus avoiding identification with any of the sacred sites of the mentioned communities). The function of the priestly ritual world and the fictional Aaronide priesthood is, thus, to form a reservoir of identity to which each and every group may relate themselves. The actual practice of the ritual cult may in fact be different. Thus the puzzling question of whether the rituals in the book of Numbers were practices along the lines of the ritual scripts of the biblical texts, is wrongly put, if the primary function of textualization is not the preservation of a certain practice. Nor do the rituals in Num 5 – 6 exactly mirror a practice in the temple cult, nor do they prescribe such a practice. One cannot be sure (particularly if one reflects on the appearance of ritual in the Qumran evidence), but it appears that neither Num 6:24 – 26 nor Num 5:11 – 31 nor Num 19:1 – 22 were practiced in the Second Temple cult (at least in the form in which they were transmitted in the text). The same holds true for the confession of misconduct in Num 5:5 – 10. The texts are innovating rather than reproducing established practice.

The textualization of rituals has used ancient and traditional rituals as well as composing "new" ones from elements of common ritual practice. Although it may be difficult to corroborate this hypothesis, the homogenizing function would fit very well to the overall function of Torah in the identity processes of the late 5th and early 4th centuries BCE as it is seen in recent discussions. However, to make things clear, this context shall not be understood as the one and only explanation for the textualization of rituals, but simply as one aspect, which needs further consideration.

I mentioned two aspects of innovation earlier: the first was that ritual makes an innovative statement by commenting on a legal or ritual text. The second was the amendment of a norm or a ritual by the addition or transformation of certain elements, sequences of acts or patterns of interpretation, which could be borrowed from other contexts. Both aspects seem to be two sides of the same coin in biblical ritual texts. The composition of Num 5 – 6 in particular, which will be examined in a moment, combines the two aspects impressively.

7. The Ritual-Composition Num 5 – 6

If we examine the commentaries on Numbers, the use of the label "composition" for Num 5 – 6 already suggests something too systematic. There is no need to collect the opinions for chaos, disorder, or contingency in Num 5 – 6 here in detail. I just quote two voices out of the many. Martin Noth's statement was influential in German research for a long time: "In ch. 5 – 6 several ordinances of very varied scope and very varied contents have been juxtaposed, with no recognizably close relationships, as far as subject-matter is concerned, either with each other or with what precedes and follows".[35] Different, but not in contrast to Martin Noth, is the assessment of Baruch Levine. He begins his exegesis by minimizing the rationale of textual order, too: "As is true of certain other sections of Numbers, chapter 5 is not a coherent unit but rather a collection of diverse laws and rituals. There are, to be sure, suggestive thematic links pertaining to such subjects as impurity and betrayal, but as a whole Numbers 5 is best seen as a repository of priestly legislation".[36] A repository is a more or less jumbled assemblage

---

35 Martin Noth, *Numbers: A Commentary*, OTL (London: SCM Press, 1968), 44.
36 Baruch A. Levine, *Numbers 1 – 20: A New Translation with Introduction and Commentary*, AB 4 (New York: Doubleday, 1993), 181.

without systematic order or focus. While the bulk of material in Num 5–10 was seen by Horst Seebass as preparation for the wilderness wandering, he considered Num 5–6 to be three intrusive additions which emphasize priestly competence and authority against the background of the appreciation of the Levites in Num 3–4.[37]

In my view these statements have to be reconsidered beginning with the striking fact that Num 5–6 is the most "ritualistic" passage in the entire Torah (the *sôta* of Num 5:11–31, the ritual of the Nazirite vow in Num 6:1–21 and the priestly blessing ritual in Num 6:22–27). These rituals are well chosen and form an elaborate *composition*. As I have shown elsewhere, the compositional function of Num 5:1–4 is crucial by bridging across Leviticus and Numbers with the three demands for expulsion out of the camp: cases of skin disease, bodily discharge and defilement by corpses.[38] The concrete content is insignificant because it functions as a reference to the broader context. The disorder is to be shifted from centre to periphery and beyond. They shall keep their camps clean by exclusion of impurity out of the camp (ולא יטמאו את־מחניהם אשר אני שכן בתוכם Num 5:3). The purity of the camp, which is constituted by the presence of the Lord, is to be kept by expulsion of the impure. It is important that this perfect state is breached by the three cases that follow, starting with the bold heading: people who commit sins that are common to men (כי יעשו מכל־חטאת האדם; Num 5:6). These people should be expelled from the community too, just as the woman who committed adultery and the Nazîr who defiled his vow by touching a corpse. But they are not! In contrast, the centrifugal movement of expelling is contrasted to centripetal actions: the em-

---

37 "Dagegen sind 5,5–10; 5,11–31 und 6,1–21 drei Ergänzungen zu den Marschvorbereitungen unter dem Gesichtspunkt, priesterliche Kompetenzen nach der massiven Vorstellung des Levitismus Num 3–4 hervorzukehren, ohne dass ein Bezug zur Marschvorbereitung erkennbar wäre" (Horst Seebass, *Numeri. Kapitel 1,1–10,10*, BKAT [Neukirchen-Vluyn: Neukirchener, 2012], 90, cf. 106).
38 See for a description of the sophisticated character of Num 5:1–4: Christian Frevel, "Purity Conceptions in the Book of Numbers in Context", *Purity and the Forming of Religious Traditions in the Ancient Mediterranean World and Ancient Judaism*, ed. Christian Frevel and Christophe Nihan, Dynamics in the History of Religions 3 (Leiden: Brill, 2013), 369–411. Thus, the suggestion of R. Achenbach, that Num 5–6 forms a catechetical compendium for teaching the ordinary people ("daß hier ein einheitlicher, als Kompendium gedachter Text mit Beispielen für die katechetische Unterweisung des Volkes vorliegt") is not compelling. Similarly regarding Num 5:11–31: "Dem Text geht es ja um die prinzipielle Reinerhaltung der Heiligtumsgemeinde" (Reinhard Achenbach, *Die Vollendung der Tora. Redaktionsgeschichtliche Studien zum Numeribuch im Kontext von Hexateuch und Pentateuch*, BZABR 3 [Wiesbaden: Harrassowitz, 2003], 508). But this is true only on a very general level. The focus is much more the intermediate state of undiscovered defilement which will afflict the sanctuary indirectly only in the longer run.

bezzler comes to the sanctuary to confess and to refund; the woman is brought to the entrance of the tent of meeting; the defiled Nazîr moves to this liminal area, too, to renew his vow. It is a community of individuals, which is described as a fragile order; human individuals – men as well as women (note that all three cases emphasize both genders) – unsettle the stability by misbehaviour.

Num 5:1–4 Num 5:5–6:22 Num 6:22–27

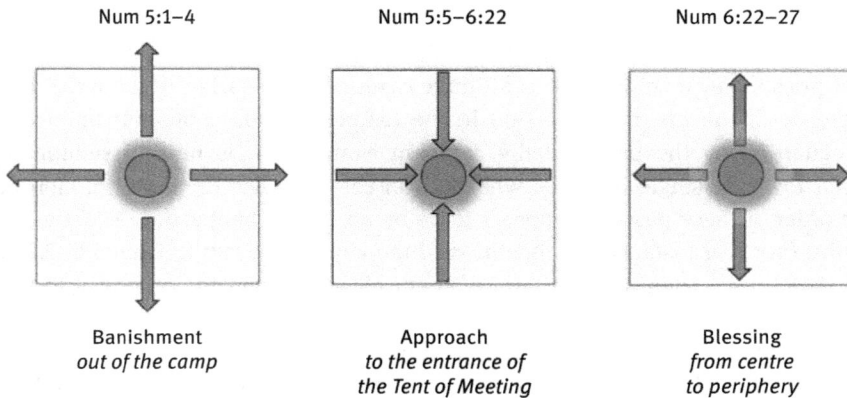

Banishment	Approach	Blessing
out of the camp	*to the entrance of*	*from centre*
	the Tent of Meeting	*to periphery*

Fig. 1: Spatial Order in Num 5 – 6

The demand for purity within the camp forms the background of the composition of Num 5:5 – 6:22 only in an implicit manner. This is not the dominant rationale as it is often noted. "Verunreinigung, Veruntreuung und Ehebruch bedrohen die Heiligkeit und Integrität des Raumes gleichermaßen und sind in ihrer Häufigkeit gleichermaßen exemplarisch."[39] But one has to face the fact, that neither the embezzler nor the adulteresses are explicitly expelled at the moment he or she is convicted. So, too, the unclean Nazirite is not explicitly excluded from the camp. If this is right, the rationale of the composition in Num 5 – 6 goes beyond the implicit defilement of the camp by misappropriation, adultery or notfulfilment of a vow. Thus, the compilation of Num 5:5 – 10; 5:11 – 31; 6:1 – 21 is not just exemplary for important issues of impurity, as R. Achenbach noted,[40] but rather for handling the tension between unseen jeopardy by concealment

---

39 Achenbach, *Vollendung*, 504.
40 "Im Anschluß an die Lagerordnung sind damit modellhaft die wichtigsten Fälle möglicher Unreinheit (Num 5) und besonderer Reinheit (6,1 – 21) im Volke am Heiligtum exemplarisch geregelt worden" (Achenbach, *Vollendung*, 511).

and responsibility through confession and compensation. Not only the priests (Lev 10:10), but the ordinary people are required to look after the holiness and to long for purification through the assistance of the priests.

It is not by chance that these movements are completed by a centripetal one again: the blessing of wellbeing, prosperity, shelter – in short שלום (Num 6:26) – emits from the centre and reaches to the periphery and all Israelites (Num 6:22–27). In the literarily constructed sacred space in the composition of Num 5–6, the blessing becomes "the verbal extension of the temple".[41] The consecrating power of God is mediated by priests to the people (note that it is by no means by chance that priests play a crucial role in all three cases of ritual earlier in the unit). The presence of the life-providing God in the temple,[42] whose potential impact is safeguarded by the purity of the camp in Num 5:1–4, is here disseminated again to every single Israelite, who lives in the presence of this God. Hence, the order of these passages appears to be by no means haphazard or just associative (note for instance the repetition of the key phrase מעל in Num 5:6,12,27). All three cases comprise men and women; all are related in some way to the sanctuary, and all address hidden impairment of the order that affects God; all integrate human responsibility in a substantial manner.

If we are allowed to read Num 5:5–10 in light of Lev 5:20–26, then all go with a particular sort of oath/vow and its potential or actual breach: (a) Num 5:5–10 a person committing perjury; (b) Num 5:11–24 the oath of a wife who did or did not commit adultery; and, finally, (c) Num 6:1–21 a person who made a vow willingly, but is hindered from fulfilling it, because he or she was defiled by a corpse. In all three passages something implicit is made explicit: the person who has embezzled property, will confess his or her fault (within the sanctuary); the woman who is suspected of committing adultery will make explicit her deeds; the Nazirite who has defiled herself or himself by contact with a corpse will cut his or her hair as a public sign of determination regarding his or her vow. In all three cases the alternative option is concealment or implicitness. In sum: there is more than a superficial order to Num 5–6, rather content and structure form a *coherent unity:* the camp is not the perfect world which it appears to be in Num 1–4. It is threatened by everyday situations and its holiness is endangered by humans.

---

41 Jeremy D. Smoak, *The Priestly Blessing in Inscription and Scripture: The Early History of Numbers 6:24–26* (Oxford: Oxford University Press, 2015), 134.
42 See the relation of the temple and blessing rituals which is emphasized by Smoak, *Blessing*, 112–13, 131.

8. Aspects of Ritual Innovation

To address aspects of ritual innovation in Num 5–6 we have to go a bit deeper into the text. I will concentrate on the relation to Lev 5 which is most interesting *in all three passages*, not only in Num 5:5–10 with regard to Lev 5:20–26, which has been constantly noted in scholarship. Already August Knobel (1861) viewed Num 5:5–10 "as a supplement to Lev 5:14–26; 7:1–10",[43] and Heinrich Holzinger (1903) noted that "vv. 5–8 are an addition to Lev 5:20–26, not only in terms of substance, but also in terms of form".[44] But the relation between Num 5 and Lev 5 does not only consist of misappropriation, but rather concerns all the cases in Num 5. In seeking to demonstrate this claim, I will not go into every detail of the exegesis of the following passages:

a) The Case for Num 5:5–10 Supplementing Lev 5

Beginning with Num 5:5–10, it seems difficult to speak of *ritual* innovation because Num 5:5–10 is not a ritual in the strictest sense. While the exact meaning of the misdeed in vv. 6–7 remains unclear, the last verse of the passage especially appears to concern priestly dues in general (cf. Num 18). The insistence that every gift/donation/offering – and modern versions differ significantly in the translation of כל־תרומה לכל־קדשי בני־ישראל [45] – should belong to the priest resembles Lev 22:2,15; Num 18:8,19,32. The passage begins with "when a man or a woman *wrongs another*, breaking faith with the LORD, that person incurs guilt" (following NRSV's translation), but the Hebrew text reads כי איש או־אשה יעשו מכל־חטאת האדם למעל מעל ביהוה ואשמה הנפש ההוא, and it is not clear whether sins in general ("sins of humans", "any wrong") or the wronged party ("sins against humans") are being addressed. And it is quite unclear how these trespasses are מעל, "sacrilege, unfaithfulness, or embezzlement", against YHWH. Is ואשמה הנפש ההוא the apodosis or an additional condition of the protasis

---

43 August Knobel, *Die Bücher Numeri, Deuteronomium und Josua erklärt nebst einer Kritik des Pentateuch und Josua* (Leipzig: S. Hirzel, 1861), 19: "Die Verordnung über die Ablieferung unrechtmäßigen Eigenthums an Jehova erscheint als ein Nachtrag zum Schuldopfergesetze Lev. 5,14–26; 7,1–10 und betrifft den besonderen Fall, dass der Beeinträchtigte nicht mehr vorhanden ist und die Erstattung nicht in Empfang nehmen kann".

44 Holzinger, *Numeri*, 17: "5–8 ist eine Ergänzung zu Lev. 5,20–26 nicht nur sachlich, sondern auch formell".

45 Septuagint reads καὶ πᾶσα ἀπαρχὴ κατὰ πάντα τὰ ἁγιαζόμενα and links the passage more tightly to Num 18.

("than this person incurs guilt" or "and/or that person incurs guilt")? As already observed, Num 5:5 – 8 is closely related to Lev 5:20 – 26. Most of the text in Numbers consists of an abridgement of the more detailed text. Leviticus 5 encompasses "fraud, embezzlement, and misuse of belongings entrusted to one's keeping"[46] which are identified as "sacrilege against the Lord" מעל ליהוה, because the person has committed a perjury concealing the true property relations or liability. Thus, it is generally agreed that Num 5:5 – 10 should be read against the background of Lev 5:20 – 26.[47] Three aspects can be viewed as amendments or innovations. First, by generalizing the wronged party the law is not restricted to the compatriot (עמיתו) anymore. Secondly, Num 5 adds the explicit confession of misdoing v. 7, and, finally, it adds the regulation of cases in which the wronged party has no legal successor (vv. 8 – 10). By using the verb ידה, which is rare in the Torah (Lev 5:5; 16:21; 26:40), it is signalled that the confession has been borrowed from Lev 5:5 (והיה כי־יאשם לאחת מאלה והתודה אשר חטא עליה). Acts, which were committed unwittingly, but later recognized as guilty, are to be confessed publicly. While Lev 5:20 – 26 may also *imply* a confession,[48] this is made explicit in Num 5:7. Besides the verb ידה, Num 5:7 resorts to Lev 5:23 by using שוב *hiphil* for the repayment demand. "The wording of this law appears to compress the statements of Lev 5:20 – 26".[49] The three aspects of innovation are summarized by Jacob Milgrom:

> First, it generalizes whereas Leviticus also cites specific cases, thus confirming that *ma'al* applies to all cases of defrauding man by means of an oath. Second, it adds the stipulation that in the case wherein the defrauded man dies and leaves no kin, the reparation belongs to the officiating priest. The third innovation is most crucial: restitution must be preceded by confession.[50]

---

46 Levine, *Numbers*, 187. Cf. Nihan, *Torah*, 250 – 52 with reference to the history of research.
47 In contrast to the majority of scholars Calum Carmichael has suggested that Num 5:5 – 10 is *not* a supplement to Lev 5:20 – 26, and does not even relate to it. Instead he presumes both texts to refer to different contexts in the Book of Genesis. "I contend that the rules are similar not because there has been updating but because each is a response to two different issues arising on two separate occasions recounted in Genesis 37 – 50" (Calum Carmichael, *The Book of Numbers. A Critique of Genesis* [New Haven: Yale University Press, 2012], 45). While Lev 5 addresses the Joseph story, Num 5 relates to the Judah-Tamar account. See Carmichael, *The Book of Numbers*, 44 – 53.
48 See the discussion in Milgrom, *Leviticus 1 – 16*, 301, 344 – 345; Milgrom considers the necessity of a confession primarily with deliberate sins: "confession is never required for inadvertencies but only for deliberate sins" (301). Cf. the explicit confession in Lev 5:5 which is phrased with ידה, too, see below.
49 Levine, *Numbers 1 – 20*, 190.
50 Milgrom, *Leviticus 1 – 16*, 368.

Commentators are unanimous that in comparison to Lev 5 a novel aspect is found in Num 5:8.[51] If there is no redeemer of the aggrieved, the reimbursement passes over to God and from his title down to the priest (cf. Lev 23:20). Levine is correct in pointing to Num 18 for a systemizing perspective: "Whatever went to God, with the exception of sacrifices entirely consumed on the altar, actually went into the temple treasury, or was otherwise uses in support of the priesthood. This system is summarized in Numbers 18".[52] That the wording of the innovation in v. 8 is related to Lev 5, too, is corroborated by the unique expression "ram of atonement" (איל הכפרים; Num 5:8) which is comprehensible only as abbreviation of Lev 5:25–26.[53] In sum, Num 5:5–10 has recourse to both Lev 5:20–26 *and* Lev 5:5, thus already presupposing the final composition of Lev 5.

b) The Case of the *Sôta* and Its Relation to Lev 5

Numbers 5:11–31, the *sôta* case, is different in terms of innovation. Although ordeal practice in cases of conjugal suspicion was common in the Ancient Near East as already evinced in article §131 and §132 in the Codex Hammurabi, we do not have templates or older versions of the ritual itself. It may have been compiled by reference to traditional material, but we have none of that. The alternative view, that the ritual was designed for the present context, remains a matter of speculation. We cannot decide on ritual innovation in terms of performance.[54] Hence, with reference to the given text, the ordeal itself is innovative as are the specific practices of taking the dust from the floor or wiping writing into the ritual agent, which is "holy water" (מים קדשים; v. 16). Compared to the sacrificial practice in Leviticus, the *minḥāh* of the suspected adulteress is different from other אשם-offerings. It is to consist of barley flour (קמח שערים) instead of wheat (סלת), and no oil shall be poured on it and no frankincense shall be

---

51 This aspect is often singled out as the only innovation: "8a ist das einzig Neue in den Versen 6–8 gegenüber Lev 5" (Kellermann, *Priesterschrift*, 66). "Einzig 8a enthält eine Neuregelung" (Seebass, *Numeri*, 115).
52 Levine, *Numbers 1–20*, 191.
53 Cf. Holzinger, *Numeri*, 18: "Dass Lev 5,22 ff. dabei formell vorausgesetzt wird, beweist der Artikel in אֵיל הַכִּפֻּרִים v. 8, der Lev 5,25 f. zitiert".
54 Interestingly enough, the emphasis on script and its magic effect is present in various cultures still today. I mention for instance the so called Taweez or Ta'wiz in Muslim societies. For the practice to write verses of the Quran on a piece of paper, and then drinking the water, see Margaret A. Mills, "Islam", in *South Asian Folklore: An Encyclopedia. Afghanistan, Bangladesh, India, Nepal, Pakistan, Sri Lanka*, ed. Margaret A. Mills et al.: New York and London: Routledge, 2003), 294–97 (here 294).

laid on it. This sort of offering can be understood only in relation to other *min-ḥāh*-offerings (Lev 2). The offering is specifically called "a cereal offering of jealousy" (מנחת קנאת) three times (Num 5:15,18,25) and two times "a cereal offering of remembrance" (מנחת זכרון; Num 5:15,18). The unmixed flour is strange as offering material in this context. Again, we are directed to Lev 5, where in v. 11 a specific sort of purification offering (*ḥaṭṭa't*) is mentioned for the poor:[55] one-tenth of an ephah of choice flour for a purification offering instead of two turtle-doves. But no oil is to be put on it, and no frankincense shall be laid on it, "for it is a purification/sin offering" and not a *minḥāh* (עשירת האפה סלת לחטאת לא ישים עליה שמן ולא יתן עליה לבנה כי חטאת היא). By contrast in Num 5 the oil is not "poured out" over (לא-יצק in Num 5:15) instead of not "laid upon" (לא-יישים Lev 5:11). However, the phrase לא יתן על לבנה is identical in both texts.[56] Hence, as in Num 5:5–10, the ritual innovation in the *sôṭa* may not be coined independently from Lev 5. This again corroborates the assessment above that Num 5–6 is a text that relies on Lev 5 as a prior composition.

c) Innovation in the Case of the Nazirite and Its Relation to Lev 5

Num 6:1–21 has innovative aspects in respect to its ritual as well. That approaching or touching a corpse[57] inadvertently nullifies the vow is comprehensible only by assuming the defiling power of death which is developed in the Torah in Lev 21 (esp. vv. 1 and 11); 22:4; Num 5:2; 9:6–14; and extensively in the ritual in Num 19.[58] The issue is reckoned a very serious one in these texts, insofar as it post-

---

55 For the חטאת in Lev 5:1–13 see Jacob Milgrom, "The Graduated Ḥaṭṭā't of Leviticus 5:1–13", *JAOS 103* (1983), 249–54; Milgrom, *Leviticus 1–16*, 292–318.
56 Milgrom, *Leviticus 1–16*, 306, mentions the parallel, but gives a different explanation: "Oil and frankincense are also deliberately omitted from the cereal offering of the suspected adulteress (Num 5:11). Thus it seems that both ingredients were considered signs of a joyous occasion, and their omission would accentuate the somber nature of the offerings". Even if this holds true, the special kind of cereal offering parallels both cases. Watts, *Leviticus*, 365, does not mention the parallel and considers the difference to be mindful of the social status of the sacrificer, who may not be able to finance the costly frankincense. This makes sense but does not fit as explanation for Num 5.
57 See Frevel, "Purity Conceptions", 373, for narrowing Num 6 to the *indirect* contact.
58 Cf. in addition Num 31:19–20 (implementation of Num 19 in the Midianite war); Lev 10:4–7 (avoidance of corpse contact by priests and prohibition of mourning rituals); Ezek 44:25–27 (restrictions for priests and handling of ritual impurity caused by corpse contact); Hag 2:13 (impurity by corpse contact in general). For the rationale of Num 19 see Christian Fre-

pones the date of the Pesach or justifies expulsion from the camp. In Num 6 contact with a corpse requires two turtle-doves or two young pigeons, one as a חטאת and one as a עלה in order to expiate the candidate after seven days uncleanness (Num 19:11,14,16). The priest shall make atonement for him, for he has incurred guilt or was defiled by reason of the corpse (מאשר חטא על־נפש). The combination of two turtle-doves or two pigeons is the regular substitute for a sheep (Lev 12:8), the ritual purification of the mother after giving birth (Lev 14:22), as a substitute within the ritual of cleaning the cured leprous person, מצרה, and finally as a regular offering after a bodily discharge (Lev 15:13,29). Although all cases are related to the completion of a period of seven days of uncleanness (Lev 14:10,23; 15:14,29), they do not match fully, because the Nazirite has neither given birth nor is he or she unclean due to a bodily discharge.[59] Nevertheless, there is one other case with the two pigeons, which is close to the issue here. It is Lev 5:7, 11, the cases of something hidden which require as a minor purification offering (חטאת) a female head of the flock regularly (Lev 5:4), or, as a substitute of less value, two pigeons.[60] The four cases in Lev 5 are: a) withholding witness; b) uncleanness by touching carcasses unwittingly and becoming aware of it later; c) defilement by "any kind of human uncleanness",[61] which is the usual interpretation of כי יגע בטמאת אדם;[62] and, finally, d) a person who swears an oath imprudently that cannot be kept, but he is unaware of this fact. The cases have in common the fact that the "implications [...] are not realized at the moment when they are performed".[63] It is especially the case in c) and d) which concern corpse impurity. While at first hand, Lev 5:1–13 fits best with the case of the Nazirite (Num 6:10), two differences are both obvious and striking: the *explicit confession* in Lev

---

vel, "Struggling with the Vitality of Corpses: Understanding the rationale of the Ritual in Numbers 19", *Les vivants et leurs morts*, OBO 257 (ed. Jean-Marie Durand et al.; Göttingen: Vandenhoeck & Ruprecht; Fribourg: Presses Universitaires, 2012), 199–226.

59 Thomas Hieke interprets the offering of the two doves as related to the breaching of the vow: "Sodann sind am achten Tag ein Entsündigungs- und ein Brandopfer (von Tauben) erforderlich, um den 'Bruch' des Gelübdes, der gewiss unabsichtlich geschah, aber dennoch ein Faktum ist, zu überwinden und dieses von Gott trennende Ereignis (das in einer sehr erweiterten Begrifflichkeit als 'Sünde' bezeichnet wird, ohne dass es um moralische Schuld geht) zu beseitigen (6,10–11)" (Thomas Hieke, "Unreinheit der Leiche nach der Tora", in *The Human Body in Death and Resurrection*, ed. T. Nicklas, F. Reiterer, and J. Verheyden, Deuterocanonical and Cognate Literature Yearbook [Berlin: de Gruyter, 2009], 43–65 [here 50–51]).

60 For the socially induced lowering of tariffs in Ancient Near Eastern cultic laws see Watts, *Leviticus*, 362.

61 Nihan, *Priestly Torah*, 241.

62 Cf. Lev 7:21.

63 Nihan, *Priestly Torah*, 241–42.

5:5 is lacking in the case of the Nazirite, and instead of offering a female animal from the flock, the requirement is lowered to two turtle doves or two pigeons as the standard offering. How are we to interpret this "innovation"? The lack of a confession may be due to the inadvertence of the defilement (v. 9), but this is not the only way to understand the difference. The Nazirite comes to the tent of meeting to settle the old vow and to renew it. His response is as public as a confession and it may have been seen as a substitute. Everybody can acknowledge that the Nazirite's outward appearance demonstrates that their vow has been broken since they have cut their hair. The renewal of the vow of the Nazirite is to be accompanied by an additional sacrifice as an אשם, namely a male lamb a year old (כבש בן־שנתו; Num 6:12[64]). The sacrificial tariff in Leviticus differentiates between female and male of the flock. Male sheep are mentioned explicitly in Lev 14 in the אשם rite in Lev 14:12,13,21,24,25, and once in Lev 12:6 in a חטאת (in contrast to Lev 4:32). Thus, in sum, the Nazirite has to invest more to restore his ritually purity than ordinary people. Besides the purity ritual of the מי נדה of Num 19, which fills in the period of seven days uncleanness (Num 19:11,14,16), and appears to be assumed in Num 6, there is no further requirement for the person who has been defiled by corpses. The need for a "higher degree" of purity agrees with the fact that the Nazirite must not be defiled by relatives, even if they are close family. The Nazirite "differs from any other corpse-contaminated person" and he "approximates the greater sanctity of the high priest".[65] It is striking that the phrase נפש מת is paralleled only by נפשת מת in Lev 21:11.

9. Summary – Practicing Rituals in a Textual World

The first part of this essay elaborated on ritual and the issue of innovation. While biblical rituals are textual, and not ritual scripts that match ritual practice, ritual innovation beyond the textuality of rituals is difficult to discern. Imaginable innovation in the performance of biblical rituals, be it by altering the ritual sequence, modifying ritual mastery, or changing contexts can no longer be observed. Hence ritual innovation in biblical rituals has to be discussed in textual form. Ritual innovation can particularly be described if various aspects of rituals can be examined comparatively on a textual level. We took as a case study the ritual composition of Num 5–6 which was first introduced in terms

---

64 The phrase כבש בן־שנתו is attested only in Lev 12:6 and Num 6:12,14.
65 Milgrom, *Leviticus 1–16*, 279–80.

of the space, ritual participants, and purposes of the individual rituals. Then the rituals were compared to Lev 5 as an antecedent composition. All three cases showed a specific relation to Lev 5 and differed with regard to the matter of *ritual innovation*. Num 5:5 – 10 was comprehensible only as amendment of Lev 5:20 – 26. Novel aspects were generalization, public confession and the absence of a legal successor. Each of these were added by drawing on the phraseology of Lev 5 in particular. The *sôta* drew on Lev 5 in terms of sacrificial systematics and the related ritual practices. This was also true with the law of the Nazirite in Num 6. In addition, the consequences of the unwittingly broken vow were developed by analogy with Lev 5:1 – 10. While Num 5:5 – 10 was obviously formulated for the present context, this solution is not compelling for the *sôta* (Num 5:11 – 31) or the law of the Nazirite (Num 6:1 – 21). There are good reasons to assume that both are not entirely ritual innovations coined completely for the context of Num 5 – 6. Certainly, it is not by chance that the literary unity of the *sôta* is so much discussed in exegesis.[66] This may indicate that the ordeal had a longer prehistory, which is generally accepted in scholarship.[67] The same holds true for the Nazirite vow, which is not a late Persian innovation,[68] but is rather accentuated in the late post-exilic period. But it was striking that all the innovative aspects of the Nazirite law were related to the specific situation in vv. 6 – 12, which was dedicated to the danger of the vow's defilement. However, it was conclusive that both the instructions for the *sôta* and the Nazirite were formulated with reference to Lev 5. The textual horizon of the Nazirite law was even wider, including both the requirement for priestly purity in Lev 21 and the ritual of Num 19 as well.

We have considered the rituals of Num 5 – 6 as a composition, which was well orchestrated with regard to its content, its spatial conceptions, and its function within the larger context. Num 5:1 – 4 functions as a compositional anchor that relates the rituals to the textual section Lev 11–Num 19.[69] The rituals in

---

66 See, for instance, Sarah Shectman, "Bearing Guilt in Numbers 5:12 – 31", *Gazing on the Deep: Ancient Near Eastern and Other Studies in Honor of Tzvi Abusch,* ed. Jeffrey Stackert, Barbara Nevling Porter and David P. Wright (Bethesda: CDL Press, 2010), 479 – 93; Jaeyoung Jeon, "Two Laws in the Sotah Passage", *VT 57* (2007): 181 – 207. For a more reluctant position see Achenbach, *Vollendung,* 507 – 8.

67 See, for instance, Achenbach, *Vollendung,* 508.

68 See Ludwig Schmidt, "Nasiräer", *Wibilex.* https://www.bibelwissenschaft.de/stichwort/28839/. Or, Achenbach, *Vollendung,* 509: "Der Text bietet die redaktionelle Ausarbeitung eines auf älteren Regeln beruhenden Instituts."

69 As an aside, if this section Lev 11–Num 19 is accepted, Lev 10 and Num 20 are related by framing this section. While Lev 10 narrates the transgression of the sons of Aaron and its lethal consequences, Num 20 recounts the transgression of Moses and Aaron, and the death of Aaron.

Num 5–6 "take place" in the wilderness presuming the camp as a virtual space. In literary respects, they presuppose Lev 5 in particular. Even the Holiness Code with its legal considerations on the purity of priests and the high priest, and Num 19 (and probably Num 18, too), are presupposed. As a consequence we have to attribute the composition of Num 5–6 to a relatively late stage of literary growth in the Pentateuch. We should consider not only H as Jacob Milgrom and Israel Knohl did,[70] but rather the post-H priestly literary discourses (which are labelled *Theokratische Bearbeitung II* by Achenbach) as background. Christophe Nihan has suggested that Lev 5 is part of "the growing involvement of priestly scribes in legal matters during the Persian period".[71] Its "complexity and, indeed, sophistication [...] suggest an erudite work rather than a composition with a primarily practical design".[72] However, this is exactly the impression we got in Num 5–6, but on the next textual level of adaptation, cross-linkage, and interpretation. The performance of the rituals may have had a practical background, but they are now embedded in a textual world, which has an autonomous character and functions on the textual level. Thus, ritual innovation can take place in a textual world.

This is compositionally significant and underlines that the books Leviticus and Numbers were not seen as separate units although they were divided into "books".

70 Milgrom, *Leviticus 1–16*, 368–69.
71 Nihan, *Priestly Torah*, 255.
72 Nihan, *Priestly Torah*, 255–56.

Ian Werrett
Walking over the Dead: Burial Practices and the Possibility of Ritual Innovation at Qumran

In 1948, shortly after the discovery of the Dead Sea Scrolls, the venerable Israeli archaeologist and Biblical scholar Eleazar Sukenik posited that the halakhic interpretations and organizational principles recorded in the scrolls from Cave 1 appeared to be synonymous with the ancient Jewish sect known as the Essenes, as described by Josephus, Philo and Pliny.[1] Soon after the publication of Sukenik's hypothesis, Bedouin shepherds and archaeologists with the American School of Oriental Research succeeded in locating additional manuscript caves and hundreds of scrolls in the same vicinity as the finds from Cave 1. Of particular interest was the discovery of a document known as the *Community Rule*, copies of which were found in Caves 1, 4, and 5, thereby suggesting a relationship between the various textual deposits. And when Roland de Vaux unearthed a cylindrical jar at a nearby archaeological site – a jar with the same typology as those that were recovered from Cave 1 – he and his colleagues began to interpret the scrolls, the caves, and the site of Khirbet Qumran as being contemporaneous and interconnected.

Since the late 1940s the archaeological site of Khirbet Qumran and its cemetery have become the focal point for what has come to be known as the Qumran Essene hypothesis. Although de Vaux's initial soundings of the site and its environs suggested that Khirbet Qumran may have once been a Roman fort,[2] subsequent excavations yielded material culture that placed the occupation of Qumran, and those who were interred within the adjacent cemetery, within the Second Temple period. Some sixty-five years have passed since de Vaux first opened Tombs 1 and 2[3] and the vast majority of scholars working in the field of Dead Sea Scrolls research continue to interpret Qumran and the cemetery as being interrelated. And while there may be compelling evidence connecting

---

1 Eleazar Sukenik, *Megillot Genuzot. Sequira Rishona* (Jerusalem: Mossad Bialiak, 1948).
2 Roland de Vaux, *Archaeology of the Dead Sea Scrolls* (London: The British Academy, 1973), 36–44.
3 Unfortunately, the field notes for Tombs 1 and 2 have gone missing and are not available for inspection. Jean-Baptiste Humbert and Alain Chambon, eds., *The Excavations of Khirbet Qumran and Ain Feshkha: A Synthesis of Roland de Vaux's Field Notes* (trans. S. Pfann; Fribourg: University Press; Göttingen: Vandenhoeck & Ruprecht, 2003), 73.

the cemetery to the site, such as their proximity to one another and their relative chronological dates,[4] there are equally compelling reasons for us to be cautious when attempting to interpret the evidence from the cemetery through the lens of the Qumran Essene hypothesis, the witness of the scrolls, and/or the archaeological record of Qumran.[5] In the ensuing discussion I will endeavour to discuss two separate, yet related, topics with regard to the cemetery at Qumran. First, I will examine how scholars have interpreted the supposedly idiosyncratic burial architecture at Qumran over the last six decades. And, second, I will try to determine whether any ritual innovations can be detected with regard to the construction and architecture of the shaft graves at Qumran.

1. The Qumran Cemetery – Not as Unique as We Once Thought

Although de Vaux was not the first to conduct excavations in the cemetery at Qumran,[6] he explored more of its graves than any other archaeologist before or since and he is responsible for some of our best information regarding the cemetery. Of the 1,177 graves that have been identified at Qumran, de Vaux excavated a total of 43.[7] Shortly after his death in 1971 an English translation of a lec-

---

4 Humbert and Chambon, *The Excavations of Khirbet Qumran and Ain Feshkha*, 73 – 79.
5 "In the main cemetery and the secondary ones", notes de Vaux, "we have marked down more than 1,200 tombs. Of these we have opened 43, and this number is quite inadequate to establish any valid statistical evidence." (de Vaux, *Archaeology of the Dead Sea Scrolls*, 128). Similarly, Gideon Avni has observed: "The archaeological data from the graves is insufficient to pinpoint the social and religious identity of those buried in it, their occupation or lifestyle, whether they lived only in the neighbouring settlement or roamed the Judean Desert highlands and the Dead Sea area. Thus the archaeological and environmental arguments from the cemetery are in themselves insufficient to resolve the disagreements among scholars about the nature of the Qumran settlement during the Second Temple period." (Gideon Avni, "Who Were Interred in the Qumran Cemetery? On Ethnic Identities and the Archaeology of Death and Burial", in *Qumran Revisited: A Reassessment of the Archaeology of the Site and its Texts*, ed. D. Stacey and G. Doudna [London: Archaeopress, 2013], 125 – 36 [here 130 – 31]).
6 Lieutenant Claude R. Conder and Charles Tyrwhitt-Drake excavated one grave at Qumran in 1873 shaft tomb, niche to the side, mud brick covering, head to south – and Charles Clermont Ganneau excavated a second grave, identical in form, in 1874; See Claude R. Conder and Horatio H. Kitchener, *The Survey of Western Palestine, 3: Judea* (London: Palestine Exploration Fund, 1883), 210 – 11; Charles Clermont-Ganneau, *Archaeological Researches in Palestine During the Years 1873 – 1874*, 2 vols. (London: Palestine Exploration Fund, 1896), 2:14 – 16.
7 Hanan Eshel, Magen Broshi, Richard Freund, and Brian Schultz, "New Data on the Cemetery East of Khirbet Qumran", *DSD* 9 (2002): 135 – 65 (here 135 – 43).

ture series that de Vaux delivered at the British Academy in 1959 was published under the title *Archaeology and the Dead Sea Scrolls*. In this publication, which is as close as de Vaux ever came to publishing an official report on the excavations of Qumran, he describes the basic structure of the cemetery and one of its unusual characteristics:

> To the east of the ruins, and separated from them by an empty space of nearly fifty metres, extends a vast cemetery containing about 1,100 tombs. It takes up all the rest of the plateau and the tombs are arranged in regular and closely ordered rows divided into three areas separated by alleys. This careful ordering is in contrast to the disorder usual in the ancient cemeteries of Palestine.[8]

Beyond the "careful ordering" of the cemetery, the burial architecture of the individual graves at Qumran was unlike anything that had been previously seen in Jewish burials from the Second Temple period. Whereas the interments in Jerusalem and Jericho from this period were either (1) primary burials on benches in loculus tombs, (2) primary burials in loculus tombs followed by the transferal of bones to communal charnels, or (3) secondary burials in ossuaries within family tombs,[9] the graves at Qumran are individual shaft burials descending 1.5–2.5 metres into the earth.[10] Oriented primarily in a north/south direction, loculi, or niches, have been fashioned at the bottom of the graves, to the east of the main shaft, and the corpses were laid to rest on their backs; heads pointing south, arms folded across the pelvis or at their sides.[11] After the corpse had been placed into the loculus it was sealed with flat stones or mud-bricks, thereby encasing the body in a pocket of air, while the main shaft was backfilled with stones, dirt, and potsherds.[12] The graves are indicated on the surface by an oval pile of stones – occasionally with a slightly larger stone at the head of the grave. As Rachael Hachlili has observed:

> The graves in [the Qumran] cemetery are very well organized, carefully dug, thoughtfully arranged, and are evidently not family tombs. These differences in grave form and burial customs reflect an out of the ordinary, distinctive community that no doubt deliberately used different customs.[13]

---

8 De Vaux, *Archaeology of the Dead Sea Scrolls*, 45–46.
9 Rachel Hachlili, *Jewish Funerary Customs and Rites in the Second Temple* Period. SJSJ 94 (Leiden: Brill, 2005), 450–51.
10 de Vaux, *Archaeology of the Dead Sea Scrolls*, 45–47.
11 Avni, "Who Were Interred in the Qumran Cemetery?", 126.
12 Humbert and Chambon, *The Excavations of Khirbet Qumran and Ain Feshkha*, 73–79.
13 Hachlili, *Jewish Funerary Customs*, 476.

Although Hachlili's observations are compelling, the seemingly idiosyncratic nature of the Qumran community's burial practices have, until recently, been somewhat exaggerated. In 1968, the much maligned journalist-cum-amateur-archaeologist, Solomon Steckoll, claimed that the burial architecture at Qumran is "different from that in vogue in Palestine during the Second Temple Period and reflects a more primitive culture or attitude towards the dead".[14] But neither the latter theory nor Steckoll's hypothesis that the Qumran community subjected the recently deceased to a literal "baptism of fire" have gained any traction in the field of Dead Sea Scrolls research.[15]

Yet another way in which the Qumran cemetery has enjoyed a unique status within the scholarly community involves the excavation and interpretation of subsequent "Qumran-style" graves in the Dead Sea region and beyond. After excavating 18 shaft graves at the Dead Sea site of 'En el-Ghuweir, which displayed the same burial architecture and orientation of graves as the cemetery at Qumran, the archaeologist Pesach Bar-Adon claimed "there is no doubt about the close social and religious affinity between the two settlements...one can assert that the inhabitants of 'En el-Ghuweir and Qumran belonged to the same Judean Desert sect."[16] Several years later, at the site of Haim el-Sagha, Hanan Eshel and Zvi Greenhut excavated 2 graves that had been constructed in the so-called "Qumran-style" leading Eshel and Greenhut to conclude that the site "contained graves of tent living nomads whose (burial) ideology was similar to that of the Qumran sect".[17] In 1982 and 1994, three graves in the "Qumran-style" were unearthed in Jerusalem in the East Talpiyot neighbourhood[18] and in Mamilla[19] respectively, while in 1996 upwards of 50 "Qumran-style" graves were discovered

---

14 Solomon Steckoll, "Preliminary Excavation Report in the Qumran Cemetery", *RevQ* 6 (1968): 323–44 (here 331).

15 According to Steckoll: "we may conclude that the evidence of fire inside most of the Qumran graves shows that the Community of the Scrolls practiced a ceremony of baptism or purification of the dead by fire. Like John [the Baptist] they taught and practiced a three-fold system of purification: water for the remission of sins, fire after death and by the Holy Spirit, as mentioned in the *Serek ha'yahad* scroll 4.21." (Solomon Steckoll, "The Community of the Dead Sea Scrolls", in *Atti del Convegno internazionale sui metodi della citta antica* 5 [1973–74], 199–244 [here 216]).

16 Pesach Bar-Adon, "Another Settlement of the Judean Desert Sect at 'En el-Ghuweir on the Shores of the Dead Sea", *BASOR* 227 (1977): 1–25 (here 20).

17 Hanan Eshel and Zvi Greenhut, "Haim El-Sagha. A Cemetery of the Qumran Type, Judaean Desert", *RB* 100 (1993): 252–59 (here 258–59).

18 Amos Kloner and Joseph Gat, "Burial Caves in East Talpiot", *Atiqot* 8 (1982): 74–76.

19 Ronny Reich, "The Ancient Burial Ground in the Mamilla Neighborhood, Jerusalem", in *Ancient Jerusalem Revealed*, ed. H. Geva (Jerusalem: Israel Exploration Society, 1994), 111–18 (here 117).

at a site in southern Jerusalem called Beit Safafa.[20] After excavating 41 of the Beit
Safafa graves, half of which were oriented east/west and half north/south, Boas
Zissu observed that "the shaft graves of Beit Safafa are identical to those of Qumran, both in their design and in their size."[21] Zissu concluded his initial article on
Beit Sefafa by citing several references in Josephus and the Dead Sea Scrolls indicating that there may have been an Essene presence in Jerusalem during the
late Second Temple period.[22] In a subsequent publication, Zissu takes the latter
idea even further when he claims that the discovery of the Beit Safafa graves
"suggest that if the inhabitants of Qumran were Essenes, then there must have
been a contingent of Essenes living in Jerusalem."[23]

The biggest challenge to the purportedly unique status of the grave architecture at Qumran came in the form of an accidental discovery at the Jordanian site
of Khirbet Qazone. In 1994, during a project to widen the al-Mazra'a as-Safi high-
way, which runs along the eastern side of the Dead Sea, construction crews discovered a massive cemetery containing 3,500 graves dating to the first and second centuries CE.[24] Archaeologists were eventually summoned to conduct rescue
excavations at the site in 1996, but in the two years after its initial discovery,
grave robbers had aggressively and systematically emptied the cemetery of its
contents. Of the remaining undisturbed graves, 23 were excavated by teams
from the Jordanian Department of Antiquities and the British Museum, and
their findings were subsequently published by the director of the excavations,
Konstantinos Politis. According to Politis, not only were all 3,500 graves oriented
north/south, but the grave architecture was identical to that of Qumran: shaft
graves 1.5 to 2.5 meters in depth, individual burials with no signs of reburial,
and loculi at the bottom of the shaft; each sealed virtually air tight with large
slabs of mud brick. Unlike at Qumran and the cemeteries mentioned above, however, none of the grave goods or artefacts from Khirbet Qazone were identifiably
Jewish. Rather, argues Politis, the archaeological evidence from Khirbet Qazone
suggests that the graves belonged to "ordinary [men,] women and children,

---

20 Boas Zissu, "'Qumran Type' Graves in Jerusalem: Archaeological Evidence of an Essene
Community?", *DSD* 5 (1998): 158–71.
21 Zissu, "'Qumran Type' Graves", 170.
22 Zissu, "'Qumran Type' Graves", 170–71.
23 Boas Zissu, "Odd Tomb Out", *BAR* 25/2 (1999): 50–55.
24 Konstantinos Politis, "Rescue Excavations in the Nabataean Cemetery at Khirbet Qazone
1996–1997", *Annual of the Department of Antiquities* 42 (1998): 611–14; Konstantinos Politis,
"The Nabataean Cemetery at Khirbet Qazone", *NEA* 62 (1999): 128; Konstantinos Politis, "The
Discovery and Excavation of the Khirbet Qazone Cemetery and its Significance Relative to Qumran", in *Qumran, the Site of the Dead Sea Scrolls: Archaeological Interpretations and Debates*, ed.
J.B. Humbert, STDJ 57 (Leiden: Brill, 2006), 213–19.

largely characterized as Nabataean".[25] Given the presence of shaft graves at Khirbet Qazone and at other Nabataean sites in Jordan, such as Ain Sekine, Haditha, and Feifa,[26] Politis offers a rather sobering and judicious conclusion:

> It is not immediately apparent that they [shaft burial-type] belong to the Essenes or even Jews, for that matter. In fact, they are not exclusive to any ethnic or religious group. Therefore, shaft burials should be viewed as a feature of the multicultural society prevalent in the Dead Sea area during [the] later Roman Empire.[27]

If Politis is right about the shaft-style burial not being exclusive to the Jews or the Essenes, and I believe that he is, then the implied relationship between the Qumran cemetery and other cemeteries with shaft-style burials all but evaporates.[28] And while there may yet be additional evidence connecting the sites where shaft-style burials have been unearthed, a statistical analysis of the data suggests that there is far more work to be done. Of the 4,767 graves that have been identified at Khirbet Qazone (3,500), Khirbet Qumran (1,177), Bait Safafa (50), Haim el-Sagha (20), 'En el-Ghuweir (17), East Talpiyot (2) and Mamilla (1), a grand total of 151 have been excavated. With only 3% of the known graves from the aforementioned sites having been explored, it is not an overstatement to say that our ability to generalize from the sample size to the entire collection of graves is severely hampered.[29] In point of fact, it is undoubtedly rash to make

---

25 Politis, "The Discovery and Excavation of the Khirbet Qazone Cemetery", 218.

26 Konstantinos Politis and Hero Granger-Taylor, "Nabataeans on the Dead Sea Littoral", in *Petra Rediscovered: The Lost City of the Nabataean Kingdom*, ed. G. Markoe (New York: Harry N. Abrams in association with the Cincinnati Art Museum, 2003), 110–12.

27 Politis, "The Discovery and Excavation of the Khirbet Qazone Cemetery", 219.

28 "First", notes Politis, "single shaft burials are not only very common at Petra and elsewhere in Nabataea, but can also be found at sites west of the Dead Sea, such as 'Ain el-Ghuweir and Hiam es-Sagha. Second, the variety of burial types in Qumran, as well as at Beit Safafa, argues against one single 'Qumran-type' burial at these 'Jewish-Essene' sites. Clearly shaft burials can neither be attributed to any particular ethnic group nor be used to identify a specific religious practice." (Politis, "The Discovery and Excavation of the Khirbet Qazone Cemetery," 219).

29 According to de Vaux, "the small number of tombs excavated [at Qumran] does not permit us to draw any statistics from them which can validly be applied to the cemetery as a whole" (de Vaux, *Archaeology and the Dead Sea Scrolls*, 47). Similarly, Rachel Hachlili observes: "It would be doubtful that the excavation of 43 tombs out of 3,500 [at Khirbet Qazone] would be a representative sample from which one would draw far-reaching conclusions" (Rachel Hachlili, "The Qumran Cemetery Reassessed", in *The Oxford Handbook of the Dead Sea Scrolls*, ed. T. Lim and John J. Collins [Oxford: Oxford University Press, 2010], 70). Finally, John Collins has observed: "The archaeological data are mute, and require a theory about the beliefs of the sect to explain them. They cannot themselves provide that theory, in the absence of written evidence." (John J. Collins, *Apocalypticism in the Dead Sea Scrolls* [London: Routledge, 1997], 124).

any bold inferences about the shaft-style burials, or the cemetery at Qumran for that matter, but there may yet be some profit in exploring the various hypotheses that have been forwarded to explain the burial practices at Qumran.

2. Ritual Innovation and the Scholarly Imagination

One of the first individuals to forward a hypothesis concerning the orientation and burial style of the graves at Qumran was Jozef Milik.[30] According to Milik, whose theory has subsequently been championed by Emile Puech,[31] the north/south orientation of the graves at Qumran was intended to point the feet of the deceased in the direction of Paradise. The basis for this argument, claims Milik, is rooted in the *Book of the Watchers*, which loosely describes the geographical locations of the divine throne, the tree of life, the Garden of Righteousness, and the resting places of the dead as being to the north (1 Enoch 22.1; 24 – 25; 32). Given that numerous copies of *1 Enoch* were found at Qumran, and that there would appear to be an identification between Paradise and the northern mountains in the Book of the Watchers, Puech argues "it is certain that for an Essene, Paradise was situated in the north."[32] Building upon this theory, Puech attempts to shed light on the individual shaft burials at Qumran by tying this practice to the Qumran community's belief in the resurrection of the body (cf. 4Q437 2):

> At the resurrection of the elect, lying in their tombs, head to the south but looking north… [the Essenes] will be facing the Paradise of righteousness and the divine abode; those lying with their head to the west even facing south, when resurrected, will look at the Sun of Justice and his bright light.[33]

In spite of the ingenuity of Milik and Puech's hypothesis, there are several factors that undermine it. First, as John Collins has rightly noted, the *Book of the Watchers* is not entirely clear about the direction of Paradise or the divine throne and nowhere in *1 Enoch* are these locations specifically described as being in the

---

30 Jozef Milik, "Henoch au pays des aromates. Fragments arameens de la grotte 4 de Qumran", *RB* 65 (1958): 70 – 77.
31 Emile Puech, "The Necropolises of 'Khirbet' Qumrân and 'Ain el-Ghuweir and the Essene Belief in Afterlife", *BASOR* 312 (1998), 21 – 36.
32 Puech, "The Necropolises of 'Khirbet' Qumrân", 30.
33 Puech, "The Necropolises of 'Khirbet' Qumrân", 36.

north.[34] Second, although the vast majority of the 1,177 graves at Qumran are oriented north/south, 54 are oriented east/west. And notwithstanding Joe Zias' compelling argument that the east/west graves in Qumran's Southern Cemetery are, by and large, later Bedouin intrusions,[35] a handful of east/west graves in the main cemetery at Qumran have been tentatively identified as being from the Second Temple period.[36] Given the presence of these anomalies, Puech has countered that the remaining east/west burials may be from the first generation of inhabitants at Qumran who were interred in the period before the Temple was deemed to have been defiled and/or prior to the creation of a standardized plan for their cemetery.[37] Finally, the discovery of 3,500 Nabataean graves at Khirbet Qazone, which are overwhelmingly north/south in orientation, indicates that the orientation of the graves at Qumran may have less to do with the parochial beliefs of a small Jewish sect than they do with the burial practices of the wider Dead Sea region.

Taking a slightly different tack to Milik and Puech, Joan Taylor has suggested that the Qumran community rejected the prevailing Jewish burial styles that were in vogue during the Second Temple period (i.e., burial in family tombs and/or subsequent reburials in communal charnels or ossuaries) so as to adopt a practice that is customarily associated with those of a lower socio-economic standing.[38] But as Boas Zissu has observed, not all "poor" or "field" burials are created equally. Where shallow graves of no more than half a metre were typically used by those who could not afford to purchase a tomb of their own, shaft graves, with a side loculus at its base, required a great deal of effort to construct and could be used only once, thereby indicating a greater amount of wealth.[39] In response to this two-tiered classification system, Taylor has remarked:

> We do not know whether poor burials might themselves fall into two types, one deeper type with loculus, and one shallower type without. The data are simply insufficient. While it is possible that the graves with loculi are sectarian, it remains unproven that all these graves

---

34 Collins, *Apocalypticism in the Dead Sea Scrolls*, 124.
35 Joseph Zias, "The Cemeteries of Qumran and Celibacy: Confusion Laid to Rest?", *DSD* 7 (2000): 220–53.
36 Humbert and Chambon, *The Excavations of Khirbet Qumran and Ain Feshkha*, 73; Puech, "The Necropolises of 'Khirbet' Qumrân", 28.
37 Puech, "The Necropolises of 'Khirbet' Qumrân", 26.
38 Joan Taylor, "The Cemeteries of Khirbet Qumran and Women's Presence at the Site", *DSD* 6 (1999): 285–323.
39 Zissu, "'Qumran Type' Graves in Jerusalem", 166–67.

in the Graeco-Roman period are Essene; they may simply reflect customs of burial among the poor that the people of Qumran adopted.[40]

If Qumran did indeed adopt the burial practices of the poor, it may well shed some light on the sectarian character of those who were buried in the adjacent cemetery. As Taylor has observed, the notion that the Qumranites were "buried as poor people, when they themselves might not have been – collectively – poor",[41] is compelling from a sociological perspective and suggests that the Qumran community may have embraced some of the same organizational principles in death as they did in life (i.e., shared property/no individual wealth). There is, however, precious little evidence in the scrolls, or the graves themselves, to support Taylor's hypothesis.

In an unpublished Master's thesis, Jonathan Norton offers two halakhically-inspired theories to account for the presence of shaft-cut graves to the east of Khirbet Qumran.[42] The first, which is tangentially related to Taylor's "collectively poor" argument, involves the decision not to use the caves in cliffs to the west of Qumran to bury their dead. After all, if the Qumranites were literally poor, one might expect the inhabitants to use the nearby caves as makeshift tombs in order to save time and money, but they did not. By way of an explanation, Norton suggests that the caves were not used for burials in that any tombs in the surrounding hills would have rendered the Qumran community's main water supply, and the aqueduct that transported it, ritually impure. In support of this argument, Norton cites a Pharisaic criticism of the Sadducees in the *Mishnah*, which accuses the Sadducees of incorrectly ruling that channels of water flowing through burial grounds were clean (m. Yad. 4:7). Norton's second argument, which is also supported by the witness of the Rabbinic material, claims that the caves were not used as tombs because they would have rendered those who were residing in the cliffs above Qumran impure. And although the Rabbinic passage cited by Norton indicates that corpse impurity does not penetrate the walls of a tomb (*m. 'Ohal.* 7:1), Norton follows the lead of Hannah Harrington by claiming that the halakhic interpretations of Qumran are consistently more severe than those of the Rabbis:

---

40 Taylor, "The Cemeteries of Khirbet Qumran", 312–13.
41 Taylor, "The Cemeteries of Khirbet Qumran", 313.
42 Jonathan Norton, "A Fresh Look at the Qumran Cemetery: The limits and Potential of the Material Evidence" (MA thesis, Oxford University, 1996). https://heythrop.academia.edu/Jonathan-Norton.

In almost all cases where an issue is raised in halakhic texts from Qumran, which is also raised in Rabbinic sources, the Qumran halakhah rules more strictly than the Rabbis were to do. Therefore, if the Yahad at Qumran concluded, unlike the Sages did, that the sides of a rock-cut tomb were not clean, it would explain why tombs were not cut into the marl cliffs or the rock cliffs at Khirbet Qumran in terms of halakhah.[43]

I have written elsewhere about the challenges that are inherent in assuming that Qumran is consistently more stringent than the Rabbis,[44] so I will refrain from doing so here. As for Norton's theories concerning the absence of tombs in the caves to the west of Qumran, it is difficult to offer a judgment. While Norton has raised some interesting possibilities, there are, by his own admission, "no halakhic rullings in the scrolls, which directly account for the burial form witnessed in the Qumran cemetery"[45] making it all the more difficult to offer an opinion about why the inhabitants of Qumran did not engage in other forms of burials.

One of the more counterintuitive interpretations forwarded thus far can be credited to Jonathan Klawans.[46] Citing a 2001 survey of the Qumran cemetery that employed ground-penetrating radar,[47] Klawans notes that 37 previously undiscovered voids (i.e., possible graves) were detected in the marl terrace, much closer to the eastern wall of Khirbet Qumran than previous thought. Given that the Rabbinic sources mandate that there be a distance of at least 50 cubits, or 23 metres, between burial sites and places of habitation (m. B. Bat. 2:9), the discovery of over three dozen possible graves, located some 10 to 15 metres from the settlement of Qumran, presents us with a possible halakhic dilemma.

In order to overcome the problem of having graves closer than 50 cubits from the cemetery wall at Qumran, Klawans offers two solutions. The first alternative, and by far and away the least convincing, is the possibility that the Qumran community considered their members and initiates to be so righteous that, when they died, they did not convey corpse impurity. Unfortunately, there is no evidence from the Second Temple period of Jews treating corpses, or portions thereof, like the sacred relics of Christian saints, which makes it difficult to accept this theory. Moreover, the Dead Sea Scrolls repeatedly emphasize the con-

43 Norton, "A Fresh Look at the Qumran Cemetery", 38.
44 Ian C. Werrett, *Ritual Purity and the Dead Sea Scrolls*, STDJ 72 (Leiden: Brill, 2007).
45 Norton, "A Fresh Look at the Qumran Cemetery", 38.
46 Jonathan Klawans, "Purity in the Dead Sea Scrolls", in *The Oxford Handbook of the Dead Sea Scrolls*, ed. T. Lim and John J. Collins (Oxford: Oxford University Press, 2010), 377–402.
47 Eshel, Broshi, Freund, and Schultz, "New Data on the Cemetery East of Khirbet Qumran", 135–65.

taminating power of corpses and their ability to render even the smallest of objects impure,[48] which represents a greater level of severity than we find in Num 19, or anywhere else in the Torah for that matter.

Klawans' second hypothesis suggests that the rift between Qumran and the Temple priesthood created a situation whereby corpse impurity had become an irresolvable problem. Take, for example, the Red Heifer rite. If the Qumran community disagreed with the Jerusalem priesthood and its interpretation of this ritual, as the Dead Sea Scrolls would seem to suggest (4Q269 8 ii 3b–6; 4Q394 3–7 i 16b–19a; 4Q277 1 ii 0–7a), then it may have motivated the Qumranites to hold the Red Heifer rite in abeyance until the ritual could be performed to their own exacting standards, just as Hannah Harrington has argued.[49] Without the waters of the מי נדה the Qumran community would have been unable to cleanse themselves, their buildings, or their belongings from corpse impurity. "If that were the case", notes Klawans, "then the problem of the cemetery's proximity finds a solution not in the group's stringency, but in their (albeit forced) leniency."[50] In other words, since the Qumranites had no way to combat corpse impurity, there was no need for them to worry about the contaminating presence of the graves or the cemetery.

Although I find some of Klawans' comments to be appealing, the end result of his theories is that the repeated and highly detailed references to corpse impurity, the Red Heifer rite, and the sprinkling of the מי נדה in the Dead Sea Scrolls amount to little more than wishful thinking or scholarly fantasy. But if everyday life at Qumran was so diametrically opposed to what we find in the Dead Sea Scrolls, then what, if anything, can we say for certain about the authors of these documents? And is there a way for us to determine with absolute certainty what is real and what is theoretical in the scrolls? The short answer, of course, is "no", but there may well be a way to straddle this fault-line by reading the archaeological record in conjunction with the textual witness from Qumran so as to formulate a theory that can account for the most evidence possible.[51]

---

48 See CD 12.15b–18; 4Q251 1–2 6; 4Q265 7 3; 4Q269 8 ii 3–6; 4Q274 2 ii 2–3a; 4Q277 1 ii 2, 5b–10; 4Q394 3–7 i 16b–19a; 4Q414 2 ii, 3, 3 2, 1 5; 4Q512 1–6 xii 5–6; 11Q19 49.5–21, 50.4b–51.5a.
49 Hannah K. Harrington, *The Purity Texts*, Companion to the Qumran Scrolls (London: T&T Clark, 2004), 83.
50 Klawans, "Purity in the Dead Sea Scrolls", 392.
51 As John J. Collins notes, "The archaeological data are mute, and require a theory about the beliefs of the sect to explain them. They cannot themselves provide that theory, in the absence of written evidence." (*Apocalypticism in the Dead Sea Scrolls*, 124).

Despite being highly speculative, the sealed loculus in the shaft graves at Qumran may yet be connected to the idea of ritual purity. As Zissu describes it: "The long burial niche, dug parallel to the shaft and covered by stone slabs, apparently bears witness to the desire to create an 'air pocket' which would prevent the exit of impurity."[52] Although impossible to prove, the number of passages in the Dead Sea Scrolls dealing with corpse impurity is quite high, thereby suggesting that the authors and redactors were acutely aware of the contaminating force of corpses and graves. Furthermore, not only do the Scrolls' rulings about corpse impurity often exceed the rigour of the Torah, such as when the Temple Scroll and the Damascus Document claim that a corpse in a house contaminates everyone and everything within the house, no matter its size or if it was sealed with a lid (CD 12.17b–18; 11Q19 49.11–16a; cf. Num 19:14–15), but the authors of the Scrolls spend a disproportionate amount of time talking about who can prepare and sprinkle the מי נדה (i.e., clean men who have waited until evening to be clean, and no boys – 4Q269; 4Q276; 4Q277; 4Q394; 11Q19) and when it should be sprinkled (i.e., never on the Sabbath – 4Q251; 4Q265; 4Q274). In point of fact, the Dead Sea Scrolls have more to say about corpse impurity and the Red Heifer rite than nearly all other forms of ritual purity/impurity combined,[53] which suggests that it was of great concern to the Qumranites and not simply an exaggeration on the part of modern scholars.

Putting aside for the moment the question of whether or not the Qumran community participated in the Red Heifer rite, it seems unlikely that they would have abandoned their beliefs and admitted that corpse impurity was an unresolvable problem, as Klawans and Harrington have suggested. If impurity has a cumulative effect on the sanctuary, as Jacob Milgrom has convincingly argued,[54] then it stands to reason that the Qumran community would have avoided adding to this problem, especially if they were keen to convince the Temple priesthood to come around to their way of thinking or if they considered themselves to be a physical replacement for the Temple (cf., 1QS 8 – 9; 4Q174). Moreover, if the 37 voids detected by ground-penetrating radar near the eastern wall of Qumran are indeed graves, then the Qumran community may have tried to deal with the issue of corpse impurity in some other way than by ignoring it. Namely, creating a new burial style, or reinterpreting a preexisting one, whereby the contaminating miasma of a corpse is contained in an airtight loculus at the bottom of a shaft grave. But while this would theoretically solve the problem of

---

52 Zissu, "'Qumran Type' Graves in Jerusalem", 167 n.20.
53 Werrett, *Ritual Purity and the Dead Sea Scrolls*, 288 – 91.
54 Jacob Milgrom, "Israel's Sanctuary: The Priestly Picture of Dorian Gray", *RB* 83 (1976): 390 – 99.

the graves being too close to the site of Qumran, there is simply not enough evidence to prove that the shaft graves at Qumran were interpreted in a manner that would mark them out as being unusual or different from any other shaft graves dating to this period.[55]

Before bringing this discussion to a close I would like to discuss one final theory for the presence of shaft burials at Qumran. As mentioned above, the prevailing burial style for Jews during the Second Temple period typically involved a corpse's interment in loculus or family tombs with later reburial in communal charnels or ossuaries. By contrast, the shaft graves at Qumran were designed for individual bodies and primary burials. Although Milik[56] and Puech[57] have claimed that individual shaft burials facilitated the act of resurrection, and Zias[58] has asserted that the practice was an outgrowth of the Qumran community's supposed predisposition towards celibacy, shaft burials may well be nothing more than tacit criticism of the popular practice of reburial in communal charnels and ossuaries. According to the Temple Scroll,

> Any man in an open field who touches the bone of a dead person...let him purify himself by the procedure of the ordinance already described. (11Q19 50.4–5)

Similarly, 4QMMT reads:

> Concerning [the impurity] of the dead, we have determined that every bone, whether [a piece] or the whole, is considered according to the commandment of the dead or the slain. [...] (4Q396 1–2 iv 1b–3)

Given that the authors of the Temple Scroll and 4QMMT are keen to specify that the bones of the dead, regardless of their size, transmit corpse impurity, it stands to reason that the Qumran community was opposed to the vogue of reburial among the Jewish elite during the Second Temple period. While highly specula-

---

55 The Temple Scroll maintains that those who "touch" a grave are ritually defiled and must be cleansed (11Q19 50.6). By contrast, the Copper Scroll states: "At the grave of the common people – it is ritually pure – in it: fourteen votive vessels, and their inventory list is next to them" (3Q15 11:9–11). And while it is hypothetically possible that the burial architecture at Qumran enabled people to walk over the graves without becoming unclean so long as they did not "touch" the grave, and that the "grave of the common people" was a ritually clean burial style, there is simply not enough evidence in the scrolls or in the archaeological record to prove that this was the case.
56 Milik, "Henoch au pays des aromates", 70–77.
57 Puech, "The Necropolises of 'Khirbet' Qumrân", 21–36.
58 Zias, "The Cemeteries of Qumran and Celibacy", 220–53.

tive, it is difficult to think of another situation in which a person would regularly come in contact with the bones of the dead, pieces or otherwise, thereby necessitating the creation of a new legal position.[59] If this interpretation is accurate, then what better way to keep a corpse from being reburied, or preventing animals from scavenging bones, than to bury it in a single-use-grave, 2.5 metres below the surface, in an airtight pocket that has been sealed shut with mudbrick. Although this theory is not without difficulties of its own, the hypothesis that the loculi in the graves at Qumran prevented or mitigated the transmission of corpse impurity, or that it functioned as a tacit criticism against those who were engaging in the vogue of secondary reburial, appears to correspond with the witness of the Dead Sea Scrolls and the meagre evidence from the cemetery. Yet, in spite of these correspondences, and the fact that this hypothesis is both intellectually compelling and theoretically plausible, its appeal has far more to do with the scholarly imagination than it does with the archaeological record from Qumran or the actual burial practices of the wider Dead Sea region before, during, and after the Second Temple period.

3. Conclusion

The archaeological evidence from Khirbet Qazone and Jerusalem, not to mention that of 'En el-Ghuweir, Haim el-Sagha and half a dozen other sites, argues against the notion that the Qumran Community reinterpreted a popular burial style so as to mitigate the contaminating effect of graves. Similarly, the extant evidence from the scrolls and Khirbet Qumran fails to prove that the inhabitants of Qumran were criticizing those Jews who were participating in secondary reburials by engaging in primary burials in shaft graves. Not only do the limited number of excavated graves at Qumran and elsewhere in the region prevent us from saying anything certain about the Qumran cemetery, but there is absolutely no proof that the shaft-style burial architecture with side niches was used for a different purpose at Qumran than it was at other sites.

In what may come to be regarded as the definitive article on the Qumran cemetery, Gideon Avni concludes:

> Even though many scholars have examined the cemetery and its findings, there is nothing in the their studies to reinforce the view that the Qumran cemetery is exceptional in its

---

59 Reburials in charnels and ossuaries required the retrieval of bones from loculi tombs after the flesh of the deceased had disappeared. Moreover, loculi tombs and ossuaries appear to have been used almost exclusively by those at the higher end of the socioeconomic spectrum.

structure and finds. It is more likely that it should be attributed to the large body of cemeteries consisting of simple shaft graves dug into the ground, which are widespread throughout history in many locations in the eastern Mediterranean and its peripheral desert regions.[60]

As opposed to being unusual or unique, it turns out that the burials at Qumran are not terribly dissimilar from those of other cemeteries in the region. And while we may yet discover evidence that the shaft-style burials at Qumran are emblematic of some form of ritual innovation, the archaeological data would appear to be pointing us in a different direction. This is not to say, however, that we should refrain from forwarding theories to account for the evidence at our disposal. Rather, as we continue to refine our hypotheses about the Dead Sea Scrolls and Khirbet Qumran, we must be honest about the limitations of our knowledge and careful to differentiate between the archaeological record, the textual evidence, and the scholarly imagination.

---

60 Avni, "Who Were Interred in the Qumran Cemetery?", 132.

Contributors

Reinhard Achenbach, Professor of Old Testament, Westfälische Wilhelms-Universität Münster

Christian Frevel, Professor of Old Testament Studies, Ruhr-University Bochum and Extraordinary Professor at the Department of Old Testament Studies, University of Pretoria

Roy E. Gane, Professor of Hebrew Bible and Ancient Near Eastern Languages, Andrews University

Nathan MacDonald, Reader in the Interpretation of the Old Testament, University of Cambridge and Fellow of St John's College

Saul M. Olyan, Samuel Ungerleider Jr. Professor of Judaic Studies and Professor of Religious Studies, Brown University

Jeffrey Stackert, Associate Professor of Hebrew Bible, University of Chicago

James W. Watts, Professor of Religion, Syracuse University

Ian Werrett, Director of the Spiritual Life Institute and Associate Professor of Religious Studies, Saint Martin's University

Subject Index

Index of names